ALL THE PRES

Carl Bernstein
Bob Woodward

IDENT'S MEN

A TOUCHSTONE BOOK
Published by Simon & Schuster
New York   London   Toronto   Sydney   Tokyo   Singapore

First Touchstone Edition, 1987

Published by Simon & Schuster, Inc.
Simon & Schuster Building
Rockefeller Center
1230 Avenue of the Americas
New York, NY 10020

TOUCHSTONE and colophon is a registered trademark of
Simon & Schuster, Inc.

Designed by Edith Fowler

Manufactured in the United States of America

10 9 8 7   Pbk.

Library of Congress Cataloging in Publication data

Bernstein, Carl, date.
  All the President's men.

  (A Touchstone book)
  Includes index.
  1. Watergate Affair, 1972–1974. 2. Bernstein,
Carl, date. 3. Woodward, Bob. 4. Washington
Post (1877) I. Woodward, Bob. II. Title.
[E860.B47   1987]   364.1′32′0973   87-12938

ISBN 0-671-64644-3 Pbk.

Acknowledgments

Like the *Washington Post*'s coverage of Watergate, this book is the result of a collaborative effort with our colleagues—executives, editors, reporters, librarians, telephone operators, news aides. Since June 17, 1972, we have had their assistance, support and advice. Some persons stand out. Our particular gratitude to Katharine Graham, Benjamin C. Bradlee, Howard Simons, Harry M. Rosenfeld, Barry Sussman, Leonard Downie, Jr., Lawrence Meyer, Larry Fox, Bill Brady, Douglas Feaver, Elisabeth Donovan, Philip Geyelin, Meg Greenfield, Roger Wilkins and Maureen Joyce.

Others contributed their time, energy and counsel to the preparation of this book. We are indebted to Taylor Branch, Mary Graham, Elizabeth Drew, Haynes Johnson and David Obst for their help and kindness. To Nora Ephron, Barbara Cohen and Richard Cohen, special affection and thanks.

Richard Snyder and the staff of Simon and Schuster—in particular Chris Steinmetz, Elise Sachs, Harriet Ripinsky and Sophie Sorkin, who prepared the manuscript for production—extended us enormous tolerance as deadlines were missed, production schedules altered and complicated technical problems accommodated. Throughout, the staff, especially Dan Green, Milly Marmur, Helen English and Terry Mincieli, was a source of enthusiasm and, more important, friendship.

This book would not have been possible without the work of Robert Fink, who assisted us in the research, lent us his ideas and gently offered us his criticism.

And most of all, our appreciation and respect to Alice Mayhew, our editor, whose thought and guidance are reflected on every page.

CARL BERNSTEIN
BOB WOODWARD

Washington, D.C.
February 1974

To the President's other men and women—
in the White House and elsewhere—
who took risks to provide us
with confidential information.
Without them there would have been
no Watergate story told by the Washington Post.

And to our parents.

Cast of Characters

THE PRESIDENT OF THE UNITED STATES

RICHARD M. NIXON

THE PRESIDENT'S MEN

ALFRED C. BALDWIN III	Security guard, Committee for the Re-election of the President (CRP)
ALEXANDER P. BUTTERFIELD	Deputy Assistant to the President; aide to H. R. Haldeman
JOHN J. CAULFIELD	Staff aide to John Ehrlichman
DWIGHT L. CHAPIN	Deputy Assistant to the President; appointments secretary
KENNETH W. CLAWSON	Deputy Director of Communications, the White House
CHARLES W. COLSON	Special Counsel to the President
KENNETH H. DAHLBERG	Midwest Finance Chairman, CRP
JOHN W. DEAN III	Counsel to the President
JOHN D. EHRLICHMAN	Assistant to the President for Domestic Affairs
L. PATRICK GRAY III	Acting Director, FBI
H. R. HALDEMAN	Assistant to the President; White House Chief of Staff
E. HOWARD HUNT, JR.	Consultant to the White House
HERBERT W. KALMBACH	Deputy Finance Chairman, CRP; personal attorney to the President
HENRY A. KISSINGER	Assistant to the President for National Security Affairs

9

RICHARD G. KLEINDIENST   Attorney General of the United States

EGIL KROGH, JR.   Deputy Assistant to the President for Domestic Affairs; aide to Ehrlichman

FREDERICK C. LaRUE   Deputy Director, CRP; aide to John Mitchell

G. GORDON LIDDY   Finance Counsel, CRP; former aide on John Ehrlichman's staff

CLARK MacGREGOR   Campaign Director, CRP

JEB STUART MAGRUDER   Deputy Campaign Director, CRP; former Haldeman aide and Deputy Director of White House Communications

ROBERT C. MARDIAN   Political Coordinator, CRP; former Assistant Attorney General

JOHN N. MITCHELL   Campaign Director, CRP; former Attorney General

POWELL MOORE   Deputy Press Director, CRP; former White House press aide

ROBERT C. ODLE, JR.   Director of Administration and Personnel, CRP; former White House staff aide

KENNETH W. PARKINSON   Attorney, CRP

HERBERT L. PORTER   Scheduling Director, CRP; former aide to Haldeman

KENNETH RIETZ   Youth Director, CRP

DONALD H. SEGRETTI   Attorney

DEVAN L. SHUMWAY   Director of Public Affairs, CRP; former White House press aide

HUGH W. SLOAN, JR.   Treasurer, CRP; former aide to Haldeman

MAURICE H. STANS   Finance Chairman, CRP; former Secretary of Commerce

GORDON C. STRACHAN   Staff assistant to Haldeman

GERALD WARREN   Deputy Press Secretary to the President

DAVID R. YOUNG   Staff assistant, National Security Council; aide to Henry Kissinger, John Ehrlichman

RONALD L. ZIEGLER   Press Secretary to the President

THE BURGLARS

BERNARD L. BARKER
VIRGILIO R. GONZALEZ
EUGENIO R. MARTINEZ
JAMES W. McCORD, JR.
FRANK A. STURGIS

THE PROSECUTION

HENRY E. PETERSEN	Assistant Attorney General
EARL J. SILBERT	Assistant U.S. Attorney for the District of Columbia; chief prosecutor
DONALD E. CAMPBELL	Assistant U.S. Attorney
SEYMOUR GLANZER	Assistant U.S. Attorney

THE JUDGE

JOHN J. SIRICA	Chief Judge, U.S. District Court for the District of Columbia

THE WASHINGTON POST

KATHARINE GRAHAM	Publisher
BENJAMIN C. BRADLEE	Executive Editor
HOWARD SIMONS	Managing Editor
HARRY M. ROSENFELD	Metropolitan Editor
BARRY SUSSMAN	District of Columbia Editor

THE SENATOR

SAM J. ERVIN, JR.	Chairman, Senate Watergate Committee

1

JUNE 17, 1972. Nine o'clock Saturday morning. Early for the telephone. Woodward fumbled for the receiver and snapped awake. The city editor of the *Washington Post* was on the line. Five men had been arrested earlier that morning in a burglary at Democratic headquarters, carrying photographic equipment and electronic gear. Could he come in?

Woodward had worked for the *Post* for only nine months and was always looking for a good Saturday assignment, but this didn't sound like one. A burglary at the local Democratic headquarters was too much like most of what he had been doing—investigative pieces on unsanitary restaurants and small-time police corruption. Woodward had hoped he had broken out of that; he had just finished a series of stories on the attempted assassination of Alabama Governor George Wallace. Now, it seemed, he was back in the same old slot.

Woodward left his one-room apartment in downtown Washington and walked the six blocks to the *Post*. The newspaper's mammoth newsroom—over 150 feet square with rows of brightly colored desks set on an acre of sound-absorbing carpet—is usually quiet on Saturday morning. Saturday is a day for long lunches, catching up on work, reading the Sunday supplements. As Woodward stopped to pick up his mail and telephone messages at the front of the newsroom, he noticed unusual activity around the city desk. He checked in with the city editor and learned with surprise that the burglars had not broken into the small local Democratic Party office but the headquarters of the

Democratic National Committee in the Watergate office-apartment-hotel complex.

It was an odd place to find the Democrats. The opulent Watergate, on the banks of the Potomac in downtown Washington, was as Republican as the Union League Club. Its tenants included the former Attorney General of the United States John N. Mitchell, now director of the Committee for the Re-election of the President; the former Secretary of Commerce Maurice H. Stans, finance chairman of the President's campaign; the Republican national chairman, Senator Robert Dole of Kansas; President Nixon's secretary, Rose Mary Woods; and Anna Chennault, who was the widow of Flying Tiger ace Claire Chennault and a celebrated Republican hostess; plus many other prominent figures of the Nixon administration.

The futuristic complex, with its serpent's-teeth concrete balustrades and equally menacing prices ($100,000 for many of its two-bedroom cooperative apartments), had become the symbol of the ruling class in Richard Nixon's Washington. Two years earlier, it had been the target of 1000 anti-Nixon demonstrators who had shouted "Pigs," "Fascists" and *"Sieg Heil"* as they tried to storm the citadel of Republican power. They had run into a solid wall of riot-equipped Washington policemen who had pushed them back onto the campus of George Washington University with tear gas and billy clubs. From their balconies, anxious tenants of the Watergate had watched the confrontation, and some had cheered and toasted when the protesters were driven back and the westerly winds off the Potomac chased the tear gas away from the fortress. Among those who had been knocked to the ground was *Washington Post* reporter Carl Bernstein. The policeman who had sent him sprawling had probably not seen the press cards hanging from his neck, and had perhaps focused on his longish hair.

As Woodward began making phone calls, he noticed that Bernstein, one of the paper's two Virginia political reporters, was working on the burglary story, too.

Oh God, not Bernstein, Woodward thought, recalling several office tales about Bernstein's ability to push his way into a good story and get his byline on it.

That morning, Bernstein had Xeroxed copies of notes from reporters at the scene and informed the city editor that he would make some more checks. The city editor had shrugged his acceptance, and Bernstein had begun a series of phone calls to everybody at the Watergate he could reach—desk clerks, bellmen, maids in the housekeeping department, waiters in the restaurant.

Bernstein looked across the newsroom. There was a pillar between his desk and Woodward's, about 25 feet away. He stepped back several paces. It appeared that Woodward was also working on the story. That figured, Bernstein thought. Bob Woodward was a prima donna who played heavily at office politics. Yale. A veteran of the Navy officer corps. Lawns, greensward, staterooms and grass tennis courts, Bernstein guessed, but probably not enough pavement for him to be good at investigative reporting. Bernstein knew that Woodward couldn't write very well. One office rumor had it that English was not Woodward's native language.

Bernstein was a college dropout. He had started as a copy boy at the *Washington Star* when he was 16, become a full-time reporter at 19, and had worked at the *Post* since 1966. He occasionally did investigative series, had covered the courts and city hall, and liked to do long, discursive pieces about the capital's people and neighborhoods.

Woodward knew that Bernstein occasionally wrote about rock music for the *Post*. That figured. When he learned that Bernstein sometimes reviewed classical music, he choked that down with difficulty. Bernstein looked like one of those counterculture journalists that Woodward despised. Bernstein thought that Woodward's rapid rise at the *Post* had less to do with his ability than his Establishment credentials.

They had never worked on a story together. Woodward was 29, Bernstein 28.

The first details of the story had been phoned from inside the Watergate by Alfred E. Lewis, a veteran of 35 years of police reporting for the *Post*. Lewis was something of a legend in Washington journalism— half cop, half reporter, a man who often dressed in a blue regulation Metropolitan Police sweater buttoned at the bottom over a brass Star-of-David buckle. In 35 years, Lewis had never really "written" a story; he phoned the details in to a rewrite man, and for years the *Washington Post* did not even have a typewriter at police headquarters.

The five men arrested at 2:30 A.M. had been dressed in business suits and all had worn Playtex rubber surgical gloves. Police had seized a walkie-talkie, 40 rolls of unexposed film, two 35-millimeter cameras, lock picks, pen-size tear-gas guns, and bugging devices that apparently were capable of picking up both telephone and room conversations.

"One of the men had $814, one $800, one $215, one $234, one $230," Lewis had dictated. "Most of it was in $100 bills, in sequence. . . . They seemed to know their way around; at least one of them must have been familiar with the layout. They had rooms on the second and third floors of the hotel. The men ate lobster in the restaurant there, all at the same table that night. One wore a suit bought in Raleigh's. Somebody got a look at the breast pocket."

Woodward learned from Lewis that the suspects were going to appear in court that afternoon for a preliminary hearing. He decided to go.

Woodward had been to the courthouse before. The hearing procedure was an institutionalized fixture of the local court's turnstile system of justice: A quick appearance before a judge who set bond for accused pimps, prostitutes, muggers—and, on this day, the five men who had been arrested at the Watergate.

A group of attorneys—known as the "Fifth Street Lawyers" because of the location of the courthouse and their storefront offices—were hanging around the corridors as usual, waiting for appointments as government-paid counsel to indigent defendants. Two of the regulars—a tall, thin attorney in a frayed sharkskin suit and an obese, middle-aged lawyer who had once been disciplined for soliciting cases in the basement cellblock—were muttering their distress. They had been tentatively appointed to represent the five accused Watergate burglars and had then been informed that the men had retained their own counsel, which is unusual.

Woodward went inside the courtroom. One person stood out. In a middle row sat a young man with fashionably long hair and an expensive suit with slightly flared lapels, his chin high, his eyes searching the room as if he were in unfamiliar surroundings.

Woodward sat down next to him and asked if he was in court because of the Watergate arrests.

"Perhaps," the man said. "I'm not the attorney of record. I'm acting as an individual."

He said his name was Douglas Caddy and he introduced a small, anemic-looking man next to him as the attorney of record, Joseph Rafferty, Jr. Rafferty appeared to have been routed out of bed; he was unshaven and squinted as if the light hurt his eyes. The two lawyers wandered in and out of the courtroom. Woodward finally cornered Rafferty in a hallway and got the names and addresses of the five suspects. Four of them were from Miami, three of them Cuban-Americans.

Caddy didn't want to talk. "Please don't take it personally," he told Woodward. "It would be a mistake to do that. I just don't have anything to say."

Woodward asked Caddy about his clients.

"They are not my clients," he said.

But you are a lawyer? Woodward asked.

"I'm not going to talk to you."

Caddy walked back into the courtroom. Woodward followed.

"Please, I have nothing to say."

Would the five men be able to post bond? Woodward asked.

After politely refusing to answer several more times, Caddy replied quickly that the men were all employed and had families—factors that would be taken into consideration by the judge in setting bond. He walked back into the corridor.

Woodward followed: Just tell me about yourself, how you got into the case.

"I'm not in the case."

Why are you here?

"Look," Caddy said, "I met one of the defendants, Bernard Barker, at a social occasion."

Where?

"In D.C. It was cocktails at the Army-Navy Club. We had a sympathetic conversation . . . that's all I'm going to say."

How did you get into the case?

Caddy pivoted and walked back in. After half an hour, he went out again.

Woodward asked how he got into the case.

This time Caddy said he'd gotten a call shortly after 3:00 A.M. from Barker's wife. "She said her husband had told her to call me if he hadn't called her by three, that it might mean he was in trouble."

Caddy said he was probably the only attorney Barker knew in Washington, and brushed off more questions, adding that he had probably said too much.

At 3:30 P.M., the five suspects, still dressed in dark business suits but stripped of their belts and ties, were led into the courtroom by a marshal. They seated themselves silently in a row and stared blankly toward the bench, kneading their hands. They looked nervous, respectful and tough.

Earl Silbert, the government prosecutor, rose as their case was called by the clerk. Slight, intent and owlish with his horn-rimmed glasses, he was known as "Earl the Pearl" to Fifth Streeters familiar with his fondness for dramatic courtroom gestures and flowery speech. He argued that the five men should not be released on bond. They had given false names, had not cooperated with the police, possessed "$2300 in cold cash, and had a tendency to travel abroad." They had been arrested in a "professional burglary" with a "clandestine" purpose. Silbert drew out the word "clandestine."

Judge James A. Belsen asked the men their professions. One spoke up, answering that they were "anti-communists," and the others nodded their agreement. The Judge, accustomed to hearing unconventional job descriptions, nonetheless appeared perplexed. The tallest of the suspects, who had given his name as James W. McCord, Jr., was asked to step forward. He was balding, with a large, flat nose, a square jaw, perfect teeth and a benign expression that seemed incongruous with his hard-edged features.

The Judge asked his occupation.

"Security consultant," he replied.

The Judge asked where.

McCord, in a soft drawl, said that he had recently retired from government service. Woodward moved to the front row and leaned forward.

"Where in government?" asked the Judge.

"CIA," McCord whispered.

The Judge flinched slightly.

Holy shit, Woodward said half aloud, the CIA.

He got a cab back to the office and reported McCord's statement. Eight reporters were involved in putting together the story under the byline of Alfred E. Lewis. As the 6:30 P.M. deadline approached,

Howard Simons, the *Post*'s managing editor, came into the city editor's office at the south side of the newsroom. "That's a hell of a story," he told the city editor, Barry Sussman, and ordered it onto Sunday's front page.

The first paragraph of the story read: "Five men, one of whom said he is a former employee of the Central Intelligence Agency, were arrested at 2:30 A.M. yesterday in what authorities described as an elaborate plot to bug the offices of the Democratic National Committee here."

A federal grand jury investigation had already been announced, but even so it was Simons' opinion that there still were too many unknown factors about the break-in to make it the lead story. "It could be crazy Cubans," he said.

Indeed, the thought that the break-in might somehow be the work of the Republicans seemed implausible. On June 17, 1972, less than a month before the Democratic convention, the President stood ahead of all announced Democratic candidates in the polls by no less than 19 points. Richard Nixon's vision of an emerging Republican majority that would dominate the last quarter of the century, much as the Democrats had dominated two previous generations, appeared possible. The Democratic Party was in disarray as a brutal primary season approached its end. Senator George McGovern of South Dakota, considered by the White House and Democratic Party professionals alike to be Nixon's weakest opponent, was emerging as the clear favorite to win the Democrats' nomination for President.

The story noted: "There was no immediate explanation as to why the five suspects would want to bug the Democratic National Committee offices, or whether or not they were working for any other individuals or organizations."

Bernstein had written another story for the Sunday paper on the suspects. Four were from Miami: Bernard L. Barker, Frank A. Sturgis, Virgilio R. Gonzalez and Eugenio R. Martinez. He had called a *Miami Herald* reporter and obtained a long list of Cuban exile leaders. A *Post* reporter had been sent from the President's press party in Key Biscayne to make checks in Miami's Cuban community. All four of the Miami suspects had been involved in anti-Castro activities and were also said to have CIA connections. ("I've never known if he works for the CIA or not," Mrs. Barker told Bernstein. "The men never tell the women anything about that.") Sturgis, an American soldier-of-fortune and the only non-Cuban among them, had been recruiting militant Cubans to demonstrate at the Democratic national convention, according to several persons. One Cuban leader told Bernstein that Sturgis and others whom he described as "former CIA types" intended to use paid provocateurs to fight anti-war demonstrators in the streets during the national political conventions.

Woodward left the office about eight o'clock that Saturday night. He knew he should have stayed later to track down James McCord. He had not even checked the local telephone directory to see if there was a James McCord listed in Washington or its suburbs.

The national staff of the *Washington Post* rarely covers police stories. So, at Sussman's request, both Bernstein and Woodward returned to the office the next morning, a bright Sunday, June 18, to follow up. An item moving on the Associated Press wire made it embarrassingly clear why McCord had deserved further checking. According to campaign spending reports filed with the government, James McCord was the security coordinator of the Committee for the Re-election of the President (CRP).

The two reporters stood in the middle of the newsroom and looked at each other. What the hell do you think it means? Woodward asked. Bernstein didn't know.

In Los Angeles, John Mitchell, the former U.S. Attorney General and the President's campaign manager, issued a statement: "The person involved is the proprietor of a private security agency who was employed by our committee months ago to assist with the installation of our security system. He has, as we understand it, a number of business clients and interests, and we have no knowledge of these relationships. We want to emphasize that this man and the other people involved were not operating on either our behalf or with our consent. There is no place in our campaign or in the electoral process for this type of activity, and we will not permit or condone it."

In Washington, the Democratic national chairman, Lawrence F. O'Brien, said the break-in "raised the ugliest question about the integrity of the political process that I have encountered in a quarter-century of political activity. No mere statement of innocence by Mr.

Nixon's campaign manager, John Mitchell, will dispel these questions."

The wire services, which had carried the Mitchell and O'Brien statements, could be relied upon to gather official pronouncements from the national politicians. The reporters turned their attention to the burglars.

The telephone book listed the private security consulting agency run by McCord. There was no answer. They checked the local "criss-cross" directories which list phone numbers by street addresses. There was no answer at either McCord's home or his business. The address of McCord Associates, 414 Hungerford Drive, Rockville, Maryland, is a large office building, and the cross-reference directory for Rockville lists the tenants. The reporters divided the names and began calling them at home. One attorney recalled that a teenage girl who had worked part-time for him the previous summer knew McCord, or perhaps it was the girl's father who knew him. The attorney could only remember vaguely the girl's last name—Westall or something like that. They contacted five persons with similar last names before Woodward finally reached Harlan A. Westrell, who said he knew McCord.

Westrell, who obviously had not read the papers, wondered why Woodward wanted to know about McCord. Woodward said simply that he was seeking information for a possible story. Westrell seemed flattered and provided some information about McCord, his friends and his background. He gave Woodward some other names to call.

Gradually, a spare profile of McCord began to emerge: a native of the Texas Panhandle; deeply religious, active in the First Baptist Church of Washington; father of an Air Force Academy cadet and a retarded daughter; ex-FBI agent; military reservist; former chief of physical security for the CIA; teacher of a security course at Montgomery Junior College; a family man; extremely conscientious; quiet; reliable. John Mitchell's description of McCord notwithstanding, those who knew him agreed that he worked full-time for the President's re-election committee.

Several persons referred to McCord's integrity, his "rocklike" character, but there was something else. Westrell and three others described McCord as the consummate "government man"—reluctant to act on his own initiative, respectful of the chain of command, unquestioning in following orders.

Woodward typed out the first three paragraphs of a story identifying one of the Watergate burglars as a salaried security coordinator of the President's re-election committee and handed it to an editor on the city desk. A minute later, Bernstein was looking over the editor's shoulder, Woodward noticed. Then Bernstein was walking back to his desk with the first page of the story; soon he was typing. Woodward finished the second page and passed it to the editor. Bernstein had soon relieved him of it and was back at his typewriter. Woodward decided to walk over and find out what was happening.

Bernstein was rewriting the story. Woodward read the rewritten version. It was better.

That night, Woodward drove to McCord's home, a large two-story brick house, classically suburban, set in a cul-de-sac not far from Route 70-S, the main highway through Rockville. The lights were on, but no one answered the door.

After midnight, Woodward received a call at home from Eugene Bachinski, the *Post*'s regular night police reporter. The night police beat is generally considered the worst assignment at the paper. The hours are bad—from about 6:30 P.M. to 2:30 A.M. But Bachinski— tall, goateed and quiet—seemed to like his job, or at least he seemed to like the cops. He had come to know many of them quite well, saw a few socially and moved easily on his nightly rounds through the various squads at police headquarters: homicide, vice (grandly called the Morals Division), traffic, intelligence, sex, fraud, robbery—the catalogue of city life as viewed by the policeman.

Bachinski had something from one of his police sources. Two address books, belonging to two of the Miami men arrested inside the Watergate, contained the name and phone number of a Howard E. Hunt, with the small notations *"W. House"* and *"W.H."* Woodward sat down in a hard chair by his phone and checked the telephone directory. He found a listing for E. Howard Hunt, Jr., in Potomac, Maryland, the affluent horse-country suburb in Montgomery County. No answer.

At the office next morning, Woodward made a list of the leads. One of McCord's neighbors had said that he had seen McCord in an Air

Force officer's uniform, and another had said that McCord was a lieutenant colonel in the Air Force Reserve. Half a dozen calls to the Pentagon later, a personnel officer told him that James McCord was a lieutenant colonel in a special Washington-based reserve unit attached to the Office of Emergency Preparedness. The officer read him the unit roster, which contained only 15 names. Woodward started calling. On the fourth try, Philip Jones, an enlisted man, mentioned casually that the unit's assignment was to draw up lists of radicals and to help develop contingency plans for censorship of the news media and U.S. mail in time of war.

Woodward placed a call to a James Grimm, whose name and Miami telephone number Bachinski had said was in the address book of Eugenio Martinez. Mr. Grimm identified himself as a housing officer for the University of Miami, and said that Martinez had contacted him about two weeks earlier to ask if the university could find accommodations for about 3000 Young Republicans during the GOP national convention in August. Woodward called CRP, the Republican National Committee headquarters and several party officials who were working on convention planning in Washington and Miami. All said they had never heard of Martinez or of plans to use the university for housing Young Republicans.

But the first priority on that Monday was Hunt. The Miami suspects' belongings were listed in a confidential police inventory that Bachinski had obtained. There were "two pieces of yellow-lined paper, one addressed to 'Dear Friend Mr. Howard,' and another to 'Dear Mr. H.H.,' " and an unmailed envelope containing Hunt's personal check for $6.36 made out to the Lakewood Country Club in Rockville, along with a bill for the same amount.

Woodward called an old friend and sometimes source who worked for the federal government and did not like to be called at his office. His friend said hurriedly that the break-in case was going to "heat up," but he couldn't explain and hung up.

It was approaching 3:00 P.M., the hour when the *Post*'s editors list in a "news budget" the stories they expect for the next day's paper. Woodward, who had been assigned to write Tuesday's Watergate story, picked up the telephone and dialed 456-1414—the White House. He asked for Howard Hunt. The switchboard operator rang an extension. There was no answer. Woodward was about to hang up when the operator came back on the line. "There is one other place he might be," she said. "In Mr. Colson's office."

"Mr. Hunt is not here now," Colson's secretary told Woodward, and gave him the number of a Washington public-relations firm, Robert R. Mullen and Company, where she said Hunt worked as a writer.

Woodward walked across to the national desk at the east end of the newsroom and asked one of the assistant national editors, J. D. Alexander, who Colson was. Alexander, a heavy-set man in his mid-thirties with a thick beard, laughed. Charles W. Colson, special counsel to the President of the United States, was the White House "hatchet man," he said.

Woodward called the White House back and asked a clerk in the personnel office if Howard Hunt was on the payroll. She said she would check the records. A few moments later, she told Woodward that Howard Hunt was a consultant working for Colson.

Woodward called the Mullen public-relations firm and asked for Howard Hunt.

"Howard Hunt here," the voice said.

Woodward identified himself.

"Yes? What is it?" Hunt sounded impatient.

Woodward asked Hunt why his name and phone number were in the address books of two of the men arrested at the Watergate.

"Good God!" Howard Hunt said. Then he quickly added, "In view that the matter is under adjudication, I have no comment," and slammed down the phone.

Woodward thought he had a story. Still, anyone's name and phone number could be in an address book. The country-club bill seemed to be additional evidence of Hunt's connection with the burglars. But what connection? A story headlined "White House Consultant Linked to Bugging Suspects" could be a grievous mistake, misleading, unfair to Hunt.

Woodward called Ken W. Clawson, the deputy director of White House communications, who had been a *Post* reporter until the previous January. He told Clawson what was in the address books and police inventory, then asked what Hunt's duties at the White House were. Clawson said that he would check.

An hour later, Clawson called back to say that Hunt had worked as a White House consultant on declassification of the Pentagon

Papers and, more recently, on a narcotics intelligence project. Hunt had last been paid as a consultant on March 29, he said, and had not done any work for the White House since.

"I've looked into the matter very thoroughly, and I am convinced that neither Mr. Colson nor anyone else at the White House had any knowledge of, or participation in, this deplorable incident at the Democratic National Committee," Clawson said.

The comment was unsolicited.

Woodward phoned Robert F. Bennett, president of the Mullen public-relations firm, and asked about Hunt. Bennett, the son of Republican Senator Wallace F. Bennett of Utah, said, "I guess it's no secret that Howard was with the CIA."

It had been a secret to Woodward. He called the CIA, where a spokesman said that Hunt had been with the agency from 1949 to 1970.

Woodward didn't know what to think. He placed another call to his government friend and asked for advice. His friend sounded nervous. On an off-the-record basis he told Woodward that the FBI regarded Hunt as a prime suspect in the Watergate investigation for many reasons aside from the address-book entries and the unmailed check. Woodward was bound not to use the information in a story because it was off the record. But his friend assured him that there would be nothing unfair about a story which reported the address-book and country-club connections. That assurance could not be used in print either.

Barry Sussman, the city editor, was intrigued. He dug into the *Post* library's clippings on Colson and found a February 1971 story in which an anonymous source described Colson as one of the "original back room boys . . . the brokers, the guys who fix things when they break down and do the dirty work when it's necessary." Woodward's story about Hunt, which identified him as a consultant who had worked in the White House for Colson, included the quotation and noted that it came from a profile written by "Ken W. Clawson, a current White House aide who until recently was a [*Washington Post*] reporter."

The story was headlined "White House Consultant Linked to Bugging Suspects."

That morning at the Florida White House in Key Biscayne, presidential press secretary Ronald L. Ziegler briefly answered a question about the break-in at the Watergate by observing: "Certain elements may try to stretch this beyond what it is." Ziegler described the incident as "a third-rate burglary attempt" not worthy of further White House comment.

The next day, Democratic Party chairman O'Brien filed a $1 million civil damage suit against the Committee for the Re-election of the President. Citing the "potential involvement" of Colson in the break-in, O'Brien charged that the facts were "developing a clear line to the White House" and added: "We learned of this bugging attempt only because it was bungled. How many other attempts have there been and just who was involved? I believe we are about to witness the ultimate test of this administration that so piously committed itself to a new era of law and order just four years ago."

2

BERNSTEIN HAD been told by Sussman to take Monday and Tuesday off. On Wednesday, he set out to learn what he could about Charles W. Colson. He called a former official of the Nixon administration who he thought might be able to supply some helpful biographical data. Instead of biography, the man told Bernstein: "Whoever was responsible for the Watergate break-in would have to be somebody who doesn't know about politics but thought he did. I suppose that's why Colson's name comes up. . . . Anybody who knew anything wouldn't be looking over there for real political information. They'd be looking for something else . . . scandal, gossip."

The man knew the inner workings of the White House, of which Bernstein and Woodward were almost totally ignorant, and, better still, he maintained extensive contacts with his former colleagues.

Bernstein asked if he thought there was any possibility that the President's campaign committee or—less likely—the White House would sponsor such a stupid mission as the Watergate raid. Bernstein waited to be told no.

"I know the President well enough to know if he needed something like this done it certainly wouldn't be a shoddy job," said the former official. But it was not inconceivable that the President would want his campaign aides to have every piece of political intelligence and gossip available. He recalled that one White House political consultant "was always talking about walkie-talkies. You would talk about politics and he would talk about devices. There was always a great preoccupation at the White House with all this intelligence nonsense. Some of those people are dumb enough to think there would be something there."

This picture of the White House was in sharp contrast to the smooth, well-oiled machine Bernstein was accustomed to reading about in the newspapers—those careful, disciplined, look-alike guards to the palace who were invariably referred to as "the President's Men."

Bernstein asked about one of them, Robert Odle, presently director of personnel at CRP and a former White House aide. The committee had identified Odle as the man who had hired McCord as its security coordinator.

"That's bullshit," the former official replied. "Mitchell wouldn't let go of a decision like that. Mitchell would decide, with advice from somebody who knew something about security."

The hiring of McCord would almost certainly have involved at least one other person, he said—a Mitchell aide whom he described as the former Attorney General's right-hand man, Fred LaRue. Bernstein jotted down the name (spelling it La Roue) as he was told more about him.

"I would expect that if any wiretaps were active up to the time of the break-in, LaRue would have known about them."

The former official offered an additional thought. Murray Chotiner, the President's old friend and specialist in low-road campaign tactics since the days of Nixon's congressional campaigns against Jerry Voorhis and Helen Gahagan Douglas was in charge of something called "ballot security." Although officially undefined, the job's purpose was to prevent the Democrats from stealing the election, as the President and his loyalists (as well as some Democrats) maintained had happened in 1960.

Later that afternoon, David Broder, the *Post*'s national political reporter and columnist, gave Bernstein the name of an official of the Republican National Committee and suggested that he be contacted. Broder described the official as a "very straight guy" who might know something because he was among those engaged in planning security arrangements for the GOP convention. CRP had said that McCord had worked as a consultant on convention security.

"The truth is that McCord has never done security work of any kind for the convention," the party official told Bernstein. "What he has been doing, I assume, is taking care of security for the Committee to Re-elect. All they care about at CRP is Richard M. Nixon. They couldn't care less about the Republican Party. Given the chance, they would wreck it."

Did the party official believe the denials of involvement by John Mitchell and CRP?

The man laughed. "Bob Dole and I were talking on the day of the arrests and agreed it must be one of these twenty-five-cent generals hanging around the committee or the White House who was responsible. Chotiner or Colson. Those were the names thrown out."

Bernstein had not expected anyone closely tied to the Nixon administration to speak with such scorn and derision of the men around the President. He walked across the room to tell Sussman about it. The city editor thought the information was interesting. Then, uncomfortably, he told Bernstein he was taking him off the Watergate assignment because the Virginia desk could no longer spare one of its two political reporters in an election season.

Bernstein returned to his desk feigning unconcern but in a foul mood. The *Post* owed him almost four months of vacation. Until the break-in, he had planned to use it that summer on a cross-country bicycle trip. He decided to make a last attempt to stay on the Watergate story. He wrote a five-page memo outlining what he called the "Chotiner Theory" and sent copies to Sussman, Woodward and Harry M. Rosenfeld, the *Post's* metropolitan editor.

"It is a long shot, to be sure," the memo began, "but . . . Colson is Chotiner's successor at the White House. . . . Colson might well be tied up in some aspects of 'ballot security' with Chotiner. That could mean evaluating whatever information Chotiner is coming up with."

The next day, Rosenfeld told Bernstein to pursue the Chotiner Theory and see what else he could learn.*

At a press conference that same afternoon, June 22, President Nixon made his first public comment on the break-in. "The White House has had no involvement whatever in this particular incident," he said.

Bernstein and Woodward lingered over the phrase "this particular

---

* In spite of suggestions that Chotiner was involved in the Watergate bugging, no evidence whatsoever was ever developed to indicate that it was true. Chotiner died in early 1974.

incident." There were already too many coincidences which couldn't be dismissed so offhandedly: An attorney in Washington had said he could positively identify Frank Sturgis as one of the several men who had attacked Pentagon Papers defendant Daniel Ellsberg outside a memorial service for the late FBI director J. Edgar Hoover in May. One suspect's address book contained a rough sketch of hotel rooms that were to be used as headquarters by Senator McGovern at the Democratic convention. An architect in Miami had said that Bernard Barker had tried to get the blueprints of the convention hall and its air-conditioning system. Hunt's boss at the Mullen firm, Robert Bennett, had been the organizer of about 100 dummy campaign committees used to funnel millions of dollars in secret contributions to the President's re-election campaign. McCord had been carrying an application for college press credentials for the Democratic convention when he was arrested. He had recently traveled to Miami Beach. Some of the accused burglars from Miami had been in Washington three weeks before their arrest, when the offices of some prominent Democratic lawyers in the Watergate office building were burglarized.

Within an hour of the President's statement, reporters were told by Devan L. Shumway, the public-relations director of CRP, that John Mitchell had ordered an in-house investigation of the break-in at Democratic headquarters.

On July 1, nine days after the President's statement, Mitchell resigned as manager of the Nixon campaign, explaining that his wife had insisted he quit.

Woodward asked several members of the *Post*'s national staff, which was handling the story, if they believed the resignation was unconnected to Watergate. They did.

The next day, metropolitan editor Harry Rosenfeld frowned and told Woodward: "A man like John Mitchell doesn't give up all that power for his wife."

Shortly after the name of Charles Colson first came to Bernstein's attention, a fellow reporter told him that he had once dated a young woman who worked at the White House. In Colson's office, he thought. Bernstein reached her by telephone. She had worked for one of Colson's assistants, not Colson himself. She had come to know Howard Hunt slightly.

"I had suspicions about the whole bunch of them, especially Colson, because he was so overprotective of the President and very defensive about him," she said. "He was always rushing up and down with papers, but was very secretive." Hunt, however, "was really nice, a pleasant man, personable. He was one of the few people around who took the time to make you feel like part of it all," and occasionally he would take her to lunch. Although hired as a consultant, "he worked there almost every day. He'd take off and go to Florida once in a while . . . and there were trips to California." That was in the summer and early fall of 1971. Hunt was just as secretive as Colson, she said, "but somebody in the office told me that Howard was doing investigative work on different things, including the Pentagon Papers." She had gotten the impression that he had not been working on "declassification" of the papers, as the White House had said, but instead on finding out how they had been leaked to the press.

"At about the same time," she said, "I noticed a book on Chappaquiddick on his desk, so I asked about that. He was doing investigative work on that case, too, on Kennedy. They weren't willing . . . they never gave me a whole lot of information."

Who told her that Hunt was investigating Kennedy?

Another secretary in Colson's office. Then she had seen other papers and books on Hunt's desk dealing with Senator Kennedy and the automobile accident at Chappaquiddick. She remembered that one was a paperback, "something simple like 'Kennedy and Chappaquiddick.'" Some of the material had been checked out from the White House library, she thought. And one of Colson's aides—she couldn't remember which one—had also told her Hunt was investigating Kennedy. "It was verified up the line," she added.

Bernstein called the White House and asked for the librarian. He was put through to Jane F. Schleicher, an assistant librarian. Identifying himself as a reporter, he asked her if she remembered the name of the book on Senator Kennedy that Mr. Hunt had checked out.

"I think I do remember something about that," the librarian replied. "He took out a whole bunch of material" on the subject of Senator Kennedy and Chappaquiddick. Mrs. Schleicher added that "I thought

I had it in my notes" and asked Bernstein to call back after she had a chance to check the records.

"I think the book you probably mean is the one by Jack Olsen, *The Bridge at Chappaquiddick*," Mrs. Schleicher said on the second call. Bernstein asked when Hunt had borrowed the book. Mrs. Schleicher asked him to hold the line. When she returned to the phone a few minutes later, she sounded agitated. "I don't have a card that Mr. Hunt took that out," she said. "I remember getting this book for someone, but there is no card on Mr. Hunt taking it out." There was no card on the book at all; she had never had any requests from Hunt. She referred Bernstein to the press office. She didn't know who Hunt was.

Woodward then called her and asked about the Kennedy material. "I had no business giving that out [to Bernstein]," she replied.

Woodward dialed the White House switchboard again and asked for a young presidential aide he had once met socially. They talked for an hour. Assured that his name would not be used, the official told him that Hunt had been assigned by the White House to conduct an investigation of Kennedy's private life. He would not say who had ordered the investigation, but he left the clear impression that Colson was among those who knew of it. The official remembered that Hunt had received some material about Kennedy from the Library of Congress.

Bernstein and Woodward took a cab to the Library of Congress and found the office that handles White House requests for material in the library. Speaking to the reporters in a hallway, rather than his office, a librarian informed them politely that White House transactions were confidential. Eventually, the reporters found a more cooperative clerk and spent the afternoon in the reading room sorting through thousands of slips of paper—every request since July 1971, when Hunt was hired by the White House.

Woodward called Ken Clawson and told him about Bernstein's conversation with the librarian. When Clawson called back, he said he had talked with Mrs. Schleicher. "She denies that the conversation [with Bernstein] took place. She said she referred you to the press office both times." Hunt, he said, had never received any White House assignment dealing with Senator Kennedy. "He could have been doing research on his own," said Clawson. "You know, he wrote forty-five books." Howard Hunt wrote spy novels.

Bernstein called the former administration official and was told, "The White House is absolutely paranoid about Kennedy." The President, White House chief of staff H. R. Haldeman and Colson had been "obsessed" with the idea of obtaining information that could damage a Kennedy candidacy.

Bernstein and Woodward wrote a story reporting that Hunt had been investigating Kennedy while employed at the White House. The importance of the story, the reporters were thinking, was that Hunt was no ordinary consultant to the White House, but a political operative.

Harry Rosenfeld was enthusiastic and took the story to Benjamin C. Bradlee, the *Post*'s executive editor. Bradlee came out of his glassed-in office at the far end of the newsroom and sat down in a chair near Bernstein's desk. He was holding a copy of the story in his hands and shaking his head. It was the reporters' first encounter with Bradlee on a Watergate story. The *Wall Street Journal* once described him as looking like an international jewel thief. Bradlee, 50, had been an intimate friend of President Kennedy and was sensitive to stories about the Kennedy family.

Leaning back, he said now, "You haven't got it. A librarian and a secretary say this fellow Hunt looked at a book. That's all."

Woodward told him that a responsible White House source had explicitly said Hunt was conducting such an investigation.

It was near deadline. Other reporters were watching the scene.

"How senior?" Bradlee asked.

Woodward was a little unsure about the rules on disclosing sources to the executive editor. Do you want the source? Woodward asked unsteadily.

"Just tell me if he's at the level of Assistant to the President," Bradlee said.

Woodward didn't know much about titles. He described the person's position. Bradlee was not impressed. He took out his pen and began editing the story, changing the lead paragraph to read merely that Hunt "showed a special interest" in Kennedy and the Chappaquiddick accident. He crossed out a paragraph on the White House attitude toward a Kennedy candidacy.

Rosenfeld asked Bradlee if the story could go on page one.

Bradlee said no. "Get some harder information next time" he said as he walked off.

Meanwhile, Howard Hunt had not been seen since the day he had spoken briefly on the telephone to Woodward. The FBI had assigned 150 agents to the search. On July 7, the same day the Hunt-Chappaquiddick story appeared in the *Post,* Hunt came in from the cold. Several days later, Bernstein spoke to a Washington lawyer who knew William O. Bittman, Hunt's attorney.

Bittman, the lawyer said, had received $25,000 in cash in a brown envelope to take Hunt's case. The man was disturbed. Bittman was a highly respected member of the bar, a partner in the prestigious firm of Hogan and Hartson, a former Justice Department attorney who had successfully prosecuted Jimmy Hoffa, the former president of the Teamsters' Union.

"It's good information, that's all I can tell you about it," the man said. There was one other thing. At least $100,000 in CRP's budget was earmarked for "Convention Security," he said. "The money is the key to this thing."

Bernstein called Bittman. He would not say how he had been retained.

Had he gotten $25,000 cash in an envelope? Bernstein asked.

Bittman could not discuss any aspect of his involvement in the case, he said, but to Bernstein's surprise, he did not specifically deny it.

Nevertheless, Woodward and Bernstein could not find anyone else who had even heard the story about money in a brown envelope. They spent hours and hours getting nowhere, and not just on that question.

Officials at the White House and CRP were in the business of sending reporters on wild-goose chases. There had been leaks that the Watergate break-in was the work of anti-Castro Cubans out to prove that the Democrats were receiving contributions from Cuba.*

---

* Tales of Caribbean adventure had led the *Washington Star* to report on July 7: "A right-wing group of anti-Castro Cubans financed the break-in at Democratic National Party headquarters here, according to sources close to the investigation. . . . The sources said the anti-Castro group financed the break-in at the Watergate complex as part of a continuing effort to keep Democrats under surveillance because of fear

The Watergate story had stalled, maybe even died. The reporters could not understand why. Bernstein's administration contact, the former official, was also unable to get any useful information and joked—or so Bernstein thought—that the White House had "gone underground."

Bernstein, protesting, was shipped back to Virginia politics. Woodward decided to take a vacation.

On July 22, the day Woodward left for Lake Michigan, the Long Island afternoon paper *Newsday* reported that a former White House aide named G. Gordon Liddy, who had been working as a lawyer for the campaign committee, had been fired by Mitchell in June for refusing to answer FBI questions about Watergate.

Liddy, 42, had come from the White House as CRP's general counsel on December 11, 1971, and had later been appointed finance counsel, handling legal advice on campaign finances and contributions. Like McCord, he was an ex-FBI agent, but Devan Shumway, the committee's spokesman, said Liddy's duties were unrelated to security or intelligence gathering.

At the White House, Ken Clawson acknowledged that in late 1971 Liddy had worked there on "law enforcement" problems, as a member on the staff of John D. Ehrlichman, President Nixon's principal assistant for domestic affairs.

Three days later, on his day off from Virginia's political wars, Bernstein received a call at home from Barry Sussman. Could he come in? The *New York Times* had a front-page story reporting that at least 15 calls had been placed from Barker's phones in Miami to CRP. More than half of the calls were made between March 15 and June 16 to a telephone in an office shared by Liddy and another lawyer.

Bernstein had several sources in the Bell system. He was always reluctant to use them to get information about calls because of the ethical questions involved in breaching the confidentiality of a person's

that leading candidates for the Democratic presidential nomination are pro-Castro."

The *New York Times* assigned Tad Szulc, the paper's expert on Latin America and Spain, to the story. For almost a week, he reported about anti-Castro organizations whose members had ties to some of the suspects from Miami. However, on June 26, the *Times* ran a 3000-word wrap-up under the byline of Walter Rugaber. The story gave short shrift to the possibility of an anti-Castro plot, and reviewed some unanswered questions about the possibility of White House and Nixon campaign involvement in the break-in.

telephone records. It was a problem he had never resolved in his mind. Why, as a reporter, was he entitled to have access to personal and financial records when such disclosure would outrage him if he were subjected to a similar inquiry by investigators?

Without dwelling on his problem, Bernstein called a telephone company source and asked for a list of Barker's calls. That afternoon, his contact called back and confirmed that the calls listed in the *Times* had been made. But, he added, he could not get a fuller listing because Barker's phone records had been subpoenaed by the Miami district attorney.

You mean the FBI, or the U.S. Attorney's office, don't you?

"No, the phone company in Miami said it was the local district attorney," the man said.

Why should a local district attorney be interested in the records? Before rewriting the *Times* story, Bernstein called the U.S. Attorney in Miami, who said that he had made no such request.

Bernstein then began phoning the local district attorneys in the Miami area. On the third call, he reached Richard E. Gerstein, the state's attorney for Dade County—metropolitan Miami. His office had subpoenaed the records and was trying to determine if Florida law had been violated by persons involved in the break-in. Gerstein did not know what was in the records, but his chief investigator, Martin Dardis, would. Gerstein would instruct Dardis to cooperate if the *Post* would not reveal that it was dealing with his office. That evening, Bernstein received a phone call from Dardis.

Dardis was in a hurry and didn't want to talk on the telephone. He had subpoenaed some of Barker's telephone and bank records, and Bernstein was welcome to fly down to Miami and discuss them. Bernstein asked him if he knew the origin of a sum of $89,000* that Assistant U.S. Attorney Silbert said had been deposited in and withdrawn from Barker's bank account in Miami that spring.

"It's a little more than $89,000," said Dardis.

---

* The $89,000 had first been mentioned by Silbert during a bond hearing for the Watergate suspects in early July. At the hearing, Barker's attorney had explained that $89,000 had moved through the Miami bank account as a result of a real-estate transaction in which Barker had represented a group of Chilean investors. The investors could not be identified, Barker's attorney said, for fear of political reprisals. The deal had fallen through, and Barker had returned the $89,000 to the investors, the lawyer had explained.

More like $100,000? asked Bernstein.

"A little more."

Where had the money come from?

"Mexico City," Dardis replied. "A businessman there, a lawyer."

He would not give Bernstein the lawyer's name, but said he would discuss it if Bernstein came to Florida. He could not see Bernstein for a few days, so they agreed to meet on Monday, July 31. Sussman approved the trip.

Bernstein habitually arrived at airports moments before departure time. Monday as he ran for the plane, he grabbed a *Post* and a *New York Times* from a newsstand and sprinted for the gate. He was off the ground when he read the three-column *Times* headline: "Cash in Capital Raid Traced to Mexico." Bernstein directed his ugliest thoughts to Gerstein and Dardis. The *Times* story, under Walter Rugaber's byline, carried a Mexico City dateline. Bernstein was almost certain that Rugaber had gotten the information in Miami and then flown to Mexico to file. The story cited "sources close to the investigation" without mentioning the FBI, the federal government or the Justice Department. Rugaber had traced the $89,000 in Barker's bank account to four cashier's checks* issued at the Banco Internacional to Manuel Ogarrio Daguerre, a prominent Mexico City lawyer.

Bernstein called Sussman from the Miami airport. Should he go to Mexico City and let Woodward, who was back from vacation, deal with Dardis by phone? Sussman thought Bernstein should stay in Miami at least for the day.

Half an hour later, Bernstein checked in at the Sheraton Four Ambassadors, Miami's most expensive hotel. He asked the desk clerk for Walter Rugaber's room number.

"Mr. Rugaber checked out over the weekend," the clerk said.

The office of the state's attorney of Dade County, Florida, occupies the sixth floor of the Metropolitan Dade County Justice building,

---

* On April 20, $89,000 was deposited in Barker's account in four checks issued to Ogarrio in Mexico City, endorsed by him there and deposited in Miami, the *Times* reported. The drafts were for $15,000, $18,000, $24,000 and $32,000. Barker later withdrew the money. Ogarrio's 28-year-old son had told the *Times* that neither he nor his father had seen the four Banco Internacional drafts, and that none of the signatures on the checks resembled his father's.

directly across a narrow, palm-lined lane from the county jail. Bernstein took the elevator up, stepped into the reception room and asked for Dardis. A receptionist told him that Mr. Dardis had left his apologies but had had to go out on a case. She had no idea when he would be back. Bernstein started reading magazines.

An hour passed. Uniformed policemen, shirt-sleeved detectives with snub-nosed thirty-eights tucked into their holsters, defendants and prosecutors streamed through. Many stopped to chat with the receptionist, whose name was Ruby, and to ask how "the boss"—Gerstein—was doing in his campaigning. Ten days earlier, he had announced that he was running for an unprecedented fifth term as the local prosecutor.

Bernstein asked Ruby about Gerstein. He was a Democrat, 48 years old, a World War II bomber pilot and the biggest vote-getter in the history of the state's attorney's office. "Everybody loves him," Ruby said.

Bernstein thumbed through a local afternoon paper. "Gerstein Cracks Interstate Baby-Sale Racket," read the headline. Oh boy, Bernstein muttered to himself. The Democratic primary was scheduled for September 12. He imagined a headline for September 11: "Gerstein Cracks Watergate Case."

Another half-hour passed. Bernstein asked Ruby if she could reach Dardis by car radio.

"He's not available just now, but he'll be calling in soon," she said.

Bernstein walked across the hall to the county registrar's office and asked the clerk for copies of all the subpoenas issued by Gerstein's office during July. She returned with an accordion file arranged by days of the month. Bernstein sorted through them until he found one issued to Southern Bell, the local telephone company, demanding the return of all records of long-distance calls billed to Bernard L. Barker or Barker Associates, his real-estate firm. Another had been issued to the Republic National Bank for Barker's bank records. There were similar subpoenas to other banks and to the phone company for "any and all documents and records" pertaining to the other three Watergate suspects from Miami. Dardis' name was on each. Bernstein took notes on all the subpoenas in the file which bore Dardis' name. Then he called Woodward from a pay phone.

Woodward had not reached Ogarrio and had been unable to confirm the *Times* story anywhere else. He had picked up an interesting piece of information on Capitol Hill, however. The Miami men had bought their photo equipment and had paid for some processed film at a camera shop in a Cuban neighborhood in Miami.

Bernstein sat down with the Miami yellow pages and started calling photo shops. Another hour passed. Still no Dardis. Was his secretary in? "She's with Mr. Dardis," the receptionist said. Bernstein was trying to explain his deadline problems to Ruby when Gerstein strode past with a retinue of aides. Bernstein recognized him from the afternoon paper.

Could he please see Mr. Gerstein? It was half plea, half demand. Ruby transmitted the message. Bernstein was escorted to Gerstein's outer office. His secretary said he was in conference. Half an hour later, the door opened and Gerstein invited Bernstein in. The state's attorney was about six foot five and wore an immaculate tropical-weight tattersall suit.

"Tell me where the case stands," Gerstein began. "I can't get the FBI to tell me anything."

Bernstein replied that he would welcome the opportunity to spend a leisurely afternoon discussing Watergate with Gerstein, but it was now almost five o'clock and the *Post*'s first-edition deadline was only two hours away. (Actually, it was closer to three hours away, but Bernstein was taking no more chances.) If Bernstein could get that day's story out of the way, then they could talk. He had come to Miami expecting an appointment in the early afternoon and, presumably, information that would lead to a story. Instead, as he explained to Gerstein, the story had been in that morning's *New York Times,* and its source was off God-knows-where.

"I don't know what Dardis has," Gerstein said. "I've let Martin handle the whole thing because I've been so damn busy. I know there are some checks, but I'm not sure what they show. I'll get you in with Dardis as soon as I hear from him."

Bernstein thanked Gerstein. On his way out of the office, he thought of something. Trading information with a source was a touchy business and a last resort, but he was having no success with the photo-shop tip from Woodward. So he passed it on to Gerstein.

If anything turns up, how about a call? Bernstein asked.

"Sure," said Gerstein.

Another 45 minutes passed in the reception room. Bernstein called Woodward from the pay phone. You wouldn't believe this place, he said. I wait here all day, I finally get to see Gerstein, and he wants to ask *me* questions.

After he hung up, Bernstein turned down a hallway, opened a door marked NO ADMITTANCE and spotted Dardis' name on a door. A secretary was on the phone. "Yes, Mr. Dardis," she was saying. "Okay, I'll bring it right in."

As calmly as possible, Bernstein introduced himself and explained that he had been waiting all afternoon to see Mr. Dardis.

"Mr. Dardis is in conference," she said. "I'm sorry, but you're not allowed back here. If you'll go back to the reception room, we'll call you."

Bernstein thanked her and headed back to Ruby's domain; they were locking the doors.

He hurried back past the NO ADMITTANCE sign, walked past Dardis' office, then around the corner and into Gerstein's office. Gerstein was on his way out.

Look, Bernstein said, exploding. If there was some reason why the state's attorney's office couldn't talk about what it had or couldn't let the *Post* disclose what it had, just say so. But they had been jerking his chain all day. Dardis was in his office, he had probably been there for hours and . . .

"I'll get you in right away," said Gerstein. "I don't know what's going on. I'm sorry." He seemed genuinely apologetic. Bernstein went back to the locked reception room through an inner doorway. A few moments later, Dardis walked in. He was short, with a red face and a redder nose. His ancient blue blazer was frayed at the elbows.

Immediately, he glanced at his watch. "Christ, I've got a seven o'clock appointment," he said. "I've gotta be out of here at ten of. Can't we discuss this tomorrow? Jesus!"

Bernstein tried to stay cool. If they could just go through the checks quickly, then tomorrow they could spend some time and . . .

"Okay, okay." Dardis was irritated. "Hey, what's the idea of all this *New York Times* crap with Gerstein? You trying to get me in trouble with my boss? You were supposed to deal with me, not him. Come on back to the office. Let's do this quick."

Bernstein sat down in front of Dardis' desk as the chief investigator opened a file cabinet with a combination lock, pulled out a folder and withdrew a sheaf of telephone toll slips, stapled together. He threw them across the desk to Bernstein. "You can look through these while I sort out the bank stuff."

Bernstein started scribbling furiously.

"Hey, a guy I used to work with is with the Washington field office of the Bureau," Dardis said. "You know him? Name of . . ."

Bernstein kept scribbling, shaking his head no.

Dardis took out the bank statements and peered at them like a dealer studying his hand. He started reading aloud transactions from what he said was Barker's bank account.

"Christ, I'll never get out of here by ten of," he said.

Look, Bernstein said, you got a Xerox machine?

Dardis said he couldn't risk Xeroxing the bank statements or the checks. "Somebody could trace it back to me," he said.

Okay, suggested Bernstein, you go Xerox the rest of the phone records and I'll copy the checks.

"Fine, but hurry up, for Christ's sake," said Dardis.

The Mexican checks were exactly as the *Times* had described them—each was drawn on a different American bank and endorsed on the reverse side with an illegible signature, directly above a typed notation: "Sr. Manuel Ogarrio D. 99-026-10."

But there was a fifth check, for $25,000. It was slightly wider than the others, and was dated April 10. Bernstein copied it, as he had the other four, just as if he were drawing a facsimile. It was a cashier's check, drawn on the First Bank and Trust Co. of Boca Raton, Florida, No. 131138, payable to the order of Kenneth H. Dahlberg. Dardis returned to the room as Bernstein finished copying. The $25,000 had been deposited on April 20, along with the four Mexican checks, making a total deposit of $114,000. Four days later, Barker had withdrawn $25,000. The remaining $89,000 had been withdrawn separately.

"We're still trying to find out who this Dahlberg guy is," said Dardis. "You ever hear of him?"

Bernstein said he hadn't.

Dardis handed Bernstein the Xeroxed phone records and said, "Come back at nine tomorrow and we can talk. I've gotta run."

Thanks, said Bernstein, I really appreciate the help.

Bernstein walked down the hallway, turned the corner and then charged for the elevator. It was seven o'clock. He called Woodward from a pay phone in the lobby, told him about the fifth check and dictated all the numbers and other details. Then he went back to his hotel to look for Kenneth H. Dahlberg.

There was no answer at the bank in Boca Raton. The Boca Raton police department gave him the name and phone number of a bank officer who could be reached in emergencies. The banker had never heard of Dahlberg. The check was signed by an officer of the bank whose first name was Thomas; the last name was illegible. There were two officers at the bank named Thomas, but neither remembered the transaction. Bernstein asked the second for the name and phone number of the bank's president.

The president knew Dahlberg only slightly as the owner of a winter home in Boca Raton, and as a director of a bank in Fort Lauderdale. That bank's president was James Collins.

Yes, Collins said, Dahlberg was a director of the bank. As he was describing Dahlberg's business interests, Collins paused and said, "I don't know his exact title, but he headed the Midwestern campaign for President Nixon in 1968, that was my understanding."

Bernstein asked him to please repeat the last statement.

It was nine o'clock when Bernstein called Woodward. Sussman answered the phone. Woodward was talking to Dahlberg, he said. For Chrissakes, Bernstein shouted, tell him Dahlberg was head of Nixon's Midwest campaign in '68.

"I think he knows something about it," said Sussman. "I'll call you right back."

In Washington, Woodward had checked Boca Raton information and found a listing for Dahlberg. The number was disconnected. He, too, had called the police and had been told that Dahlberg's home was in a neighborhood which had its own gates and private security guardposts. Woodward called the guard on duty there, who would say nothing except that Dahlberg stayed there only in the winter.

Woodward asked a *Post* librarian if there was anything on Dahlberg in the clipping files. There was not. Sussman asked for a check of the picture files. A few moments later, he dropped a faded newspaper picture on Woodward's desk. It was a photograph of Senator Hubert

H. Humphrey standing next to a small man with a jubilant smile. The man was identified in the caption as Kenneth H. Dahlberg.

Was Dahlberg a Democrat? The picture had no dateline. On a chance, Woodward called information for Minneapolis, the largest city in Humphrey's home state, and got a number for a Kenneth H. Dahlberg. Not sure it was the right Dahlberg, Woodward dialed. When Dahlberg came on the phone, Woodward said he had tried him at his Florida home first. Was that a winter home?

"Yes," Dahlberg said.

About the $25,000 check deposited in the bank account of one of the Watergate burglars . . .

Silence.

The check which, as you know, has your name on it. . . .

Silence.

We're writing a story about it and if you want to comment . . .

Dahlberg finally interrupted. "I don't know what happened to it. I don't have the vaguest idea about it. . . . I turn all my money over to the committee."

The Nixon re-election committee?

"Yes."

Didn't the FBI ask you how your check ended up in Barker's bank account?

"I'm a proper citizen, what I do is proper," Dahlberg responded. His voice was tense. Then he seemed to relax for a moment and asked Woodward's indulgence. "I've just been through a terrible ordeal," he explained. "My dear friend and neighbor Virginia Piper was kidnaped and held for two days."*

Woodward asked again about the check.

Dahlberg acknowledged that it was his, refused to discuss it and hung up. Minutes later, he called back. He said he had been hesitant to answer questions because he was not sure Woodward was really a *Post* reporter. He paused, seeming to invite questions.

Whose money was the $25,000? Woodward asked.

"Contributions I collected in my role as Midwest finance chairman."

---

* Mrs. Piper, a Minneapolis socialite, had just been found handcuffed to a tree in the wilderness after her husband had paid a $1 million ransom, thought to be the largest kidnap ransom in U.S. history.

Woodward was quiet. He was afraid he might be sounding too anxious.

"I know I shouldn't tell you this," Dahlberg resumed.

Tell me, Woodward thought. Tell me.

"Okay. I'll tell you. At a meeting in Washington of the [campaign] committee, I turned the check over either to the treasurer of the committee [Hugh W. Sloan, Jr.] or to Maurice Stans himself."

Woodward couldn't wait to get off the line. Stans was Nixon's chief fund-raiser and CRP's finance chairman.

It was 9:30 P.M., just an hour from deadline for the second edition. Woodward began typing:

A $25,000 cashier's check, apparently earmarked for the campaign chest of President Nixon, was deposited in April in the bank account of Bernard L. Barker, one of the five men arrested in the break-in and alleged bugging attempt at Democratic National Committee headquarters here June 17.

The last page of copy was passed to Sussman just at the deadline. Sussman set his pen and pipe down on his desk and turned to Woodward. "We've never had a story like this," he said. "Just never."

3

Now, SIX WEEKS after Mitchell's initial statement affirming CRP's dedication to the traditional American electoral process, the committee's protestations of non-involvement in Watergate were disintegrating. Woodward telephoned Clark MacGregor, Mitchell's successor as manager of the Nixon campaign, and told him what the *Post* had learned.

"I know nothing about it," MacGregor said.

"These events took place before I came aboard," he continued. "Mitchell and Stans would presumably know about this." He sounded disgusted, less with Woodward, it seemed, than with Mitchell and Stans.

Earlier that evening, George McGovern had announced that his running mate, Senator Thomas F. Eagleton of Missouri, was withdrawing from the Democratic ticket, after his medical history had been made an issue in the campaign.* More than ever, Richard Nixon's re-election seemed assured.

The next morning, Woodward talked again to Dahlberg.

"Obviously, I'm caught in the middle of something. What it is I

---

* Six days earlier, Eagleton had revealed that he had undergone electric shock treatment for mental fatigue in the 1960s. His announcement came after he had been asked about the matter by a reporter from the Knight newspapers.

don't know," Dahlberg said. He was now certain that he had given the $25,000 check to Maurice Stans personally, on April 11.

Stans' secretary told Woodward that there would be no immediate comment. She said Stans was "agonized over the confusing circumstances" which made it impossible for him to explain what had actually happened and thus reaffirm his own integrity.

At the White House, Ron Ziegler said the President continued to have full confidence in Stans, and referred inquiries about the $25,000 to CRP. The committee's statement, issued over Clark MacGregor's name, said that further comment would not be "proper" because the matter was under investigation.

Woodward telephoned Philip S. Hughes, director of the new Federal Elections Division of the General Accounting Office—the federal auditing agency.

Unlike the Justice Department and the FBI, which are part of the Executive Branch and report to the President, the GAO is the investigative arm of Congress and therefore operates independently of the Executive. Hughes said that the story in that day's *Post* had revealed "for the first time [that] the bugging incident was related to the campaign finance law. . . . There's nothing in Maury's [Stans] reports showing anything like that Dahlberg check."

Hughes, who had worked at the Bureau of the Budget during the Eisenhower administration when Stans was its director, added: "We're going to conduct a full audit and find out what's up." The audit would be the first undertaken under the Federal Campaign Expenditures Act, which had gone into effect on April 7, establishing tighter control of campaign donations and requiring that all expenditures be reported.

A GAO investigator called Woodward that afternoon for additional information on the $25,000 check. Woodward told him that he and Bernstein had written everything they knew about it.

Before writing a follow-up on the GAO audit, Woodward tried to reach Hugh Sloan, the CRP treasurer. But he no longer worked for the re-election committee. A reporter on the city staff drove to Sloan's home in suburban Virginia: Sloan was young, about 30, polite, and refused to discuss Watergate, except to say that he had cooperated with the FBI and the grand jury.

Van Shumway told Woodward that Sloan had resigned "for personal reasons" unrelated to Watergate. "He was getting an ulcer and his wife is pregnant."

Woodward called the GAO investigator every day to learn how the audit was progressing.

"Hundreds of thousands of dollars in unaccounted cash," the GAO man said one day. "A slush fund of cash," he said the next. "A rat's nest behind the surface efficiency of computerized financial reporting," the third. With each day that Woodward did not write a story, the investigator felt freer to talk to him. Fitting these remarks together with another investigator's, Woodward was becoming convinced that the cash "slush fund" was the same "convention security money" Bernstein had heard about early in July. The fund, which totaled at least $100,000, included the money from Barker's bank account obtained from cashing Dahlberg's check, according to the investigator.

Bernstein made one of his regular calls to the former administration official and was told: "There was a large fund over which Gordon Liddy had supervision. . . . Yeah, it's the same one. The present plan is for Liddy to take the fall for everyone. The story that the re-election committee will put out has nothing to do with the truth. They'll say they were deeply concerned for the security of their convention and that they had a big fund to be sure they were secure from interference. That's the word that will trickle out. Mitchell said to get the story out. Too many guys knew about the fund."

The reporters waited. Several days later, on August 16, Clark Mac-Gregor met with a select group of White House reporters and made the first public attempt to shift the responsibility to Liddy. While serving as CRP's finance counsel, MacGregor said, Liddy had spent campaign funds on his own initiative "for the purpose of determining what to do if the crazies made an attack on the President" at the Republican convention.

Later that afternoon on the telephone, MacGregor was angered by Woodward's attempt to get a fuller explanation. "I have no idea why the departed Gordon Liddy wanted cash," MacGregor shouted. "It's impossible for me to tell. . . . I never met Liddy. . . . I don't know what's going on."

Woodward suggested that MacGregor was implying that he was out of touch with the campaign he was supposed to be running.

"If you print that, our relationship is terminated," MacGregor said, and added: "I'm not threatening you. I'm just telling you what will happen." MacGregor was one of the few Nixon administration officials who had a reputation for being friendly with the press.

On August 22, the second day of the Republican convention in Miami, the *Post*'s front page reported the preliminary findings of the GAO's audit. Based primarily on Woodward's conversations with the investigators, the story said the GAO had determined that CRP had mishandled more than $500,000 in campaign funds—including at least $100,000 maintained in an apparently illegal "security fund."

Paul E. Barrick, Hugh Sloan's successor as treasurer, responded on behalf of CRP: "*Washington Post* stories of allegations to the effect that the . . . committee has incorrectly reported or failed to report contributions and expenditures in accordance with law are entirely wrong."

The rawest nerve touched by the GAO's preliminary findings, however, was not that at least half a million dollars had been mishandled but the revelation of a "security fund" at the committee. For more than five weeks, Van Shumway, a former wire-service reporter who had come to the committee from the White House staff, had been insisting that no such fund existed. He had told Bernstein in July, "One thing I will never do is knowingly tell you something that is untrue." Now Shumway said he had since learned that there was such a fund. "I'm afraid some people here aren't telling me the truth," he added.

The GAO's report was to be released publicly the same day. An hour before it was due to go out, the GAO sent a message to the news media that there would be a delay.

Woodward called the GAO investigator. What had happened?

"You won't believe it," the investigator said. "Stans called Hughes and asked him to come down to Miami at the convention to get more material. . . . [He] of course had to go. They just didn't want that report coming out today. I don't blame them."

That evening in Miami, Richard Nixon was to be nominated by the

Republican Party for a second term as President of the United States.

Also the same day, August 22, United States District Court Judge Charles R. Richey, who was hearing the Democrats' $1 million civil suit, reversed his earlier ruling and declared that all pre-trial testimony in the case would be kept sealed and withheld from the public until after completion of the proceedings in the case. This meant that sworn statements by Mitchell, Stans and others would not be made public before the election. What was extraordinary was that Richey had reversed his own decision in the absence of any motion by the CRP lawyers. He had, he said from the bench, acted out of concern for the constitutional rights of those under investigation.

Several hours after his ruling, Judge Richey telephoned Bernstein at the *Post*. "I just wanted you to understand the basis for my decision." He explained to Bernstein the dangers of releasing testimony in the civil suit before a criminal trial.

Then Richey raised an issue that had not entered Bernstein's head, the possibility that the Judge had been approached by someone who had urged a favorable ruling for CRP: "I want it to be very clear that I haven't discussed this case outside the courtroom with anyone, and that political considerations played no part whatsoever."

Bernstein was dumbstruck. He had never met Judge Richey. The call came out of the blue.

Until the August 1 story about the Dahlberg check, the working relationship between Bernstein and Woodward was more competitive than anything else. Each had worried that the other might walk off with the remainder of the story by himself. If one had gone chasing after a lead at night or on a weekend, the other felt compelled to do the same. The August 1 story had carried their joint byline; the day afterward, Woodward asked Sussman if Bernstein's name could appear with his on the follow-up story—though Bernstein was still in Miami and had not worked on it. From then on, any Watergate story would carry both names. Their colleagues melded the two into one and gleefully named their byline Woodstein.

Gradually, Bernstein's and Woodward's mutual distrust and suspicions diminished. They realized the advantages of working together, particularly because their temperaments were so dissimilar. The breadth of the story, the inherent risks and the need for caution all argued for at least two reporters working on it. By dividing the work and pooling their information, they increased their contacts.

Each kept a separate master list of telephone numbers. The numbers were called at least twice a week. (Just the fact that a certain source wouldn't come to the phone or return calls often signaled something important.) Eventually, the combined total of names on their lists swelled to several hundred, yet fewer than 50 were duplicated. Inevitably, they crossed each other's tracks. "Don't you guys work together?" a lawyer once asked Woodward. "I just this minute hung up on Carl." On another occasion, a White House aide said, "We've been trying to figure out why some of us get calls from Bernstein and others seem to be on Woodward's list." There was no reason. The reporters wanted to avoid tripping over each other's work as much as possible. In general, they preferred to keep their contacts divided because confidential sources would feel more comfortable that way: more time could be invested in developing a personal relationship.

To those who sat nearby in the newsroom, it was obvious that Woodstein was not always a smoothly operating piece of journalistic machinery. The two fought, often openly. Sometimes they battled for fifteen minutes over a single word or sentence. Nuances were critically important; the emphasis had to be just right. The search for the journalistic mean was frequently conducted at full volume, and it was not uncommon to see one stalk away from the other's desk. Sooner or later, however (usually later), the story was hammered out.

Each developed his own filing system; oddly, it was Bernstein, by far the less organized of the two, who kept records neatly arranged in manila folders labeled with the names of virtually everyone they encountered. Subject files were kept as well. Woodward's record-keeping was more informal, but they both adhered to one inviolate rule: they threw nothing out and kept all their notes and the early drafts of stories. Soon they had filled four filing cabinets.

Usually, Woodward, the faster writer, would do a first draft, then Bernstein would rewrite. Often, Bernstein would have time to rewrite only the first half of a story, leaving Woodward's second half hanging like a shirttail. The process often consumed most of the night.

As the number of leads and components in the Watergate story increased, the reporters became almost possessed by it. And, tentatively at first, they became friends. Neither had many demands on his time. Woodward was divorced; Bernstein separated. They often remained in the newsroom until late at night, making checks, reading clippings, outlining their next steps, trading theories. Sometimes they were joined by Barry Sussman, who ultimately was detached from his regular duties as city editor and given prime responsibility for directing the *Post*'s Watergate coverage.

Sussman was 38, gentle in his manner, slightly overweight, curly-haired, scholarly in demeanor. He had been a desk man on a small-town newspaper near the Virginia-Tennessee line, a speed-reading instructor at New York University, a society editor, and then suburban editor for the *Post*—a vagabond journalist who had left Brooklyn odd-jobbing his way to Washington.

Sussman had the ability to seize facts and lock them in his memory, where they remained poised for instant recall. More than any other editor at the *Post,* or Bernstein and Woodward, Sussman became a walking compendium of Watergate knowledge, a reference source to be summoned when even the library failed. On deadline, he would pump these facts into a story in a constant infusion, working up a body of significant information to support what otherwise seemed like the weakest of revelations. In Sussman's mind, everything fitted. Watergate was a puzzle and he was a collector of the pieces.

At heart, Sussman was a theoretician. In another age, he might have been a Talmudic scholar. He had cultivated a Socratic method, zinging question after question at the reporters: Who moved over from Commerce to CRP with Stans? What about Mitchell's secretary? Why won't anybody say when Liddy went to the White House or who worked with him there? Mitchell and Stans both ran the budget committee, right? What does that tell you? Then Sussman would puff on his pipe, a satisfied grin on his face.

Sussman's passions are history and polling. His hero is Jefferson, but the reporters always imagined that George Gallup ran a close second. Almost every time there had been a big demonstration in town during the height of the anti-war movement, Sussman had sent out teams of reporters to ask demonstrators their age, politics, home towns and how many previous demonstrations they had been in. Each time, he came up with the same conclusion almost every reporter on the street had already reached—the anti-war movement had become more broad-based and less radical. Since the break-in at Democratic headquarters, Sussman had been studying the Teapot Dome scandal of the Harding administration. He had a theory about Watergate that Bernstein and Woodward did not quite understand—it had to do with historic inevitability, post-war American ethics, merchandising and Richard Nixon.

Sussman and the other editors at the *Post* were by temperament informal. The reporters were never formally assigned to work on Watergate full time. They sensed that as long as the stories continued to come, there would be no problem. If they failed to produce, anything might happen in the competitive atmosphere of the *Post* newsroom. In the weeks after the story on the Dahlberg check, Rosenfeld became noticeably nervous as Simons and Bradlee showed an increasing interest in the Watergate affair. The invariable question, asked only half-mockingly of reporters by editors at the *Post* (and then up the hierarchal line of editors) was "What have you done for me today?" Yesterday was for the history books, not newspapers.

That had been the working ethic of the *Post* since Ben Bradlee took command in 1965, first as managing editor and, in 1967, as executive editor. Bradlee had been recruited with the idea that the *New York Times* need not exercise absolute preeminence in American journalism.

That vision had suffered a setback in 1971 when the *Times* published the Pentagon Papers. Though the *Post* was the second news organization to obtain a copy of the secret study of the Vietnam war, Bradlee noted that "there was blood on every word" of the *Times'* initial stories. Bradlee could convey his opinions with a single disgusted glance at an indolent reporter or editor.

Since his return from Miami, Bernstein had become obsessed with the $89,000 in Mexican checks that had passed through Bernard Barker's bank account. Why Mexico? According to the GAO investigator, Maurice Stans had said the money had come initially from Texas. But no one at the GAO had been able to understand why $89,000 in campaign contributions were routed through Mexico.

In mid-August, Bernstein had begun calling all the employees of the Texas Committee for the Re-election of the President. A secretary at the committee's offices in Houston said that the FBI had been there to interview Emmett Moore, the committee treasurer.

"They questioned me about how money was transmitted to Mexico," Moore said. "They said there had been allegations to that effect—that money was transferred to and from Mexico."

Moore immediately sought to make clear to Bernstein that the FBI agents were not interested in his own actions, but in those of the Texas committee's chairman, Robert H. Allen, who was also president of the Gulf Resources and Chemical Co. of Houston. The agents had expressed particular interest in Allen's relationship with a Mexico City lawyer, Manuel Ogarrio Daguerre, who represented Gulf Resources' interests in Mexico.

The Mexican connection. What did it mean?

Moore, who said he had been as unnerved by the FBI's visit as by Bernstein's call, knew nothing of the reasons for moving the money across the border.

Bernstein began leaving messages for Robert Allen at his home and office. They were not answered. Finally, on the morning that Maurice Stans summoned the GAO's auditor to Miami, Bernstein got up at 6:00 A.M.—5:00 A.M. in Texas—and called Allen at his Houston home. Allen sleepily declined to discuss the matter, "because it's before the grand jury."

Using his primitive high-school Spanish, Bernstein intensified his telephone search for Ogarrio and for any information on the elusive Mexican lawyer. Gradually, the enterprise became the object of good-natured office ridicule. Bernstein was unable to construct anything other than disjointed school-book phrases in the present tense. Ken Ringle, a reporter on the Virginia staff who sat next to Bernstein, would shout, "Bernstein's talking Spanish again," and reporters and editors would walk over to offer appropriate commentary. The calls went to bankers, relatives of Ogarrio, his former law partners, his clients, Mexican banking commissioners, the police, law schools. *Nada.* The standing office joke had it that Bernstein heard the whole Watergate story and didn't understand it.

Not surprisingly, the Nixon campaign's Mexican connection was uncovered in English.

On August 24, Bernstein called Martin Dardis in Miami. The chief investigator said he was coming up with pretty good information on the Mexican checks, really weird stuff that he didn't want to talk about on the telephone. Dardis assured Bernstein that it would be worth his while to fly down to Miami again. Bernstein caught the first flight out of Washington Friday, August 25, and again spent most of the day with Ruby. Seething, he left to search again for the photo shop where the burglars from Miami supposedly had bought their film.

On the freeway, a billboard caught his eye. It pictured a handsome, thirtyish, blond man who looked like a model in a cigarette ad. "Vote for Neal Sonnett, State's Attorney, Dade County," it said. Bernstein's anger at the chief investigator turned to rage.

A couple of weeks before, Dardis had called him for a favor. "It's on a case we're working, not related to Watergate," he had told Bernstein. "You must have some friends at the Pentagon or somewhere in the military. If you could get somebody to look up the records for you . . ." Then he asked for any possible derogatory information—arrests, mental illness, history of homosexuality—in the file of a Neal Sonnett.

A Pentagon colonel had agreed to try to get Sonnett's military information for Bernstein, and just before the Republican convention Bernstein had called Dardis to tell him so. Fortunately, Dardis had said he didn't need it any more.

Bernstein called Dardis before six o'clock the next morning, August 26. Gerstein's campaign schedule, he knew, began at 7:30. Dardis picked up the phone on the first ring. "God damn it, Carl, let's get together later, I gotta run. It can wait a few hours."

Bernstein mentioned what nice posters Neal Sonnett had all over town.

"I guess I shouldn't have asked you to do that," Dardis said sheepishly.

Bernstein asked him what he had learned about the Mexican checks.

"It's called 'laundering,'" Dardis began. "You set up a money chain that makes it impossible to trace the source. The Mafia does it all the time. So does Nixon, or at least that's what this guy who's the lawyer for Robert Allen says. This guy says Stans set up the whole thing. It was Stans' idea. He says they were doing it elsewhere too, that Stans didn't want any way they could trace where the money was coming from."

Dardis said he had learned the whole story from Richard Haynes, a Texas lawyer who represented Allen. Haynes had outlined the Mexican laundry operation to Dardis this way:

Shortly before April 7, the effective date of the new campaign finance law, and the last day anonymous contributions could be legally accepted, Stans had gone on a final fund-raising swing across the Southwest. If Democrats were reluctant to contribute to the campaign of a Republican presidential candidate, Stans assured them that their anonymity could be absolutely ensured, if necessary by moving their contributions through a Mexican middleman whose bank records were not subject to subpoena by U.S. investigators. The protection would also allow CRP to receive donations from corporations, which were forbidden by campaign laws to contribute to political candidates; from business executives and labor leaders having difficulties with government regulatory agencies; and from special-interest groups and such underground sources of income as the big Las Vegas gambling casinos and mob-dominated unions. To guarantee anonymity, the "gifts," whether checks, security notes or stock certificates, would be taken across the border to Mexico, converted to cash in Mexico City through deposit in a bank account established by a Mexican national with no known ties to the Nixon campaign, and only then sent on to Washington. The only record would be jealously guarded in Washington by Stans, kept simply to make sure the contributor would not be forgotten in his time of need.

From Houston, Haynes confirmed the operation to Bernstein. An operator familiar with the rough-and-tumble of Texas politics and corporate intrigues, Haynes spoke in the breezy, swashbuckling style that had earned him the nickname "Racehorse" in courthouses from Dallas to Austin.

"Shit, Stans has been running this operation for years with Nixon," he said. "Nothing really wrong with it. That's how you give your tithe."

Robert Allen, the head of the Nixon campaign organization in Texas, was merely the conduit for the funds moving to Mexico, including the $89,000 that had gone into Barker's bank account, Haynes said. Ogarrio was the money-changer, converting the checks and notes given him by Allen into American dollars, both in cash and in dollar drafts drawn on his account at the Banco Internacional.

Haynes estimated that $750,000 raised by Stans and his two principal fund-raisers in Texas had moved through Mexico in the final weeks of the pre-April 7 campaign.

"Maury came through here like a goddamned train," said Haynes, "he was really ballin' the jack. He'd say to the Democrats, the big money men who'd never gone for a Republican before, 'You know we got this crazy man Ruckelshaus* back East who'd just as soon close your factory as let the smokestack belch. He's a hard man to control and he's not the only one like that in Washington. People need a place to go, to cut through the red tape when you've got a guy like that on the loose. Now, don't misunderstand me; we're not making any promises, all we can do is make ourselves accessible. . . .'"

But the message was indelible, said Haynes. "Maury's a right high-type fellow; he would never actually threaten any of those guys. Then he'd do his Mexican hat dance, tell them there'd be no danger of the Democrats or their company's competitors finding out about the contributing, it would all get lost in Mexico. . . . If a guy pleaded broke, Maury would get him to turn over stock in his company or some other stock. He was talking 10 percent, saying it was worth 10 percent of some big businessman's income to keep Richard Nixon in Washington and be able to stay in touch."

That was Saturday, August 26, three days after the President had been renominated. In Washington, Woodward had just received the GAO report, finally released for Sunday's papers. It listed 11 "apparent and possible violations" of the new law and referred the matter to the Justice Department for possible prosecution. It also stated that Stans maintained a secret slush fund of cash in his office totaling at least $350,000. At one time the fund included the cash that had come from the $25,000 Dahlberg check and the four Mexican checks totaling $89,000.

Woodward wrote the top portion of a story from the GAO report. From Miami, Bernstein dictated an account of the Mexican laundry and Haynes' estimate that not $89,000 but $750,000 had been washed across the border.

After several lengthy conversations, Bernstein and Woodward decided not to refer to Stans' other fund-raising tactics that Haynes had described. Both were wary of the lawyer's language. Haynes' description of the "Stans shakedown cruise," as he called it, was filed for

---

* William D. Ruckelshaus, then head of the Environmental Protection Agency.

further investigation. The GAO investigator confirmed the substance of the Mexican laundry operation to Woodward.

Three days later, Tuesday, August 29, the President scheduled a press conference at his oceanside home in San Clemente, California. Reporters waited under large palm and eucalyptus trees on a sunny morning.

"With regard to the matter of the handling of campaign funds," the President said, "we have a new law here in which technical violations have occurred and are occurring, apparently on both sides."

What are the Democrats' violations? a reporter asked.

"I think that will come out in the balance of this week. I will let the political people talk about that, but I understand that there have been [violations] on both sides," Nixon remarked calmly.

Stans, the President said, is "an honest man and one who is very meticulous." In fact, Stans was investigating the matter, the President said, "very, very thoroughly, because he doesn't want any evidence at all to be outstanding, indicating that we have not complied with the law."

The President rejected suggestions that a special prosecutor, independent of the Justice Department, be appointed, and disclosed that his counsel, John W. Dean III, had conducted a Watergate investigation: "I can say categorically that his investigation indicates that no one on the White House staff, no one in this administration, presently employed, was involved in this very bizarre incident. What really hurts in matters of this sort is not the fact that they occur, because overzealous people in campaigns do things that are wrong. What really hurts is if you try to cover it up."*

Woodward, in Washington, wrote a story from the transcript of the press conference, and listed some of the people under investigation who, as the President had been so careful to point out, were not "presently employed" in the administration: Hunt, Liddy, Stans, Sloan and Mitchell.

Bernstein was still in Florida tracking the four Miami men. That morning, he had spoken with Enrique Valledor, president of the

* John Osborne, the highly respected Nixon watcher for the *New Republic*, wrote, a week later: "The thing I'll always remember about Mr. Nixon's first 'political press conference' of 1972 was his handling of the funds and bugging matter and our failure to handle him as a vulnerable candidate should be handled. It was a lesson in the mesmerizing power of the presidency."

Florida Association of Realtors, Barker's former boss. Barker was worried about losing his real-estate license and had come to see him after being released on bond. Valledor related part of their conversation: "I said, 'What about this million-dollar [Democrats'] suit? Aren't you worried?' "

"I'm not worrying. They're paying for my attorneys," Barker replied.

"Who are *they?*"

"I can't tell you."

The incident was included in the story on the President's press conference. It was the first public hint of direct money payments to the conspirators.

Since June 17, CRP had seemed inviolate, as impenetrable as a super-secret national-security bureaucracy. Visitors were met at the door by a uniformed guard, cleared for access by press or security staffs, escorted to their appointments and led back out. The committee's telephone roster of campaign officials—a single sheet of paper with more than 100 names—was considered a classified document. A *Washington Post* researcher who obtained a copy from a friend at the committee was told, "You realize, I'll lose my job if they find out."

The managers of the committee's various divisions, the second echelon generally unknown to press and public alike, were conspicuous on the roster because they had private secretaries listed below their names. Because the floor numbers were listed next to the names and phone extensions of committee personnel, it was possible to calculate roughly who worked in proximity to whom. And by transposing telephone extensions from the roster and listing them in sequence, it was even possible to determine who worked *for* whom.

Studying the roster became a devotional exercise not unlike reading tea leaves. None of the key people would talk when reached by telephone. Divining names from the list, Bernstein and Woodward, in mid-August, began visiting CRP people at their homes in the evenings. The first-edition deadline was 7:45 P.M., and each night they would set out soon afterward, sometimes separately, sometimes together in Woodward's 1970 Karmann Ghia. When traveling alone, Bernstein used a company car or rode his bicycle.

The first person on whose door Bernstein knocked pleaded with him to leave "before they see you." The employee was literally trembling. "Please leave me alone. I know you're only trying to do your job, but you don't realize the pressure we're under." Bernstein tried to get a conversation going, but was told, "I hope you understand I'm not being rude; please go," as the door closed. Another said, "I want to help," and burst into tears. "God, it's all so awful," she said, as the reporter was shown to the door.

The nighttime visits were fishing expeditions. There was, however, one constant lead that was pursued on all the visits: It concerned Sally Harmony, Gordon Liddy's secretary at CRP. Mrs. Harmony had apparently not told everything she knew to the FBI and the grand jury. Bernstein had first heard this in late August from a reporter on another newspaper. He had jotted down the tip on the back of a telephone message slip and filed it away in the mountain of papers, trash, books and cups of stale coffee that covered his desk. ". . . lied to protect Jeb Magruder . . . dep. campaign mgr.," he had written.

A Justice Department attorney had confirmed that the Watergate prosecutors were suspicious of Mrs. Harmony's testimony, but said they lacked evidence to charge her with perjury. Her lack of candor seemed common knowledge at campaign headquarters. But either no one knew or no one was willing to say what she had lied about, beyond vague references to "protecting others." Gradually, a pattern started to emerge about the bugging affair from the fragments of information they picked up on their nighttime visits. Several committee employees spoke of wholesale destruction of records that took place in the days immediately after the Watergate break-in, although they said they had heard it secondhand and knew no specifics.

Persons in critical positions who might know details of the bugging operation, particularly secretaries, seemed not to have been interviewed by the FBI. The FBI had conducted all interviews of campaign personnel at the committee's headquarters, instead of at employees' homes, where they might feel more free to speak out; the interviews were always held in the presence of a lawyer for the committee, or Robert C. Mardian, the political coordinator of the committee and former Assistant Attorney General in charge of the Justice Department's Internal Security Division. A few persons said Mardian and others had told them not to volunteer any information to the agents unless asked a specific question they could not evade—especially regarding committee finances.

What information the reporters were getting at this point came in bits and pieces, almost always from people who did not want to discuss the matter. Their fright, more than anything else, was persuading Woodward and Bernstein that the stakes were higher than they had originally perceived. Indeed, they too were unsettled by the reactions to their visits.

The trick was getting inside someone's apartment or house. There, a conversation could be pursued, consciences could be appealed to, the reporters could try to establish themselves as human beings. They always identified themselves immediately as reporters for the *Washington Post,* but the approach that seemed to work best was less than straightforward: A friend at the committee told us that you were disturbed by some of the things you saw going on there, that you would be a good person to talk to . . . that you were absolutely straight and honest and didn't know quite what to do; we understand the problem—you believe in the President and don't want to do anything that would seem disloyal.

Woodward could say that he was a registered Republican; Bernstein could argue a sincere antipathy for the politics of both parties.

Sometimes it worked. People wanted to know who at the committee had given the reporters their names. Which was fine, because Woodward and Bernstein then could explain the necessity of protecting confidential sources, reassuring whomever they were talking to that he or she would be similarly shielded. Once inside, notebooks were never used.

Then, working around the edges: . . . Has the FBI talked with you? ("I can't understand it; they never asked.") Have things gotten any better since John Mitchell left? ("Left? He might have quit, but he's in there three times a week telling Fred LaRue and Bob Mardian what to do.") Little pieces: "Jeb [Magruder] acts really scared, like the roof is going to fall down on him tomorrow." . . . "Somebody told me that MacGregor wanted to write a report and tell everything there was to know, but the White House said no." . . . "The prosecutors kept asking me if I knew about any other buggings, maybe McGovern headquarters." . . . "*Top copy,* that's the phrase they kept asking. Had I ever heard anything about the top copy [of wiretap logs] going to the White House?" . . . "The FBI wanted to know if I saw anybody using the shredder." . . . "I heard from somebody in finance that if they ever got a look at the books it would be all over, so they burned 'em." . . . "Sally [Harmony] said Gordon [Liddy] would never talk and neither would she, that she had a bad memory." . . . "From what I hear, they were spying on everybody, following them around, the whole bit.". . . "Please don't ever call me on the telephone—God, especially not at work, but not here either. Nobody knows what they'll do. They are desperate."

From one incident in early September, the reporters were made aware that the fears were not groundless.

They had picked up a copy of the committee's latest expenditure report, which listed the names of all salaried employees. Bernstein noticed the name of someone he had once met and called her for lunch. He suggested half a dozen places where they could meet and not be seen, but she insisted on a sandwich shop where dozens of Nixon campaign workers were at the tables. When they sat down, she explained: "I'm being followed. It's open here and doesn't look like I'm hiding anything. People won't talk on the phones; it's terrible."

Bernstein asked her to be calm. He thought she was overdramatizing.

"I wish I was," she said. "They know everything at the committee. They know that the indictments will be down in a week and that there will only be seven. Once, another person went back to the DA because the FBI didn't ask her the right questions. That night her boss knew about it. I always had one institution I believed in—the FBI. No more.

"I've done my duty as a good citizen. I went back to the DA, too. But I'm a fatalist now. It'll never come out, the whole truth. You'll never get the truth. You can't get it by reporters talking to just the good people. They know you've been out talking to people at night. Somebody from the press office came up to our office today and said, 'I sure wish I know who in this committee had a link to Carl Bernstein and Bob Woodward.'

"The FBI never even asked me if I was at the committee over the weekend of the break-in. I was there almost the whole time. Odle didn't tell them everything he knew. He kept removing records. I don't know if he destroyed them or not. He would tell everybody to get out of the room and then close the door. Then he'd leave with the records.

"Everything else I know is hearsay," she said. "I've done my duty, I told the DA. . . . The whole thing is being very well covered up and nobody will ever know what happened."

The Prince George's County Police Department could do a better job than the FBI, and she was through with presidential politics forever. She asked Bernstein to walk back to the office with her, to avoid any appearance of furtiveness. While they were waiting to cross the street at 17th Street and Pennsylvania Avenue, Maurice Stans pulled up to 1701, across the avenue, in his limousine.

"He was an honest man before all this started," she said. "Now he's lying too."

Bernstein studied Stans from across the street as the Secretary entered the building.

"Okay," she said, "I'll tell you, but it won't do any good. And don't ever call me, or come to see me or ask any questions about how I know. LaRue, Porter and Magruder. They all knew about the bugging, or at least lied to the grand jury about what they knew. And Mitchell. But Mitchell is mostly speculation. Take my word on the other three. I know."

Frederick LaRue, Herbert L. Porter and Jeb Stuart Magruder had all left the White House staff to join CRP.

About five o'clock, the woman telephoned Bernstein. She sounded almost hysterical. "I'm in a phone booth. When I got back from lunch, I got called into somebody's office and confronted with the fact that I had been seen talking to a *Post* reporter. They wanted to know everything. It was high up; that's all you have to know. I told you they were following me. Please don't call me again or come to see me."

Later that night, Bernstein went to her apartment and knocked on the door.

"Go away," she said, and Bernstein and Woodward went off to bang on other doors.

About the same time, Clark MacGregor called the *Post*'s executive editor, Ben Bradlee, to complain about the visits. Bradlee did not tell the reporters about it until months later, but he recalled that Mac-Gregor had asked for an appointment with him and Katharine Graham, the publisher of the *Post*. The appointment was made for the next day, but was canceled by MacGregor. "He wanted to talk about your excesses. There were five women in CRP, he said, who had been harassed by you two. And I said, 'That doesn't sound like my boys at all.' And he gave me the names. . . . I said, 'Well, how did they harass them?' and MacGregor said, 'They knocked on the doors of their apartments late at night and they telephoned from the lobby.' And I said, 'That's the nicest thing I've heard about either one of them in years.' "

On the evening of September 14, Bernstein knocked at the front door of a small tract house in the Washington suburbs. Ever since he had lunched with the woman from CRP, he had had a feeling that the owner of this house was the person who had gone back to the prosecutors. He had asked around. "She knows a lot," he was told. The woman worked for Maurice Stans.

A woman opened the door and let Bernstein in. "You don't want me, you want my sister," she said. Her sister came into the room. He had expected a woman in her fifties, probably gray; it was his image of a bookkeeper, which is what she was. But she was much younger.

"Oh, my God," the Bookkeeper said, "you're from the *Washington Post*. You'll have to go, I'm sorry."

Bernstein started figuring ways to hold his ground. The sister was smoking and he noticed a pack of cigarettes on the dinette table; he asked for one. "I'll get it," he said as the sister moved to get the pack, "don't bother." That got him 10 feet into the house. He bluffed, telling the Bookkeeper that he understood her being afraid; there were a lot of people like her at the committee who wanted to tell the truth, but some people didn't want to listen. He knew that certain people had gone back to the FBI and the prosecutors to give more information. . . . He hesitated.

"Where do you reporters get your information anyhow?" she asked. "That's what nobody at the committee can figure out."

Bernstein asked if he could sit down and finish his cigarette.

"Yes, but then you'll have to go, I really have nothing to say." She was drinking coffee, and her sister asked if Bernstein would like some. The Bookkeeper winced, but it was too late. Bernstein started sipping, slowly.

She was curious. "Somebody is certainly giving you good information if you knew I went back to the prosecutors." Then she rattled off a few names that Bernstein tried to keep in his head; if she was mentioning them as possible sources, they must be people who either had some information or were unhappy with the way things were going down at the committee.

He went into a monologue about all the fine people he and Woodward had met who wanted to help but didn't have hard information, only what they had picked up third and fourth hand.

"You guys keep digging," she said. "You've really struck close to home."

How did she know?

"I ran the totals for the people. I have an adding machine and a deft hand." The way she said it was almost mocking, as if she knew she had been watching *Naked City* too much. She shook her head and laughed at herself. "Sometimes I don't know whether to laugh or cry. I'm an accountant. I'm apolitical. I didn't do anything wrong. But in some way, something is rotten in Denmark and I'm part of it." Then she started guessing sources again and Bernstein tried to keep the names straight in his head. She was glancing at his coffee cup. He tried not to look tense, and played with her dog. She seemed to want to talk about what she knew. But to the *Washington Post,* the enemy? Bernstein had the feeling he was either going out the door any minute or staying till she had told the whole story.

"My only loyalties are to Maurice Stans, the President's re-election and the truth," she said.

Bernstein had heard that Stans' wife was sick and in the hospital. He asked how Mrs. Stans was, and then inquired if the Secretary was going to end up a fall guy for John Mitchell.

"If you could get John Mitchell, it would be beautiful. But I just don't have any real evidence that would stand up in court that he knew. Maybe his guys got carried away, the men close to him."

What guys?

Her hands were shaking. She looked at her sister, who shrugged her shoulders noncommittally. Bernstein thought he had an ally there. The sister got up to get another cup of coffee. He took a gulp and handed his cup to her. She refilled it. Bernstein decided to take a chance. He removed a notebook and pencil from his inner breast pocket. The Bookkeeper stared at him. She was not going to say anything that they probably didn't know already, Bernstein told her, and absolutely nothing would go into the paper that couldn't be verified elsewhere.

"There are a lot of things that are wrong and a lot of things that are bad at the committee," the Bookkeeper said. "I was called by the grand jury very early, but nobody knew what questions to ask. People had already lied to them."

Sally Harmony?

"She and I have not discussed it. . . . But Sally—and others— lied." The Bookkeeper had worked for Hugh Sloan, and after he quit, she was promoted to work for Stans. "There were a few of us they were worried about who got promotions.

"Sloan is the sacrificial lamb. His wife was going to leave him if he didn't stand up and do what was right. He left because he saw it and didn't want any part of it. We didn't know before June 17, but we put two and two together on June 19 and figured it out."

She changed the subject. A few days earlier, the *Post* had reported that there was another participant in the bugging whose identity had not been disclosed; and that he had been granted immunity from prosecution and was talking.

The Bookkeeper started to speculate out loud: "Baldwin? He wasn't even on the payroll."

She tried two other names.

Bernstein shook his head. (He had no idea who it was.)

"It has to be one of those three," she said. "I'm pretty sure it's Baldwin."

Bernstein asked if she knew who had received transcripts of wiretapped conversations.

"I don't know anything about how the operational end of the espionage worked," she said. "I just know who got the money and who approved the allocations. And from what I can see, you've got all the names. Track a little upstairs and out of the finance committee," she advised. "It was the political people. . . . It won't make any difference. You've got to get the law on your side if anything is going to be done. The indictments are going to get the seven and that's it. The power of the politicians is too strong."

How many people were paid?

"Thirteen or fourteen from the fund, but only six or seven are involved. The grand jury didn't even ask if there were any payments that were extra-legal."

Did Stans know who received such payments?

"He knew less than I knew. My loyalty is to Hugh and Mr. Stans," she stressed. "For some reason, Mr. Stans feels we have to take the heat for a while." She had talked to Sloan that morning and he had mentioned a story in the *New York Daily News* that gave the impression that Sloan knew of the bugging operation. "I told him he should sue, but all he said was 'I want out.' The grand jury didn't ask him the right questions either, I guess."

Who knew all the answers to the right questions?

"Liddy and Sally Harmony. She has more information than I have. But she has never talked to me about what she knows. I urged her time and time again to do what's right. Sally got promoted, too." She was now working for Robert Odle.

Was Odle involved?

"Certainly not in knowing anything about the bugging. He's a glorified office boy, Magruder's runner. Jeb's definitely involved, of course. It was all done on the political side, that's common knowledge. All the people involved are with the political committee, not finance." But she wouldn't say who, beyond Magruder. Magruder was CRP's second-in-command. Bernstein started guessing, picking names that he remembered from the GAO list. Lang Washburn? He had forgotten that Washburn was in finance, not on the political side.

"Are you kidding? Lang's so dumb that the Monday after the bugging he called everybody in finance together to say that we had nothing to do with it. And then he asked Gordon to say a few words to the kids. At which point Gordon Liddy got up and made a speech about how this one bad apple, McCord, shouldn't be allowed to spoil the whole barrel."

Bernstein asked the sister for another cup of coffee and tried another name.

"Never. The White House got him out because he didn't like to do all the crazy things they wanted."

Who?

"Right under Mitchell," the Bookkeeper suggested.

Bernstein tried LaRue and Porter. She didn't respond. He tried again. Silence.

What evidence did she have that Mitchell's assistants were involved?

"I had the evidence, but all the records were destroyed. . . . I don't know who destroyed them, but I'm sure Gordon did some shredding."

Was it hard evidence?

"It wouldn't positively say they planned the bugging; it wouldn't necessarily implicate them with this, but it would come pretty close."

How could she tell it linked them to the bugging?

"There was a special account before April 7. Back then, they were just expenditures as far as I was concerned; I didn't have any idea then what it was all about. But after June 17 you didn't have to be any genius to figure it out. I'd seen the figures and I'd seen all the people. And there were no receipts." Liddy was among those who received the money, she said. "Gordon's a case of loyalty to the President. He'll never crack. He'll take the whole rap."

The Bookkeeper was looking at Bernstein's coffee cup again, having second thoughts. "There are too many people watching me," she said. "They know I'm privy and they watch me like a hawk." She was convinced her phones were tapped.

How much money was paid out?

"A lot."

More than half a million?

"You've had it in print."

Finally it clicked. Sometimes he could be incredibly slow, Bernstein thought to himself. It was the slush fund of cash kept in Stans' safe.

"I never knew it was a 'security fund' or whatever they called it," she said, "until after June 17. I just thought it was an all-purpose political fund that you didn't talk about—like to take fat cats to dinner, but all strictly legal."

$350,000 in dinners? How was it paid out?

"Not in one chunk. I know what happened to it, I added up the figures." There had been a single sheet of paper on which the account was kept; it had been destroyed, the only record. "It was a lined sheet with names on about half the sheet, about fifteen names with the amount distributed to each person next to the name. I saw it more than once. The amounts kept getting bigger." She had updated the sheet each time a disbursement was made. Sloan knew the whole story too. He had handed out the money.

Bernstein asked about the names again. He was confused because there were about 15 names on the sheet, yet she thought only six were involved. Which six?

"Go down the GAO report; I think they've all been before the grand jury. They're easy to isolate; a couple have been named in the press but not necessarily in connection with this."

How were the funds allocated?

Telephone calls had something to do with how the money was doled out. Only three of the six had actually received money. "The involvement of the others includes answering some telephone calls," she stated.

Who were the six? he asked again.

"Mitchell's principal assistants . . . the top echelon. Magruder is one."

He started throwing out more names. No use. He tried initials: if she told him their initials, she could truthfully say that she had never given Bernstein the names, and he would at least be able to narrow down the candidates. Early in the conversation, she had not answered when he had asked if LaRue and Porter were involved. He tried L.

"L and M and P, and that's all I'm going to give you," the Bookkeeper said.

Bernstein finished his coffee. He wanted to be able to come back, and he had already pushed too hard. Thanking her at the door, he asked who at the committee might know something and be willing to talk about it. She mentioned the name of the woman who had been followed to lunch with Bernstein.

Heading for the Beltway, Bernstein stopped at a phone booth and called Woodward at home. Between the coffee jag, the euphoria of the moment and the information he was trying to keep straight in his head, Bernstein sounded overexcited. He also didn't want to say too much on the phone—the paranoia was catching. He said he'd be right over.

Woodward typed as Bernstein dictated his notes and filled in the gaps. The implications seemed clear. The money in Stans' safe was related to the bugging operation; Liddy had received some of it; but, most important, Mitchell's assistants—including Magruder—had also gotten some of the money and were aware of the espionage operation.

Woodward had turned on the stereo full-volume, and typed at the top of the page: "Interview with X. Sept. 14."

Then he passed Bernstein a slip of paper and asked him who the information was coming from. Bernstein wrote the Bookkeeper's name on it.

Late the next day, September 15, the indictments were handed down by the grand jury. As expected, Hunt, Liddy and the five men arrested on June 17 were indicted. The seven men were charged with as many as eight separate counts each—all related to conspiracy, burglary and the federal wiretapping statute prohibiting electronic interception of oral communications. In its story, the *Post* noted that the indictments did "not touch on the central questions about the purpose or sponsorship of the alleged espionage."

Attorney General Richard Kleindienst said the indictments represented the culmination of "one of the most intensive, objective and thorough investigations in many years, reaching out to cities all across the United States as well as into foreign countries."

At the *Post,* Bernstein, Woodward and the editors had become increasingly skeptical of the federal investigation. Why weren't the $89,000 in Mexican checks, the $25,000 Dahlberg check and the Stans slush fund mentioned in the indictment? How could the indictment be so limited if the government had the same information as the *Post?*

Bernstein telephoned a Justice Department official who had been helpful occasionally and asked how the indictment squared with the Bookkeeper's testimony. Hadn't everything she said been confirmed by Sloan? Certainly the government had established through at least those two that the fund in Stans' safe was tied to the bugging and that the money had been controlled by John Mitchell's assistants.

The source was uncomfortable and evasive at first. Then, defensively, he confirmed that the information was there—including the assertions of Sloan and the Bookkeeper.

Bernstein asked indignantly why the *Post* shouldn't run a story charging the government with ignoring evidence. There was proof that the fund in Stans' safe was tied to the bugging and there were witnesses who knew which higher-ups at the committee were involved.

"You're making some bad assumptions. I'll believe you if you put your name on a story that says someone can testify to a fund going for the Watergate."

Bernstein recalled that the Bookkeeper had said her evidence did not prove conclusively that the money went to the Watergate operation. He rephrased: Wasn't there a considerable body of evidence indicating that others had knowledge of the bugging operation and that the fund was central to the involvement of others?

The source hesitated. "If what you say is true, it's gonna come out in the wash. The only new things will come out in the trial."

What about the people who had come back to offer new information to the FBI and the prosecutors?

"It happens in every investigation," the official said, and added: "There is nothing you know that we don't know. We've got all the facts. You're not telling me anything."

Then this would be the end of it?

"It can safely be said that the investigation for the present is at rest, in a state of repose. It seems highly unlikely that it will be reopened."

Bernstein overstepped good judgment. Maybe the Feds should bring Dick Gerstein and his crackerjack investigator, Martin Dardis, up to Washington to help out, he suggested.

"It pisses me off that Gerstein is a member of the bar," said the official. "We know the facts—not Gerstein, not you."

4

WOODWARD HAD a source in the Executive Branch who had access to information at CRP as well as at the White House. His identity was unknown to anyone else. He could be contacted only on very important occasions. Woodward had promised he would never identify him or his position to anyone. Further, he had agreed never to quote the man, even as an anonymous source. Their discussions would be only to confirm information that had been obtained elsewhere and to add some perspective.

In newspaper terminology, this meant the discussions were on "deep background." Woodward explained the arrangement to managing editor Howard Simons one day. He had taken to calling the source "my friend," but Simons dubbed him "Deep Throat," the title of a celebrated pornographic movie. The name stuck.

At first Woodward and Deep Throat had talked by telephone, but as the tensions of Watergate increased, Deep Throat's nervousness grew. He didn't want to talk on the telephone, but had said they could meet somewhere on occasion.

Deep Throat didn't want to use the phone even to set up the meetings. He suggested that Woodward open the drapes in his apartment as a signal. Deep Throat could check each day; if the drapes were open, the two would meet that night. But Woodward liked to let the sun in at times, and suggested another signal.

Several years earlier, Woodward had found a red cloth flag lying in the street. Barely one foot square, it was attached to a stick, the type of warning device used on the back of a truck carrying a project-ing load. Woodward had taken the flag back to his apartment and one of his friends had stuck it into an old flower pot on the balcony. It had stayed there.

When Woodward had an urgent inquiry to make, he would move the flower pot with the red flag to the rear of the balcony. During the day, Deep Throat would check to see if the pot had been moved. If it had, he and Woodward would meet at about 2:00 A.M. in a pre-designated underground parking garage. Woodward would leave his sixth-floor apartment and walk down the back stairs into an alley.

Walking and taking two or more taxis to the garage, he could be reasonably sure that no one had followed him. In the garage, the two could talk for an hour or more without being seen. If taxis were hard to find, as they often were late at night, it might take Woodward almost two hours to get there on foot. On two occasions, a meeting had been set and the man had not shown up—a depressing and frightening experience, as Woodward had waited for more than an hour, alone in an underground garage in the middle of the night. Once he had thought he was being followed—two well-dressed men had stayed behind him for five or six blocks, but he had ducked into an alley and had not seen them again.

If Deep Throat wanted a meeting—which was rare—there was a different procedure. Each morning, Woodward would check page 20 of his *New York Times,* delivered to his apartment house before 7:00 A.M. If a meeting was requested, the page number would be circled and the hands of a clock indicating the time of the rendezvous would appear in a lower corner of the page. Woodward did not know how Deep Throat got to his paper.

The man's position in the Executive Branch was extremely sensi-tive. He had never told Woodward anything that was incorrect. It was he who had advised Woodward on June 19 that Howard Hunt was definitely involved in Watergate. During the summer, he had told Wood-ward that the FBI badly wanted to know where the *Post* was getting its information. He thought Bernstein and Woodward might be followed, and cautioned them to take care when using their telephones. The White House, he had said at the last meeting, regarded the stakes in Watergate as much higher than anyone outside perceived. Even the

FBI did not understand what was happening. The source had been deliberately vague about this, however, making veiled references to the CIA and national security which Woodward did not understand.

The day after the indictments were handed down, Woodward broke the rule about telephone contact. Deep Throat sounded nervous, but listened as the draft of a story was read to him. It said that federal investigators had received information from Nixon campaign workers that high officials of the Committee for the Re-election of the President had been involved in the funding of the Watergate operation.

"Too soft," Deep Throat said. "You can go much stronger."

The Bookkeeper had been right about the money in Stans' safe. It had financed the Watergate bugging and *"other intelligence-gathering activities,"* he said. John Mitchell's top assistants were only *"among those"* who had controlled the fund. He would not say if the former Attorney General had had prior knowledge of the bugging attempt.

The wiretap logs had reached some of the same Mitchell aides who had disbursed the spying funds, he said.

Following the conversation, Woodward read his scrawled notes to Bernstein, who typed a new lead:

> Funds for the Watergate espionage operation were controlled by several principal assistants of John N. Mitchell, the former manager of President Nixon's campaign, and were kept in a special account at the Committee for the Re-election of the President, the *Washington Post* has learned.

The story also reported: the fund contained more than $300,000 earmarked for sensitive political projects; Gordon Liddy was among those who received money from the fund; records relating to the account had been destroyed; Hugh Sloan's resignation had been the result of his suspicions about Watergate. Perhaps more important than the specific details of the story was its larger meaning: The Watergate indictments had not broken the conspiracy. And some of CRP's campaign workers had the answers to many of the remaining questions.

As the 6:30 deadline for the Sunday paper approached, Woodward called Van Shumway for CRP's response. Half an hour later, Shumway called back with a statement.

There have been and are cash funds in this committee used for various legitimate purposes such as reimbursement of expenditures for advances on travel. However, no one employed by this committee at this time has used any funds [for purposes] that were illegal or improper.

The statement, taken literally, did not flatly deny what had been reported.

That afternoon George McGovern held a press conference and called the Watergate investigation a "whitewash. . . . What is involved here is not only the political life of this nation, but the very morality of our leaders at a time when the United States desperately needs to revitalize its moral standards," he said. "And that is why I shall pursue this case the length and breadth of this land."

The next day, September 17, both the reporters went to the Bookkeeper's house. It was a Sunday afternoon, and she was not inclined to talk to reporters, especially when a page-one story in the *Post* contained facts that only she and a few others at the Nixon committee knew.

But she would rather have the reporters out of view than on the doorstep, where they were imploring her to listen to some information they had. She let them inside. They wanted her to tell them exactly who "L" and "M" and "P" were. Liddy or LaRue? McCord? Mitchell? Magruder? Porter? How much money was paid out? What about the others on the list?

The Bookkeeper was scared and was having second thoughts. But she was calling Bernstein by his first name.

Woodward was silent at first. Bernstein was throwing out figures. He stopped at $700,000.

"At least that, $350,000 is what's left in the fund."

The ice seemed broken. Had she meant Liddy for the "L," or had LaRue or someone else with that initial also gotten cash?

She would not say.

They said they *knew* Liddy was the only L to be paid from the fund. She confirmed it.

An unstated agreement was in the making. She seemed willing to confirm or deny statements if the reporters remained casual and gave the impression that they simply needed confirmation, not primary information. If people were to be convinced that Sloan and Stans were innocent, they told her, it was critical that the *Post*'s reporting be precise. That was where she could help.

"Morale is terrible in finance," she said. "Those of us who know are tired of being suspected. There are little jokes all the time, like 'What'd you do with the twenty-five grand, lady?' "

Was that how much Liddy got?

She shook her head no.

More than $50,000? Woodward asked.

She nodded.

Magruder got at least that too, didn't he?

Again she nodded.

Magruder was the only M to get money, right?

Another nod. But, she indicated, there was more to know about Magruder. "Let's just say I don't trust him at all, especially where his own skin is concerned," she said. "He'll stop at nothing. The last three weeks he's turned on the charm to me something fierce."

And LaRue? The reporters said they knew he was involved, too, even though he had received no money.

"He's very elusive, he covers his tracks," she said. "He and Mitchell are like this"—she intertwined her fingers. But she would not say what LaRue knew.

"P" was Bart Porter; they were sure of that, they said.

"He got a lot of money. It was in $100 bills; everybody got $100 bills."

Bernstein reminded her of a joke she had made—"We're Republicans, you know. We deal in big figures."

Porter, too, had gotten more than $50,000, she said.

The Bookkeeper was disturbed by the narrowness of the indictments. "I went down in good faith to the grand jury and testified and obviously the results are not there. My feeling is that the FBI turns the information in and it goes upstairs. . . . I just want out now. Hugh Sloan made the wisest decision of all. He quit. Mr. Stans said, 'I begged him to stay, but he wouldn't.' "

She said that people had evaded the grand jury's questions: "Rob Odle said to me after he'd come back from the grand jury, 'Don't you feel like you've been through the wringer?' And I said, 'No, and you wouldn't feel so bad if you'd tell them the whole truth.' " She wouldn't go into what Odle might have concealed.

"The propaganda since the break-in has been, 'We have nothing to do with this and hold your head up high,' " she told the reporters as they left.

Back at the office, Woodward went to the rear of the newsroom to call Deep Throat. Bernstein wished he had a source like that. The only source he knew who had such comprehensive knowledge in any field was Mike Schwering, who owned the Georgetown Cycle Sport Shop. There was nothing about bikes—and, more important, about bike thieves—that Schwering didn't know. Bernstein knew something about bike thieves: the night of the Watergate indictments, somebody had stolen his 10-speed Raleigh from a parking garage. That was the difference between him and Woodward. Woodward went into a garage to find a source who could tell him what Nixon's men were up to. Bernstein walked in to find an eight-pound chain cut neatly in two and his bike gone.

The tone of the conversation that Sunday afternoon was ominous. When Deep Throat heard Woodward's voice, there was a long pause. This would have to be their last telephone conversation, he said flatly. Both the FBI and the White House were determined to learn how the *Post* was getting its information and to put a stop to it. The situation was far more dangerous than Woodward realized. The story about Mitchell's aides had infuriated the White House.

The call clearly was a mistake. His friend was displeased, even angry at him. But what struck Woodward even more was how frightened Deep Throat seemed. The fear had been building, but Woodward had not recognized it until now. Only a part of it was personal. It had more to do with the situation, the facts, the implications of what he knew about. Woodward had never known him to be so guarded, so serious. At their last meeting, he had seemed weighed down. If Woodward was reading his friend right, something was horribly amiss.

Woodward told him what he and Bernstein had heard from the Bookkeeper about Magruder and Porter.

"They're both deeply involved in Watergate," Deep Throat responded. He sounded resigned, dejected.

Woodward asked him to be more exact.

"Watergate," he repeated. Then he paused and added, "The whole thing."

He confirmed that Magruder and Porter had received at least $50,000 from Stans' safe. And Woodward could be damned sure that the money had not been used for legitimate purposes—that was fact, not allegation. That was all he would say. From there, Woodward and Bernstein would be on their own for a while.

A touch of his old good humor returned: "Let's just say I'll be willing to put the blossoming situation in perspective for you when the time comes." But there was disgust in the way he said it.

Bernstein was already sparring with the typewriter. Woodward glanced at the lead:

> Two of President Nixon's top campaign officials each withdrew more than $50,000 from a secret fund that financed the bugging of Democratic headquarters, according to sources close to the Watergate investigation.

Woodward reached Powell Moore, the deputy press director of CRP, and told him in general terms what the *Post* intended to report in Monday's paper. Moore was a jocular 34-year-old Georgian who had worked in the White House communications office before the campaign.

"Thanks a lot," Moore said. "That's just what I need on a Sunday." He was sure the story was untrue—the reporters were getting bad information somewhere, he didn't know where, but he wished they would come off this crusade and check out these things better before putting them in the paper.

Woodward saw a lever. The reporters were sure of their facts, he told Moore. They had verified the information with sources in enough different places. But there was always the possibility of some explanation that they might be unaware of. If Moore would get Magruder to call him and discuss the allegations substantively, Woodward would agree to hold the story until after Magruder had his say. And if Magruder could convince the reporters that the story was in any way wrong, or based on some misunderstanding, they would continue to hold it until everything was checked out.

Moore agreed. It was a breakthrough, the reporters felt: an opportunity to penetrate the committee's haze of anonymous and ambiguous statements. Magruder called about half an hour later and said it was "absolutely untrue" that he received any money from any secret fund. "I only received my salary and expense account," he told Woodward.

Then how did he account for the fact that the federal investigation had determined he had received at least $50,000 from the fund in Stans' safe?

"I was questioned about it, but it was discarded . . . and it was agreed by all parties that it is incorrect." The FBI had questioned him extensively. "That's on background," he added as an afterthought.

Woodward told him he should know better than to try to put something on background *after* saying it. Magruder had served as the number-two man in the White House communications office before becoming deputy campaign manager.

"But you've got to help me," Magruder pleaded. "I'll get in trouble if I'm quoted."

Woodward told him he might put *that* statement in the paper, too. Then, at Magruder's request, they went on background. Woodward told him the *Post* intended to go ahead with the story unless Magruder could come up with a convincing reason to hold it. Magruder did not argue. But he asked Woodward to write that "government investigators," rather than the FBI, had informed Magruder of allegations against him. "You've got to help me on some of this."

It was a small point. Magruder obviously thought that an allegation attributed to the FBI sounded more serious than "government investigators." The request didn't seem unreasonable. Woodward agreed. Magruder's tone had made more of an impression on Woodward than his words. He was second in command at CRP. His job at the White House had been to deal with the press. But his voice had been shaking as he talked to Woodward.

A section of the story was about Hugh Sloan. Deep Throat had said that Sloan had had no prior knowledge of the bugging, or of how the money was to be spent. He had quit as treasurer of CRP shortly after the bugging because he "wanted no part of what he then knew was going on." The story quoted the Bookkeeper anonymously. "He didn't want anything to do with it. His wife was going to leave him if he didn't stand up and do what was right."

There was one problem in writing the story. Deep Throat had been explicit in saying the withdrawals financed the Watergate bugging. But the Bookkeeper—who suspected as much—could not confirm it. The reporters conferred with Sussman and Rosenfeld, who decided to fall on the cautious side and say the money was used to finance widespread "intelligence-gathering activities against the Democrats." Gradually, an unwritten rule was evolving: unless two sources confirmed a charge involving activity likely to be considered criminal, the specific allegation was not used in the paper.

The next morning, the *New York Times* did not mention the secret-fund stories. At the White House, Ron Ziegler was not asked about them. The networks carried neither of the stories, and most papers didn't either. On Capitol Hill, the Republican leader of the Senate, Hugh Scott of Pennsylvania, told an informal morning press conference that the Watergate case was not of concern to the average voter but of interest to "just Senator McGovern and the media." "Nobody is paying any attention to what you're writing," he said. In the newsroom, Bernstein and Woodward waited for the first edition of the afternoon *Washington Star-News* to arrive. The only Watergate story was about a George Washington University law professor who had filed a motion in federal court seeking the appointment of a special prosecutor in the case.

Late that afternoon, Bernstein signed out a company car and drove to McLean, in the Virginia suburbs, to visit Hugh Sloan, the former treasurer of CRP. The trip, ordinarily half an hour's drive, took more than an hour and a quarter in the rain; Sloan lived in a new development, and Bernstein had trouble finding it.

The development consisted of imitation Tudor houses clustered along little concrete-and-grass pedestrian lanes. The place was doubtless designed for families with young children; traffic and parking areas were safely isolated and almost every house seemed to have a tricycle or some form of hobbyhorse overturned on the lawn. Bernstein got soaked as he searched on foot for Sloan's house.

Mrs. Sloan answered the door. She was very pretty and very pregnant. Bernstein introduced himself and asked for Sloan. He was downtown and would not be home until 7:30 or so. She was friendly, and asked where Bernstein could be reached. Bernstein was looking for a way to talk to her at least for a while. She had worked at the White House as a social secretary, he knew, and she had been an important influence in her husband's decision to quit the Nixon campaign.

He guessed she was about 30. There was a softness about her good looks that seemed to suit the idea of becoming a mother. She had big brown eyes. Bernstein thought these must be awful days for the Sloans —a former assistant on the President's staff, out of work and under a cloud of suspicion, and his wife expecting their first child. At this time when they should be happiest, his name was showing up in the papers every day in a way usually associated with mobsters . . . she spent her time waiting for him to come back from the grand jury . . . FBI agents were talking to their friends and neighbors . . . reporters were knocking on their door at all hours . . .

Bernstein shared these thoughts with her, trying to dissociate himself from the hordes.

She sensed his discomfort. She understood he was only trying to do his job, she said. Like her husband. "This is an honest house." It was a declaration, proud, firm.

Had she read the *Post*'s story? Mrs. Sloan nodded. She had been pleased; it had been a relief finally to see what she knew in print. Bernstein told her the *Post*'s staff had no preconceived notions. And there were some people who were not concerned about the truth, he added, much less about what happened to her husband.

"I know," she replied. It was spoken sadly. Her husband had been let down by people he believed in, people whose principles and values they had both thought were the same as their own. But the values of many of the others had been hollow. There was a flash of anger as she spoke, but mostly sorrow.

Bernstein wanted to move the conversation away from generalities. They had established a common ground philosophically, and seemed to like each other. He certainly liked her.

What had her husband's reaction been when he realized what he was being asked to hand out money for? Bernstein was trying to cross the line slowly but she recognized it immediately.

That was something he would have to talk to her husband about. It wouldn't be appropriate for her to say. She asked for his phone number again and Bernstein wrote it on a page from his notebook. He had another appointment in McLean that evening, he lied; if it ended early enough, would it be all right to come back and talk to her husband?

Bernstein was welcome to come back, but she did not know if her husband would talk to him.

Maybe she could convince him? Bernstein smiled, trying to suggest a good-natured conspiracy.

She laughed. "We'll see," she said.

There was a pretty fair bike shop in McLean, and Bernstein drove there to kill a couple of hours and look halfheartedly for a replacement for his beloved Raleigh. But his mind was on Jeb Magruder. He had picked up a profoundly disturbing piece of information that day: Magruder was a bike freak. Bernstein had trouble swallowing the information that a bicycle nut could be a Watergate bugger. And Magruder really was a card-carrying bicycle freak who had even ridden his 10-speed to the White House every day. Nobody would ever steal Jeb Magruder's bike, at least not there. Bernstein knew that, because he had ridden his bike to the White House on July 14—not the Raleigh, but a Holdsworth that he had had built in London—and as he went through the gate he knew no one would get near it.

So Bernstein had rested his bike against the wall of the little guard-house at the entrance and not bothered to lock it. He was there to hear Vice President Agnew talk about cutting red tape to get help to victims of the Great Flood caused by Hurricane Agnes. And he had run into Ken Clawson in the hallway.

"You guys back at the *Post* are going to bark up the wrong tree one too many times on Watergate," Clawson had said.

A few hours later, Hugh Sloan answered the door, looking as if he had just stepped out of the pages of *Management Intern News*. Thirty-ish, slim, hair nicely trimmed just long enough, blue blazer, muted shirt, rep tie, quite handsome, maybe too thin.

"My wife told me to probably expect you," he said, and let Bernstein step out of the rain and into the hallway. He left the door open. "As you know, I haven't talked to the press." It was stated apologetically. That was a good sign. One eye on the open door, Bernstein decided to shoot for the moon. The morning's story had changed the situation, he argued. People now knew that Sloan was not guilty in Watergate. But Sloan knew who was, or at least he knew things that could lead to the guilty. Now that part of the story had come out, Sloan should put the rest on record, clear his own name and let people know the truth. Maybe there was a legitimate explanation for the cash handed over to

Liddy and John Mitchell's aides. If there was, and that was the whole story, so be it. Maybe things were a lot worse even than that day's story had suggested. If they were worse . . .

"They're worse," Sloan interrupted. "That's why I left, because I suspected the worst." Suddenly he looked wounded. There seemed to be no vengeance, only hurt. He was shaking his head.

Then why not tell what he knew? Now. Publicly. To keep others from getting hurt. In the long run, it would help Nixon, Bernstein argued, because the President was going to be hurt badly if the cover-up lasted much longer.

Sloan nodded. He would like to, he said. He really would. But his lawyers had advised against it; whatever he said publicly might be used against him in any civil suit arising from his role as treasurer of the Nixon campaign.

Bernstein resisted the temptation to advise Sloan to get a new lawyer; that's what he would do if he were innocent and in Sloan's place—get a new lawyer and sue CRP.

Sloan had also pledged to the prosecutors that he would not make any public statement before the Watergate trial. So he was twice bound to remain silent, he said.

How sure was Sloan that the prosecutors were on his side?

He thought they were, he said, but he didn't have much faith in anybody any more.

Because only seven people had been indicted?

"Because of the whole situation."

Bernstein remembered that the Bookkeeper had said that lawyers for the committee had been present during all FBI interviews with CRP employees.

That was true, said Sloan.

Had the lawyers told Sloan what to say, or to stay away from certain areas?

"We were never told in so many words, 'Don't talk,' " said Sloan. "But the message was clear. It was always 'Hold ranks,' or 'Keep the ship together.' "

Did that mean to lie?

Bernstein could draw his own conclusions, Sloan said. But it was not an unreasonable assumption.

Who had conveyed the message? The lawyers? Mardian? LaRue?

Well, Mardian and LaRue had been chosen by John Mitchell to develop the committee's response to the Watergate bugging. So they would certainly know about it, Sloan said; they had "engineered the response."

Was that another way of saying "covering up"?

It definitely didn't mean devising a plan for coming forward and telling the truth, Sloan said.

Did Mitchell know of the bugging before it took place? Did LaRue? Mardian?

Mitchell knew of the bugging and a lot of other things before they took place, Sloan said, but he had no absolute proof of this beyond the money, secondhand information and his knowledge of the personalities involved and how the committee worked. "Mitchell had to know of the funds. You just don't give out that kind of money without the head of the campaign knowing what it's going for, especially when his people are getting the cash."

LaRue was Mitchell's aide-de-camp, Sloan explained. He was probably involved in everything, too. He was less certain about Mardian, who had come to the committee from the Justice Department on May 1, after the money had been passed around. After June 17, however, there was no question that Mardian, who had been political coordinator at CRP, had learned all there was to know. Then he and LaRue had started running the show, in consultation with Mitchell.

Including the destruction of records?

That was part of it.

The Bookkeeper had seemed to imply that the records of the secret account in Stans' safe had been destroyed immediately after the new campaign law took effect on April 7. But Sloan said they had been destroyed right after the arrests in the Watergate, along with a lot of other financial records. These included six or seven ledger books, each about half an inch thick, that listed all campaign contributions received before the new disclosure law took effect. There had been a house-cleaning after the bugging.

They were still standing in the hallway. Sloan kept glancing at the open door and Bernstein kept trying not to notice. Sloan was uncomfortable. He kept repeating that he was going further with Bernstein than he wanted to go without having some time to think about it.

Bernstein was impressed by Sloan's thoughtfulness. Sloan seemed convinced that the President, whom he very much wanted to see re-elected, had known nothing of what happened before June 17; but he was as sure that Nixon had been ill-served by his surrogates before the bugging and had been put in increasing jeopardy by them ever since. Sloan believed that the prosecutors were honest men, determined to learn the truth, but there were obstacles they had been unable to over-come. He couldn't tell whether the FBI had been merely sloppy or under pressure to follow procedures that would impede an effective in-vestigation. He believed the press was doing its job, but, in the absence of candor from the committee, it had reached unfair conclusions about some people. Sloan himself was a prime example. He was not bitter, just disillusioned. All he wanted now was to clean up his legal obliga-tions—testimony in the trial and in the civil suit—and leave Washing-ton forever. He was looking for a job in industry, a management position, but it was difficult. His name had been in the papers often. He would not work for the White House again even if asked to come back. He wished he were in Bernstein's place, wished he could write. Maybe then he could express what had been going through his mind. Not the cold, hard facts of Watergate necessarily—that wasn't really what was important. But what it was like for young men and women to come to Washington because they believed in something and then to be inside and see how things worked and watch their own ideals disintegrate.

He and his wife believed in the same things they had before they came to Washington. Many of their friends at the White House did, too, but those people had made a decision that you could still believe in the same things and yet adapt yourself. After all, the goals were unchanged, you were still working for what you believed in, right? People in the White House believed they were entitled to do things differently, to suspend the rules, because they were fulfilling a mission; that was the only important thing, the mission. It was easy to lose perspective, Sloan said. He had seen it happen. He and his wife wanted to get out of Washington before they lost theirs.

Bernstein didn't think Sloan would be saying these things unless he was convinced the White House was involved in the bugging and the cover-up of the true story.

"I don't know anything hard about what went on across the street [meaning the White House]," Sloan said. "But judging from who's involved in the committee, it wouldn't surprise me."

In any case, Sloan said, the question was largely semantic: Since the bugging, the White House and the President himself had talked as if CRP were a private company set up by supporters of Richard Nixon who were intent on drafting him for re-election and contracting his campaign to a consulting firm. But the Committee for the Re-election of the President *was* the White House, wholly its creation, staffed by the White House, reporting only *to* the White House.

Bernstein asked if the names of any persons still working for the White House had been on that single sheet of paper used to account for withdrawals from the fund in Stans' safe. Sloan wouldn't say. But Liddy and Porter were a "logical grouping," and there had been no withdrawals of amounts comparable to theirs.

Bernstein thought, from what the Bookkeeper had indicated, that Liddy and Porter had received considerably more than $50,000 apiece: $50,000 was merely where she had cut off the guessing game.

Sloan confirmed his suspicions. The total was closer to $300,000. The fund had been in existence for more than 18 months, and had represented *cash* contributions to the Nixon campaign. Whatever cash had come into committee headquarters was simply shoveled into Stans' safe. At any given moment, there would probably have been about $700,000 in the safe.

Before June 17, Sloan added, nobody had told him of any specific purpose for the funds.

What about "convention security" or the term "security fund"?

Sloan had heard of neither until after the Watergate break-in. Then the story began making the rounds at CRP that the money withdrawn by Liddy, Porter and Magruder had been for convention security, and that Liddy had misappropriated his share, using it to pay for the bugging. But it didn't make sense to Sloan. Legitimate security expenditures were all carefully budgeted, he said, paid for by check and accounted for in reports filed with the GAO. If that had been the purpose of the expenditures, Sloan would have been told when they were made. He was the treasurer, after all.

Bernstein asked the obvious question. But Sloan would not say who had ordered him to make the secret payments. He wanted more time to think about Bernstein's suggestion that he go on the record. Bernstein said the *Post* would let him establish the ground rules; how about a taped interview? If Sloan wanted his lawyer present, that was fine, and Sloan could review the transcript and delete anything his lawyer said might give him legal problems, as long as his omissions did not distort the facts.

Bernstein wanted to come back with Woodward. If they could get Sloan to relax and to trust them, there was a good chance he might talk unguardedly. Much of what Sloan had said was ambiguous and unclear, but it suggested a broader conspiracy than he was willing to talk about at this point.

Sloan asked Bernstein to call him the next day—he would give him an answer about the interview. And if that were not possible, maybe the three of them could get together on some other basis.

They chatted easily for a few more minutes, about the baby—any day now, Sloan said—the campaign, the newspaper business. Sloan wondered if newspapers weren't a little hypocritical, demanding one standard for others and another for themselves; he doubted that reporters had any idea of the anguish they could inflict with only one sentence. He wasn't thinking of himself so much, he said. But his wife, his parents—it had been very rough on them.

Driving back to the office, Bernstein kept thinking about what Sloan had said in those last minutes.* Woodward and he had talked about the problem. Suppose that Magruder and Porter were only fall guys, that someone at the committee or the White House had wanted that day's story so they could pounce on the *Post?* Or suppose that Magruder and Porter were being fingered to protect somebody else?

Bernstein telephoned an FBI agent who was assigned to the Watergate case. He knew the man only slightly, and the agent was not happy to hear from him. The weekend stories on the secret fund, and on Bart Porter and Jeb Magruder, had caused trouble in the Bureau, he said. L. Patrick Gray III, acting director of the FBI, had personally called the head of the Washington field office and ordered him to make sure the *Post* was not getting its information from agents there.

"I don't know how you guys are doing it, but you've got access to

* Sloan was never identified as a source in the *Post* stories; he had been guaranteed anonymity. For this book, he agreed to allow the use of his name for the first time.

the 302s," the agent said, "and some people think you're getting them from us." FBI forms 302 were the interview reports filed by agents immediately after talking to witnesses.

"Now you come in through the switchboard, give your name to the girl and ask for me. Thanks a lot," he said.

Bernstein suggested that the agent announce loudly that he couldn't talk to any reporters and call him back. He did.

Bernstein read to him from his notes: Robert Odle had removed documents during the weekend of the Watergate arrests and perhaps destroyed some. Somebody, not necessarily Odle, had destroyed memos describing the wiretapped conversations of Democratic Party officials. Robert Mardian and Fred LaRue, beginning on June 19, had directed the response to the bugging and were aware of the destruction of some records: it was part of the response. LaRue and Mardian had told CRP employees to avoid certain areas when questioned by investigators—particularly as they related to any records that might have been destroyed. Mitchell had selected Mardian and LaRue to take charge of CRP's response.

The agent was furious. There was only one place the information could have come from and that was the 302s, he said. It was against the law for Bernstein to have these files, or copies of them, and if the *Post* published a story so clearly based on the 302s, the agent would attempt to have Bernstein and Woodward subpoenaed and ordered to turn over all documents belonging to the government.

It was an odd confirmation, but that's what it was.

How substantial were the allegations?

The agent would not say.

That was the trouble with the 302s, Bernstein knew. They were raw reports, unevaluated, unsubstantiated. Anybody could say any damn thing to the FBI and it went straight into the 302—facts, fourth-hand information, personal suspicions, gripes. Using a 302 as the sole basis for a story was unthinkable.

The agent's indirect confirmation on Odle, Mardian and LaRue, and on the destruction of records in general, meant only that the FBI had received the same raw information the reporters had. It wasn't enough.

Bernstein called Sloan, but he was too busy to see them, or even to talk on the phone. Bernstein could call him back later in the day.

While Woodward made the day's telephone checks, which often took hours, Bernstein began a draft of a story. Bernstein had become convinced that a tangible accounting could be assembled which would prove that an organized attempt had been made to conceal the facts of Watergate. Woodward was skeptical.

He was not alone. Rosenfeld had called Woodward into his office a few days earlier to tell him that Bernstein's thinking frequently moved one step ahead of the facts. Bernstein's theories were often right, Rosenfeld said, and he did not wish to discourage him. "But you've got to make sure none of that gets into the paper unless it's fully supported," Rosenfeld implored.

Bernstein's draft reported that John Mitchell's principal associates at CRP, Mardian and LaRue, had directed a "massive housecleaning" in which records were destroyed and staff members were instructed to "close ranks" in response to the Watergate arrests. And that the "house-cleaning" had immediately followed Mitchell's personal selection of LaRue and Mardian to direct the committee's response.

The draft described some of what had gone on at CRP during those days after the break-in at the Watergate. The wholesale destruction of documents—wiretap memos, the single-sheet accounting of the secret fund (including the withdrawals by Porter, Magruder and Liddy) and as many as seven ledger books listing campaign contributors and the amounts they gave before April 7—was accomplished. Mardian and LaRue had begun a search for incriminating evidence on June 19, and the relevant records no longer existed by the time the FBI began its examination of CRP's files. Robert Odle had spent the weekend after the Watergate break-in taking an inventory of the committee's files and removing records. After the destruction of the records he had been assigned by CRP to provide the FBI with the documents it requested.

Further, that Mardian, LaRue and the committee's lawyers had advised certain individuals "to stay away from certain areas" when questioned by the FBI, the prosecutors and the grand jury. Sloan was quoted anonymously as saying that campaign workers were "never told in so many words, 'Don't talk.' . . . It was always 'Hold ranks' or 'Keep the ship together.' " And, still further, that other employees had said their superiors suggested specific responses to questions that would be asked by investigators. FBI interviews were conducted in the presence of either the committee's lawyers or Mardian. Several employees with knowledge of damaging information were suddenly promoted in the weeks immediately following the Watergate arrests. Employees of the committee had been forbidden to talk to the press without specific clearance, even so much as to state their job titles. One employee had said she had been followed to a luncheon appointment with a reporter, and had been interrogated afterward about their conversation.

After Bernstein had finished, he reached Sloan by phone and read him the draft. Sloan confirmed virtually the entire story.

Bernstein added a few details, including an account of Liddy's "bad apple" speech to his colleagues on the Monday after the break-in.

Woodward and Bernstein took the draft to Rosenfeld. At 44, Rosenfeld had been a foreign editor of the *New York Herald Tribune* and the *Washington Post*. Brash and tough at times, he is extremely skillful at locating holes in stories written by his reporters. Since the week following the Watergate break-in, Rosenfeld had been the hard-sell artist, persuading Bradlee and the other senior editors (after satisfying himself) that the reporters had touched every base in their stories. From the day in 1970 when he moved from the foreign desk to become metropolitan editor, Rosenfeld's mission had been to raise the local staff from its second-class citizenship at the *Post*. Seizing on the potential of the Watergate story, he had fought for it to remain with the metropolitan staff and had won—resisting attempts by the national editors to take over.

Rosenfeld runs the metropolitan staff, the *Post*'s largest, like a football coach. He prods his players, letting them know that he has promised the front office results, pleading, yelling, cajoling, pacing, working his facial expressions for instant effects—anger, satisfaction, concern.

He was born in pre-Nazi Berlin and came to New York City when he was ten. He made a successful effort to forget his German and speaks English without any trace of an accent. Rosenfeld went to work for the *Herald Tribune* after his graduation from Syracuse University and has always been an editor, never a reporter. He was inclined to worry that too many reporters on the metropolitan staff were incompetent, and thought even the best reporters could be saved from self-destruction only by the skills of an editor. His natural distrust of reporters was particularly acute on the Watergate story, where the risks were very great, and he was in the uncomfortable position of having to trust Bernstein and Woodward more than he had ever trusted any reporters. Aware that much of the story was out of his hands, he tried to exercise what control he could: he hovered around the reporters' typewriters as they wrote, passed them questions as they talked on the phone to sources, demanded to be briefed after they hung up or returned from a meeting. Now, gulping down antacid tablets, Rosenfeld grilled Bernstein and Woodward to find out how solid this latest story was. He was reassured by Bernstein's conversation with the FBI agent. At least the FBI had the same allegations on paper. Rosenfeld always felt better when he knew that somewhere, no matter how inaccessible, there was a piece of paper that could support a story.

And it was a dangerous story. The *Post* was, in effect, making its own charges—not only against the campaign officials, but also concerning the thoroughness of the FBI and grand-jury investigations. The charges were, in some ways, more serious than those handed down in the indictment, four days earlier.

His interrogation completed, Rosenfeld approved the story. Bernstein called CRP for its ritual comment. The notation "Insert Denial" was marked between paragraphs two and three—right after the descriptions of Mardian and LaRue as the head housecleaners.

The committee's press office did not respond for more than an hour and a half. The reporters were certain that there would be, at least, some assertion that Fred LaRue and Robert Mardian had been models of probity in their efforts to re-elect the President.

Bernstein had a healthy fear of Mardian, having spent several years covering the New Left, the anti-war movement, demonstrations, riots, freaks, flower children, druggies, crazies, old and new radicals, during the time Mardian was head of the Internal Security Division of the Justice Department.

It was the division in charge of government wiretapping. And Mardian had supervised the unsuccessful prosecutions in many of the administration's celebrated conspiracy or "political" trials, in which defendants and lawyers alike had been placed under electronic and other means of surveillance.

Finally, Van Shumway called with CRP's response to the story. "The sources of the *Washington Post* are a fountain of misinformation," he said.

Bernstein waited. That was the whole statement.

Because the story's implications were the opposite of the message contained in the indictments, Bernstein and Woodward expected it would receive considerable attention. But, for the most part, the nation's major news outlets either ignored it or focused on denials by Mardian, who refused to talk to the *Post*.

The *Los Angeles Times* quoted Mardian's description of the *Post* story as "the biggest lot of crap I have ever heard in my life." The *Washington Star-News* carried three paragraphs on the end of another Watergate story, and quoted Mardian as calling the *Post* story "a lie" and denying that he or other campaign officials had conducted a "housecleaning" to destroy documents.

Clark MacGregor told an audience in New Hampshire that it was "important the press not discuss this [Watergate] in such great detail as to possibly prejudice any trial."

On Public Television's *Thirty Minutes With*, Richard Kleindienst was questioned by Elizabeth Drew, the Washington correspondent of the *Atlantic*, about the *Post*'s story. The Attorney General didn't know if any records had been destroyed; he hadn't any idea why anybody at CRP would want to tear up documents. If Mardian and LaRue had destroyed records, he said, an obstruction of justice might indeed have taken place.

5

BERNSTEIN AND WOODWARD thought that signs were beginning to point unmistakably toward John Mitchell, former Attorney General of the United States. Since his original declaration of CRP's innocence on June 18, Mitchell had been a subject of almost continual inquiry by the reporters, and they now knew that the prevailing opinion at the committee was that Mitchell was involved.

After his resignation as Nixon's campaign manager, Mitchell had continued to help direct the re-election effort. A CRP official had told the reporters that Mitchell helped draft many of the non-denial denials which were being issued in response to their stories. Mitchell had been questioned by the grand jury.

And there was his wife. Since June 22, when she had telephoned Helen Thomas of United Press International to say that she was "sick of the whole operation" and had threatened to leave her husband, Martha Mitchell's outbursts had been a bizarre aspect of the Watergate affair. Three days after that initial call, she had telephoned again to declare that she was a political prisoner: "I'm not going to stand for all those dirty things that go on. If you could see me, you wouldn't believe it. I'm black and blue."

The Mitchells had moved back to New York and were living at the Essex House on Central Park South. Woodward took the last night flight to New York on September 21, hoping to catch Mrs. Mitchell at home the next morning, after her husband had left for the offices of Mudge, Rose, Guthrie and Alexander, the law firm in which he and Richard Nixon had both been partners.

At nine the next morning, Woodward asked the clerk for the room number of J. N. Mitchell. No one was registered under that name.

He went to a telephone booth down the street and called the Essex House. "Give me the room where the Mitchells are staying at once, hurry," he said.

"Room 710," the switchboard operator said, ringing the extension. A man answered the phone. He asked who was calling, and Woodward identified himself as a *Post* reporter. Mrs. Mitchell couldn't come to the phone, the man said, and hung up.

A few minutes later, Woodward took the elevator to the seventh floor and walked to Room 710, which was the Marriott Suite, according to a brass plate on the white door. He moved on to the end of the hall and knocked on a door. No one answered—which was exactly what Woodward hoped: he could stand in front of the door all day, if necessary, as if waiting for someone to open it.

He had talked to Mrs. Mitchell once, in 1971, when she had called him after he had written a story about the smokestacks of a huge generating plant that were polluting the exclusive air in the vicinity of the Watergate. Checking city records, Woodward had discovered that among the formal complaints was one from Martha Mitchell, Watergate resident. He had tried to call her before he wrote the story to ask if she knew that the offending smokestacks were fed by the monster engines which supplied electrical power to the White House and the Justice Department. But he couldn't reach her. Mrs. Mitchell had called him the morning the story appeared, and Woodward had found her refreshing.

Honey, she said, she didn't care if her John and Mr. President had to work by candlelight, she had learned enough back in Pine Bluff, Arkansas, to know that human beings should not be subjected to direct hits from anybody's waste.

That had been almost a year ago. She had been considered something of a truth-teller in Washington, though a little wiggy perhaps. Now, Woodward thought, Martha Mitchell was becoming the Greek chorus of the Watergate drama—sounding her warnings to all who would hear.

Woodward had waited in the hallway for about 20 minutes when the Mitchells' security guard, a large black man, left the suite and took the elevator down. Woodward went down to a telephone booth in the lobby and called Room 710. Martha Mitchell answered. She sounded jovial and happy for the chance to chat. They talked about Washington, politics, the upcoming election, Manhattan . . . The operator broke in, saying it would take another five cents to keep talking.

"I wouldn't want Katie Graham to spend another nickel on me," Mrs. Mitchell said.

Woodward popped a quarter into the pay phone. But she was starting to sound anxious, and said she had to run. Woodward took the elevator back to the seventh floor.

After a few minutes, some hotel maids knocked on the door of 710. Martha Mitchell let them in. Woodward raced to 710 as the door was shut and knocked. Mrs. Mitchell, probably expecting another maid, opened it again. She was wearing a print blouse, blue slacks and white sandals.

"I'm so embarrassed," she said, "you caught me with grease on my face."

During a 15-minute chat, with vacuum cleaners whirring in the background, Mrs. Mitchell said she planned to write a book about her experiences in Washington and that she was much happier "making my family a non-political entity." The subject of Watergate made her visibly nervous. Each time Woodward raised a question about it, she said, "I don't know," "You tell me," or, "That comes out in the book I'm writing." And then she began fidgeting. She would not elaborate on her earlier pronouncements—made by phone to reporters in the middle of the night—about "dirty politics" or "this cops-and-robbers business."

She would talk about the upcoming election, though. She predicted that President Nixon would win the election by "the biggest landslide in the history of the country . . . getting 99.9 percent of the vote.

"I think there shouldn't be an election. If you ask me, the President should have a seven-year-term and, boom, then put him out. They start running again after they're in office two years. I don't care which party you're talking about."

Woodward wrote a brief story for the *Post*'s Style section. But it had been a wasted trip.

The Sloans' daughter, Melissa Madison Sloan, was born on September 25 at Washington's Georgetown Hospital. Bernstein talked by phone with Hugh Sloan the next day. He sounded relaxed, his mind far away from the troubles of Watergate and CRP. Bernstein had been trying to see Sloan again for days. But on the morning after the birth of his daughter, even mentioning Watergate seemed wrong. They chatted for a few minutes about the baby, her mother—she was understandably ecstatic, Sloan said—and the grandparents, who would be coming into town that week.

Perhaps sometime Sloan could find a few minutes to sit down with the reporters, Bernstein suggested. Sloan said he'd try, and suggested that Bernstein call back in a couple of days.

That afternoon Bernstein debated with himself for a while, then called a florist and ordered flowers sent to Georgetown Hospital. He was concerned that his gesture might be misunderstood. There was no denying that his motivation was touched by self-interest. But there was also the fact that he felt warmly toward the Sloans, especially Mrs. Sloan. He hoped the flowers wouldn't arrive while Maurice Stans or one of their friends from the White House was there.

Two days later, Bernstein called Sloan. Sloan might have some time the next morning, but he didn't really see how he could be very helpful. . . . Well, if the reporters had some information that he could confirm or steer them away from, that would be all right. He wouldn't be violating any trust in doing that. Could they check with him early the next morning?

Bernstein called him before eight.

Sloan said he had to clean up the house before his in-laws arrived, but if the reporters could get out to McLean quickly, they could stop by for a few minutes.

Sloan was dressed in sport clothes and, except for the broom he was holding in his hand, he still looked like the Princeton undergraduate he once had been. He shook hands with Woodward, who immediately volunteered to help clean up the house. Sloan declined the offer and offered coffee. A framed Christmas card picturing the President and Mrs. Nixon at home in the White House hung near the kitchen table. There was a scrawled message from the Chief and First Lady.

In the living room were more mementoes: another Christmas card, White House matchbooks with the Presidential Seal (Bernstein lit a cigarette and pocketed one), souvenirs from the '68 campaign.

Sloan sat in a high-backed upholstered chair, tapping his coffee cup lightly with a spoon as he talked, rarely sipping from the cup, his face drawn. He was shy.

They were discussing Maurice Stans' office—who worked there, the lines of authority. Sloan was devoted to Stans. People who thought Stans would knowingly have anything to do with political espionage did not really know the Secretary, he said. Stans was in anguish. He had allowed himself to be maligned in the press to protect the political people. He had never known what the money withdrawn by Liddy and Porter and Magruder was to be spent on.

Did that mean that Stans had known of the outlays beforehand?

Sloan hesitated. He was trying to plead Stans' case and instead was getting him in deeper.

The Bookkeeper had refused to say whether Stans knew of the withdrawals when they took place. Bernstein tried playing devil's advocate, suggesting that Stans would have been derelict had he not asked to be kept informed of disbursals of money from his own safe. Sloan agreed. Then he said that Stans had given his approval before Liddy, Porter and Magruder were authorized to make withdrawals from the fund. But that he had *not* given his authorization until after he had received assurances from the political managers of the campaign that they wanted the money disbursed.

Who were these political managers?

Sloan was uncomfortable with the question. It was enough to know that Stans had not acted on his own, he said.

Woodward jumped at the opening. In other words, a group of people in the political management of the campaign had the ultimate authority to approve disbursements from the secret fund?

That was right, Sloan said, but he did not want to go into it further.

Get those names and it will all be over, Bernstein was thinking.

Sloan was more interested in talking about the Mardian-LaRue story on CRP's housecleaning. He was curious about how the reporters had gotten their information. It was consistent with his own deductions, but he was surprised that anyone in a position to know things firsthand would have talked so explicitly.

Bernstein's stomach began a slow dance of panic. He had been under the impression that Sloan had confirmed almost the whole story on the basis of firsthand knowledge, not deduction. Other sources had confirmed the underpinning of the story, true, but much of it rested primarily on what Sloan had said, and now he seemed to be backing off. They went through the story again, handicapped by not having it in front of them. As they took it point by point, Woodward and Bernstein relaxed a bit. Very little, if anything, that Sloan had said before was deduction. He was not sure that he would have characterized all the specifics in the story as evidence of a "housecleaning," but that was a matter for the reporters' judgment. He hadn't known much about Odle; that, however, was of small concern because that information had come from somewhere else. Nothing in the story was at variance with what he understood to be true, Sloan said finally.

The discussion kept moving around the edges of the secret fund. Was there any chance that the money had been authorized for legitimate activities? For routine intelligence-gathering projects, such innocuous tasks as recording the opposition's speeches and clipping newspapers? To almost every question dealing with the fund, Sloan would answer that circumstances had forced him to "assume the worst," and then would ask the reporters what *they* thought. He had been at the White House, at CRP, and had worked in campaigns before, but maybe they knew things that would cause him to redirect his thinking.

They did not. Their thinking was directed toward the political side of the committee, particularly John N. Mitchell. Bernstein reminded Sloan of his remark that Mitchell had almost certainly known of the cash outlays from the secret fund. Was he one of those "authorized," as Sloan had put it a few minutes earlier, to approve disbursements?

"Obviously," Sloan said. There were five people with authorizing authority over the fund, and Mitchell was one of them. Stans was another.

Had Mitchell known of the disbursements that had gone to Magruder, Porter and Liddy?

Sloan nodded. But that was not proof Mitchell had known of the bugging. There was a remote possibility that the three had gone off on their own and spent the money on unauthorized projects, although Sloan doubted it. He was being careful.

How had it worked? How had Mitchell exercised his authority over the fund? By voucher?

It was a routine procedure, Sloan said, and in the context of a campaign with a budget of over $50 million, it had seemed insignificant at the time. When Sloan had first been approached for money, he had simply picked up the telephone and called Mitchell at the Justice Department. It only took a few seconds. Mitchell would tell him to give the money out. There had been a number of phone calls, beginning in 1971.

The reporters avoided looking at each other. While he was Attorney General of the United States, John Mitchell had authorized the expenditure of campaign funds for apparently illegal activities against the political opposition. They wanted to be sure they had heard Sloan correctly.

They had. Not only was Mitchell one of the five people with control over the fund, but he had exercised it frequently. Indeed, initially he had been the sole person to authorize the expenditures. Later, the authority had been passed to others. Magruder was among them, said Sloan.

The Bookkeeper's account of the fund was beginning to make sense. She had said that about six people were involved. But only three that she knew of—Porter, Liddy and Magruder—had received money. The others, she had said, had simply gotten phone calls. It was all coming together. The other names were those who could authorize payments. They had been called by Sloan before the cash was handed out. Magruder had initially received money from the fund on Mitchell's authorization. Eventually, he had been given authority to approve payments to others as well.

Mitchell, Stans and Magruder—that left two others who could authorize the payments, by Sloan's account. Were they also on the political side at CRP?

Neither worked for the re-election committee, Sloan said, but he would go no further.

Even aside from the names, the reporters still did not fully understand the purpose of the fund. Who else would have received cash from

Stans' safe? Would they necessarily have known about the bugging?

Sloan had no reason to believe the other recipients were involved or that the money they received had financed anything illegal or improper. Only Porter, Liddy and Magruder had received large amounts of money. There were no comparable payments to others.

How could Sloan be so sure that the money withdrawn by those three had been put to illegal or improper use, if the remainder of the money was spent legitimately?

Again Sloan said he was assuming the worst. But it was more than guesswork. He had heard a lot, seen a lot.

Woodward, who had not met Sloan before, was impressed by his care and his unwillingness to mention the names of persons he had no reason to think had done anything wrong. Sloan's credentials as a source seemed impeccable. He was thoroughly committed to the re-election of Richard Nixon and seemed convinced that the President had known nothing of the indiscretions committed by his campaign staff.

And he seemed to understand how they had occurred. Overzealousness, overkill, a desire to leave nothing to chance in the effort to re-elect the President—he had seen it all at the White House. One breathed a rarefied air when one was in the President's service. And Sloan thought the White House might be involved in the bugging.

The other two persons authorized to approve payments from the fund, were they members of the White House staff?

Only one, said Sloan. The other was not an official in either the campaign or the administration, not a Washingtonian.

The reporters suggested that only three persons at the White House seemed likely to have had control over the fund: H. R. Haldeman, Charles Colson, and John Ehrlichman. Their money was on Colson.

Sloan shook his head. That wasn't the way Colson operated, he said. Chuck was too crafty, too careful to put himself in jeopardy that way. If it had been Colson, he would have done it through someone else, and that hadn't happened.

The only reason the reporters had mentioned Ehrlichman was because of his high position at the White House. If Stans and Mitchell had had to be consulted before the money could be disbursed, someone of similar stature at the White House must have been involved. Ehrlichman had no major role in the campaign, as far as the reporters knew. Haldeman, because he was the overseer of CRP, and because of his reputation, seemed a more logical choice.

Haldeman, known to the reporters by little more than his reputation for autocratic control of the White House staff, was the President's eyes and ears in the campaign, Sloan confirmed. Through his political aide, Gordon Strachan, Haldeman was kept informed of every major decision made at CRP. Magruder was Haldeman's man at the committee, installed there to make sure that John Mitchell did not run the committee without proper input from the White House.

Still Sloan would not say yes or no. But he said nothing to steer the reporters away from Haldeman, as he had with Colson. They were almost convinced it was Haldeman.

That left one more person—someone who worked for neither the White House nor CRP.

Murray Chotiner?

No, said Sloan.

Bernstein threw out a name Woodward had never heard before: Herbert Kalmbach, President Nixon's personal lawyer. It was a guess. Sloan looked surprised.

Bernstein had remembered reading a piece in the *New York Times* the previous February that referred to Kalmbach as "Nixon's personal attorney on the West Coast" and said that prospective clients who had business with the government couldn't talk to him for less than $10,000. It related that his law practice had mushroomed and that he was second only to Maurice Stans on Nixon's national fund-raising team. He was secretary of the Nixon Foundation, which was planning the Nixon Library. The story said he also worked frequently on private projects for the President and the White House.

Sloan said he didn't want to get into a guessing game. The reporters could not tell whether this was because Kalmbach was a lucky guess or a ridiculous one. That could wait. Haldeman was the important name—if it *was* Haldeman.

The reporters had already helped themselves to three cups of coffee, going back to the kitchen to refill their cups. Sloan had been glancing at his watch and reminding them that he had to clean up the house. They had been there for more than two hours. It would be senseless to overstay their welcome. They tried once more on Haldeman.

If it was not Haldeman, then why not say so?

"I just don't want to get into it," said Sloan, doing nothing to shake the reporters' belief that they were on the right track.

After a few more minutes of general talk about the campaign, the three of them walked to the door.

"Someday maybe you'll be President," Woodward told Sloan.

Bernstein was astonished at the remark, for it did not sound as if it had been made lightly. Woodward had meant it as a form of flattery, but there was an element of respect in it. And more—a hope that Sloan would survive the mess.

It was past noon when the reporters got to the office. Woodward placed a quick call to a source working on the federal investigation. By then, the reporters checked regularly with a half-dozen persons in the Justice Department and FBI who were sometimes willing to confirm information that had been obtained elsewhere. The sources rarely went further, often not that far.

This time Woodward was lucky. Sloan had told the whole story of the fund to investigators; so had the Bookkeeper. Mitchell, Stans, Magruder. That was right. The source would not volunteer the names of the other two persons who had controlled the fund. It was certain that the money had paid for espionage against the Democrats; whether it had financed the Watergate operation was unclear, depending on whom you believed. The details about the fund's operation were as described by Sloan and the Bookkeeper, he said.

Haldeman?

The source would not say.

A few minutes later they met with Bradlee, Simons, Rosenfeld and Sussman in Bradlee's office, a comfortable carpeted room with a picture window looking out into the newsroom, a modern oval rosewood table instead of a desk, and a black leather couch. During discussions in his office, Bradlee frequently picked up an undersize sponge-rubber basketball from the table and tossed it toward a hoop attached by suction cups to the picture window. The gesture was indicative both of the editor's short attention span and of a studied informality. There was an alluring combination of aristocrat and commoner about Bradlee: Boston Brahmin, Harvard, the World War II Navy, press attaché at the U.S. Embassy in Paris, police-beat reporter, news-magazine political reporter and Washington bureau chief of *Newsweek*.

Simons, as restrained as Bradlee could be hard-charging and obstreperous, liked to tell of watching Bradlee grind his cigarettes out in a demitasse cup during a formal dinner party. Bradlee was one of the few persons who could pull that kind of thing off and leave the hostess saying how charming he was.

Hardly unaware of his image, Bradlee even cultivated it. He delighted in displaying his street savvy, telling a reporter to get his ass moving and talk to some real cops, not lieutenants and captains behind a desk; then rising to greet some visiting dignitary from *Le Monde* or *L'Express* in formal, flawless French, complete with a peck on each cheek.

Bradlee listened attentively as Woodward ran down what details the reporters had about the secret fund, its control by Mitchell and Stans and the probability of Haldeman's authority over it as well. Bradlee focused on Mitchell and the context in which Sloan had described Mitchell's involvement with the fund.

Bernstein and Woodward thought they were on the verge of finding out the names of all five persons who controlled the secret fund and perhaps more about the individual transactions. Then they planned to write what would be a definitive account—who controlled the money and precisely how it related to Watergate.

They started to explain their plan to Bradlee and noticed that he was doodling on a sheet of paper on his desk—a sign that he was becoming a trifle impatient. He interrupted with a wave of his hand, then got to the point.

"Listen, fellas, are you certain on Mitchell?" A pause. "Absolutely certain?" He stared at each of the reporters as they nodded. "Can you write it now?"

They hesitated, then said they could. The reporters understood Bradlee's philosophy: a daily newspaper can't wait for the definitive account of events.

Bradlee stood up. "Well then, let's do it."

And, he presumed aloud, the reporters realized the implications of such a story, that John Mitchell was not someone to be trifled with, that now they were playing real hardball? Bradlee was not interrogating them. He was administering an oath.

They nodded, aware that they were about to take a bigger step than either of them had ever taken.

"Good story, good story," Simons said, repeating an office cliché, and they all laughed.

"Go," Bradlee said, waving everybody out of his office.

Bernstein was disappointed to see the meeting end. The editor had pushed his left sleeve up and Bernstein had seen a tattoo of a rooster. Bernstein momentarily forgot about Watergate. Bradlee, whom he regarded with an unhealthy imbalance of respect, fear, anger and self-pity (Bradlee did not *understand* him, he had decided long before), was always amazing him. He wished he had gotten a better look at the tattoo.

Writing the story took surprisingly little time. It moved from Bernstein's typewriter to Woodward's, then to Rosenfeld and Sussman and finally to Bradlee and Simons. Only minor changes were made. By 6:00 P.M. it was in the composing room.

X John N. Mitchell, while serving as U.S. Attorney General, personally controlled a secret Republican fund that was used to gather information about the Democrats, according to sources involved in the Watergate investigation.

Beginning in the spring of 1971, almost a year before he left the Justice Department to become President Nixon's campaign manager on March 1, Mitchell personally approved withdrawals from the fund, several reliable sources have told the *Washington Post.*

Four persons other than Mitchell were later authorized to approve payments from the secret fund, the sources said.

Two of them were identified as former Secretary of Commerce Maurice H. Stans, now finance chairman of the President's campaign, and Jeb Stuart Magruder, manager of the Nixon campaign before Mitchell took over and now a deputy director of the campaign. The other two, according to the sources, are a high White House official now involved in the campaign and a campaign aide outside of Washington.

The rest of the story dealt with how the fund operated: Sloan's phone calls to Mitchell, withdrawals by Liddy, Porter and Magruder, and the GAO's determination that even the existence of the fund was apparently illegal because the expenditures had not been reported. The Watergate grand jury's investigation "did not establish that the intelligence-gathering fund directly financed the illegal eavesdropping," the story said. "According to the *Post*'s sources, the primary purpose of the secret fund was to finance widespread intelligence-gathering operations against the Democrats."

Bernstein called CRP for the rites of denial and reached Powell Moore. Half an hour later, Moore called back with the committee's response. "I think your sources are bad; they're providing misinformation. We're not going to comment beyond that," he said. He couldn't be budged to discuss the specifics.

Bernstein remained at the *Post* that night to pursue the apparent Haldeman connection and read the clips on Herbert Kalmbach. At about 11:00 P.M., he got another call from Moore, who had talked to John Mitchell and had a new statement:

※ There is absolutely no truth to the charges in the *Post* story. Neither Mr. Mitchell nor Mr. Stans has any knowledge of any disbursement from an alleged fund as described by the *Post* and neither of them controlled any committee expenditures while serving as government officials.

Bernstein studied the statement and underlined the soft spots. *The charges in the Post story.* What charges? *Disbursement from an alleged fund as described by the Post.* There was no denial of the fund's existence, or that money had been disbursed, only of the way it was described. *Neither of them controlled any committee expenditures.* Technically correct. Sloan had controlled the expenditures, Mitchell and Stans had only approved them.

It was the cleverest denial yet, Bernstein told Moore and tried to go over it with him. Moore wouldn't play.

The new statement would be duly recorded, along with Moore's refusal to elaborate, Bernstein told Moore. If the Nixon committee would not respond, maybe Mitchell would, he added, telling Moore he would try to reach the Attorney General.

He wrote an insert on the new statement, and dialed the number of the Essex House in New York. He asked for Room 710. Mitchell answered. Bernstein recognized the voice and began scribbling notes.

He wanted to get everything down on paper, including his own questions. Moments after the call had ended, Bernstein began to type it out. In his agitated state, it was difficult to hit the right keys.

MITCHELL: "Yes."

BERNSTEIN (after identifying himself): "Sir, I'm sorry to bother you at this hour, but we are running a story in tomorrow's paper that, in effect, says that you controlled secret funds at the committee while you were Attorney General."

MITCHELL: "JEEEEEEEEESUS. You said that? What does it say?"

BERNSTEIN: "I'll read you the first few paragraphs." (He got as far as the third. Mitchell responded, "JEEEEEEEEESUS" every few words.)

MITCHELL: "All that crap, you're putting it in the paper? It's all been denied. Katie Graham's gonna get her tit caught in a big fat wringer if that's published. Good Christ! That's the most sickening thing I ever heard."

BERNSTEIN: "Sir, I'd like to ask you a few questions about—"

MITCHELL: "What time is it?"

BERNSTEIN: "Eleven thirty. I'm sorry to call so late."

MITCHELL: "Eleven thirty. Eleven thirty when?"

BERNSTEIN: "Eleven thirty at night."

MITCHELL: "Oh."

BERNSTEIN: "The committee has issued a statement about the story, but I'd like to ask you a few questions about the specifics of what the story contains."

MITCHELL: "Did the committee tell you to go ahead and publish that story? You fellows got a great ballgame going. As soon as you're through paying Ed Williams* and the rest of those fellows, we're going to do a story on all of *you*."

BERNSTEIN: "Sir, about the story—"

MITCHELL: "Call my law office in the morning."

He hung up.

For Bernstein, the only constant had been an adrenal feeling that began with Mitchell's first JEEEEEEEEESUS—some sort of primal scream. As the cry of JEEEEEEEEESUS was repeated, Bernstein had perceived the excruciating depth of Mitchell's hurt. For a moment, he had been afraid that Mitchell might die on the telephone, and for the

---

* Edward Bennett Williams, principal attorney for the *Washington Post*.

first time Mitchell was flesh and blood, not Nixon's campaign manager, the shadow of Kent State, Carswell's keeper, the high sheriff of
Law and Order, the jowled heavy of Watergate. Bernstein's skin felt
prickly. Mitchell had escaped indictment by the grand jury, which
would keep his secrets, but the reporters had said the words out loud.
Though using the neutral language of a reporter's trade, they had
called John Mitchell a crook. Bernstein did not savor the moment.
Mitchell's tone was so filled with hate and loathing that Bernstein had
felt threatened. Bernstein was shocked at his language, his ugliness.
*Did the committee tell you to go ahead and publish that story? We're
going to do a story on all of you.* Mitchell had said "we." Once the
election was over *they* could do almost anything they damn well
pleased. And get away with it.

Bernstein was determined to get Mitchell's remarks into the paper.

When he had finished typing, Bernstein briefed Bill Brady, the night
metropolitan editor, and proposed a two-paragraph insert. Brady, who
had been rewrite man for the old *Washington Times-Herald* when it
was bought by the *Post* in 1954, was perhaps the most unflappable
person in the *Post* newsroom. But he had never heard anything like
this one and asked if Bernstein was sure he had been talking to John
Mitchell. Assured, Brady shook his head. As Bernstein had expected,
Brady was not about to render a decision on how to handle Mitchell's
commentary.

Bernstein reached Bradlee at home in bed.

The editor was stunned. "Do you know what John Mitchell just
said?" he asked his wife.

Was Mitchell drunk?

Bernstein said he couldn't tell.

There was no question that Bernstein had properly identified himself?

None.

Mitchell had understood he was talking to a reporter?

Definitely.

And Bernstein had good notes?

Right.

Bradlee asked Bernstein to read him the proposed insert for the
third time, while he considered calling Mrs. Graham. He decided the
call wasn't necessary.

"Leave everything in but 'her tit,' " Bradlee instructed, "and tell the desk I said it's okay." He rejected a mild appeal from Bernstein to run the quotation intact. People would get the message, Bradlee said.

The phone rang about five minutes later. Powell Moore wanted to know if the committee's second statement had made the paper.

Bernstein said it had, as well as Mitchell's additional comments on the matter.

Moore sounded worried. What had the Attorney General said?

Bernstein read him the insert and told him it was already being set in type.

"Oh," said Moore.

Bernstein went home, his head full of disturbing visions. He had been there for only a few minutes when the phone rang. It was Moore. Bernstein started scribbling.

MOORE: "Carl, are you sure you didn't catch Mr. Mitchell at a bad moment?"

BERNSTEIN: "I don't know."

MOORE: "You caught him at an unguarded moment. He has been a Cabinet member and so forth, he doesn't want to show up in print like that."

BERNSTEIN: "I just reported what he said."

MOORE: "If his composure is not guarded, is it fair to him to hold him accountable for what he said? I'm wondering if it's totally fair to him. He goes to bed early, you know. Did he sound sleepy?"

BERNSTEIN: "I couldn't tell. But I know that you fellows hold me accountable for what I write and what I say. So I don't think it's un-reasonable to expect any less of Mr. Mitchell. He's dealt with the press before."

MOORE: "Carl, I don't want anything printed that was said in a mo-ment when the average person is not fully alert because he was awakened in the middle of the night."

BERNSTEIN: "What time did you talk to him?"

MOORE: "It was a while ago, probably around nine—Carl, is it too late to get that out of the paper?"

BERNSTEIN: "It's in there now, I think. The only way to get it out would be to talk to my editors. It was their judgment that it should be used, and I certainly concur."

MOORE: "Who would I talk to to get it out? Is Bill Brady there?"

BERNSTEIN: "No. I would think that to get something out you would have to talk to Bradlee."

MOORE: "I certainly don't want to make an independent decision to talk to Ben Bradlee. Let me get back to you."

Five minutes later, Moore called again and asked how he could reach the editor. Bernstein said he should call the *Post* switchboard in five minutes, then he called Bradlee himself and told him to expect Moore's call.

Always the southern gentleman, Moore called Bernstein back a few minutes later to tell him that Bradlee had refused to kill the insert.

Bradlee, imitating Moore's drawl, later recalled that Moore asked him "was I sure this was a wise thing to do because we woke up the Attorney General, probably late in the mornin', and he wasn't havin' all his thoughts collected. And I remember saying, 'Which just boils down to the question, Mr. Moore, of whether he said it or not, and whether the *Washington Post* reporter identified himself as a reporter, and if he did that, all my requisites have been satisified.' "

At the *Post* the next morning, Mrs. Graham asked Bernstein if he had any more messages for her.

The night of October 4, Woodward got home at about eleven. The phone was ringing as he stepped in the door. "Ace—" it was Bill Brady. The night editor calls all the young reporters "Ace." (Brady had called Woodward "Ace" the second night he worked at the *Post,* and Woodward's head had swelled for several hours, until he heard Brady address a notorious office incompetent by the same title.)

"Ace," said Brady, "the *L.A. Times* is running some long interview with a fellow named Baldwin."

Woodward groaned, and said he'd be right in.

Alfred C. Baldwin III had seemed for a time to be one of the keys to Watergate. The reporters had learned of him while making some routine checks. Bernstein had been told that a former FBI agent had participated in the Watergate operation; that he had informed investigators that Democratic headquarters had been under electronic surveillance for about three weeks before the arrests; and that memos of the wiretapped conversations had been transcribed and sent directly to CRP. The man had also said he had infiltrated the Vietnam Veterans

Against the War, on orders from McCord. On September 11, Bernstein and Woodward had written a story about the participation of such a former FBI agent.

A week later, with help from the Bookkeeper, they had identified him as Baldwin, a 35-year-old law-school graduate who had worked as chief of security for a trucking firm before becoming a CRP employee paid in $100 bills. Baldwin was the government's chief witness—the insider who was spilling the whole story. He seemed to have unimaginable secrets to tell, and reporters were in line to hear them. Woodward had joined the queue. He began making regular phone calls to Baldwin's lawyer, John Cassidento, a Democratic state legislator from New Haven, Connecticut.

"We've got hundreds of requests for interviews, hundreds," Cassidento had told Woodward. "Everyone wants to talk to Al. There are two *Los Angeles Times* reporters camped out there. Al is getting no peace. He is followed. . . . Ugly fuckers, you reporters. Thank God *you're* not pestering us."

Taking that hint, Woodward said that he and Bernstein wouldn't join the herd.

"Fine," Cassidento said cozily. "We'll let you know if Al has anything to say. You'll get the first call."

Several days later, Cassidento called Woodward back. "Hey, Al needs some money. . . . Everyone is offering him money for his story. Just want to let you know in case you want to enter the bidding." It was rumored that a major magazine had offered $5000 for Baldwin's first-person account.

Woodward explained that the *Post* never paid for news.

"Okay, okay, I'm sorry you don't care about the story," said Cassidento. "We have other offers."

Woodward started to say that the *Post* cared very much about the story, but Cassidento had hung up.

Woodward and Bernstein told the editors about the invitation to bid on Baldwin's story. "I bid this . . ." Bradlee said, and raised the middle finger of his right hand.

Two weeks later, and without paying a penny, the *Los Angeles Times* had gotten the story that brought Woodward back to his desk the night of October 4. Baldwin's first-person account of the bugging operation, told to *Times* reporter Jack Nelson, was a vivid description of a raid on the Democratic national headquarters, and of the men who had participated in it.

From the Howard Johnson Motor Hotel across the street from the Watergate, Baldwin had monitored conversations of Democrats' phone calls. McCord had told him he would be doing the same thing at the Democratic convention in Miami. When hired, he had been handed a gun belonging to Fred LaRue. He told of an aborted attempt to break into McGovern headquarters and bug it; Gordon Liddy had suggested shooting out a street light to facilitate the entry. Baldwin described a brief stint guarding Martha Mitchell, and he related Howard Hunt's panic as he had rushed into the Howard Johnson at 2:30 A.M. on June 17 and watched the police lead five of his hirelings from the Watergate.

Bernstein and Woodward had been aced out. The story was a major break, not just because it contained a great deal of new information, but because it made the Watergate operation, and the siege mentality behind it, real.

"I would like to have had that one," Bradlee said the next day. He was not harsh, but he was grimacing, clutching his arms as he spoke, moving them quickly from side to side like a running halfback.*

In his five-hour taped interview with Jack Nelson, Baldwin had not provided the name of any individual who might have seen the wiretap memos. But two weeks before the *Los Angeles Times* interview, Bernstein had been told by a Democratic Party investigator that Baldwin had named two persons he thought had received them: Robert Odle, Jeb Magruder's intensely nervous aide-de-camp at both the White House and CRP; and William E. Timmons, Assistant to the President for congressional relations and chief White House liaison to CRP for the Republican national convention. Baldwin had seen McCord addressing the memos.

There was a third recipient, Baldwin was alleged to have said, someone whose first name sounded like a last name. Shown a list of CRP officials by federal investigators, Baldwin had picked the name of J.

---

* "Egos are tender in this business," Bradlee said months later. "You massage them, don't deflate them. . . . I can't go out and take notes for someone. I'm removed, and sometimes it frustrates the hell out of me. . . . I can't kick ass for getting scooped, but I do let it be known that I feel let down and that I hate it, just hate it. Don't forget that I hate it."

Glenn Sedam—the man who had shared an office with Gordon Liddy. But, Bernstein was told, Baldwin had not been certain about Sedam.

Bernstein suggested to Woodward that they write a story saying that Baldwin had named Odle and Timmons, and describing how he picked Sedam's name. Bernstein called a Justice Department source who confirmed the details. Woodward agreed to go ahead.

The story would be a significant advance on the *Los Angeles Times* account. It ran on October 6. There were no denunciations from CRP or the White House.

But the report was incorrect, and the decision to rush it into print was a mistake. Weeks later, Woodward and Bernstein learned that the initial FBI report had not made it clear whether the memos Baldwin had seen were of the wiretap conversations or were merely routine security memos. Eventually, the reporters became convinced that they were routine memos which had nothing to do with wiretapping.

Three men had been wronged. They had been unfairly accused on the front page of the *Washington Post,* the hometown newspaper of their families, neighbors and friends. Odle complained to the prosecutors. "He was almost in tears," one of them said later. The stigma of Watergate stayed with him, though not solely because of the story, and he had great difficulty obtaining a job. In 1973, he was hired by the Department of Agriculture as a consultant, but he was soon fired when his name continued to figure in the investigation.

Timmons was dejected about the *Post* allegations, and his wife had wanted him to quit his job on the White House staff. Only after a long conversation with the President had he decided to stay on.

6

THE NIGHT of September 28, Bernstein had been taking some good-natured complaining from the copy desk about his penchant for making late-night fixes or changes in his stories. He was not displeased when the exercise was interrupted by the phone.

The caller introduced himself as a government lawyer who had nothing to do with the Watergate investigation. He said he might have some information that might or might not have something to do with the things Bernstein and Woodward had been writing about.

Such calls were becoming more frequent, though most of the "tips" the reporters received were requests that the *Post* pursue theories about the deaths of John Kennedy, Mary Jo Kopechne, Martin Luther King and others.

As for tips related to Watergate, they had checked out dozens which had proven to be either inconsequential or without foundation.*

* They had been dismayed at the lack of first-rate information reaching them via mail or telephone tips from strangers. Jack Anderson's network of anonymous bureaucratic sources was legendary, and big ongoing stories—particularly scandals—often produced government informers who "leaked" information to newspapers on their own initiative. Watergate seemed to be the exception. No dissatisfied FBI agent or CRP employee had ever come to Bernstein or Woodward offering information. The closest they had come to observing one of these legendary fountains of information had been about a week after the indictments were handed down. The caller had said she worked for the Department of Justice and had seen files showing that Jeb Magruder and Bart Porter had lied to the grand jury, along with others. The persons in charge of the investigation had known they lied. And unusual political pressures had been brought to bear on the investigation throughout—particularly from the White House, she said. But the reporters could not keep her on the phone. She was too frightened, and they never heard from her again.

The lawyer on the phone now said he had a friend who "had been approached . . . to go to work for the Nixon campaign in a very unusual way."

Bernstein put a sheet of paper in the typewriter and began taking it down.

The caller said his friend was named Alex Shipley, an assistant attorney general of the state of Tennessee, living in Nashville. In the summer of 1971, Shipley had been asked by an old Army buddy to join the Nixon campaign.

"Essentially, the proposal was that there was to be a crew of people whose job it would be to disrupt the Democratic campaign during the primaries. This guy told Shipley there was virtually unlimited money available."

The caller didn't know the name of the man who had approached Shipley. "This guy was a lawyer. The idea was to travel around, there would be some going to towns and waiting for things to happen. For instance, some guy would be waiting to see if the Democratic candidates were renting a hall to have a rally. Then his job would be to call up the owner of the hall and say the event had been rescheduled, to fuck up the logistics."

Shipley had told the story "during a drunken conversation at a picnic" and the caller did not remember many other details. At the time Shipley was approached, he was still in the Army, stationed in Washington. He had talked to people who had worked for former Senator Albert Gore of Tennessee. "They advised him to lead this guy along while trying to figure out what was going on." The caller didn't know what had happened after that.

Reluctantly, he gave Bernstein his name and telephone number, on the condition that he never be disclosed as the source of the information. Bernstein thanked him and asked him to stay in touch.

Bernstein got Alex Shipley's number from Nashville information, but there was no answer.

The next day, Bernstein showed Howard Simons his notes and said he was convinced the information—admittedly very sketchy—was important. By itself, the Watergate bugging made little sense, particularly since it had occurred when the Nixon campaign was at its strongest. But if it had been part of something much broader, it might make some sense, Bernstein said. And there was evidence of a broader scheme, though the information was disparate. Among the things they were aware of had been the attempt to bug McGovern headquarters; Hunt's investigation of Teddy Kennedy; an investigation by McCord of Jack Anderson; the effort by Baldwin to infiltrate the Vietnam Veterans Against the War; Hunt's investigations of leaks to the news media; and McCord's rental of an office next to Muskie's campaign headquarters. Perhaps the White House had been in the political intelligence business in a much bigger way and for much longer than most people figured. Watergate could have been scheduled before the President's re-election chances looked so good and perhaps someone had neglected to pull the plug.

Simons was interested and urged Bernstein to get to Shipley fast. The managing editor shared Bernstein's fondness for doping things out on the basis of sketchy information. At the same time, he was cautious about what eventually went into print. On more than one occasion, he told Bernstein and Woodward to consider delaying a story or, if necessary, to pull it at the last minute if they had any doubts. "I don't care if it's a word, a phrase, a sentence, a paragraph, a whole story or an entire series of stories," he said. "When in doubt, leave it out."

A prize-winning science reporter, Simons had become the number-two editor at the *Post* a year before. An intent, sensitive man with a large nose, thin face and deep-set eyes, he looks like the kind of Harvard teaching assistant who carries a slide rule strapped to his belt. But he is skillful with fragile egos, and also the perfect counterpoint to Bradlee. Bradlee is more like Woodward: he wants hard information first and is impatient with theories.

Bernstein tried to stir Woodward's interest in Shipley's story, but Woodward was skeptical.

That night, Bernstein reached Shipley at home. He sounded pleasant and was surprised that a reporter would be so interested in the approach that had been made to him.

"The deal I was offered was slick," Shipley said. "We'd say we were working for So-and-so in the Democrats and really we'd be working for Nixon. Say, for instance, my job would be to go to a Kennedy rally. I'd say to one of Kennedy's people: 'I'm also with you people. We want you to go get a job in the Muskie office. And when you find out anything, you let me know and we'll get it back to Kennedy.' "

Somewhere, Bernstein had been told that the CIA did that kind of thing abroad. He had heard it called Mindfuck, but the agency called it Black Operation.

Shipley continued, "There would be as much money as needed. I was promised the pie in the sky by and by. Expenses plus salary. I'd be working for him." Shipley did not want to give the man's name until he decided to tell the whole story.

"I've been thinking about talking to somebody. About six months ago, I made a memo to myself and it's up at the office—I've got dates. And I'll give you the best of my memory."

First, however, he wanted to obtain permission from his boss before talking to the press. He thought his boss would approve. The attorney general of Tennessee was a Democrat, and so was Shipley. That was perhaps the strangest aspect of the approach in Shipley's mind.

"This guy came to me. I said, 'I'm a man with a picture of Franklin Roosevelt on the wall since I've been a child. Why me?' He said, 'It could be for purely selfish reasons—we can do a lot for you.' Liking the Democrats more, I didn't follow it up."

Beyond the man's word, Shipley had no proof that the offer was made on behalf of Richard Nixon's re-election campaign. He had known the man in the Army. "My impression was that he would not be very effective at spy stuff. But he said he was working for Nixon."

Bernstein did not want to press for the recruiter's name—yet.

He called Shipley the next evening. The Democratic attorney general of Tennessee told Shipley to do what he thought right, and Shipley had gotten his notes together. The man who had approached him was named Donald Segretti.

"The first time he called would have been 26 June, 1971. He had called and told me he would be in Washington, and he came to a dinner party at my apartment on 26 June. Nothing was said that night. On 27 June, I met him for breakfast. That's when he first mentioned the deal. He asked would I be interested, because I was getting out of the Army? Both of us were getting out shortly. We were all captains in the Judge Advocate General Corps. None of us had anything lined up. He told me he had come to Washington for an interview at the Treasury Department."

Bernstein wrote a note to himself: "Treasury—Liddy." Gordon Liddy had worked at Treasury before he joined the White House staff, at just about the time Shipley was talking about. But Shipley said he had never heard of Liddy before the Watergate break-in.

Shipley had picked Segretti up at the Georgetown Inn the morning of June 27, 1971 and driven him to Dulles Airport. "On the way to Dulles, he said, 'How would you like to work in an operation doing a little political espionage?' I said, 'What are you talking about?' He said, 'For instance, we go to a Kennedy rally and find an ardent Kennedy worker. Then you say that you're a Kennedy man too but you're working behind the scenes; you get them to help you. You send them to work for Muskie, stuffing envelopes or whatever, and you get them to pass you the information. They'll think that they are helping Kennedy against Muskie. But actually you're using the information for something else.' It was very strange. About three quarters of the way to the airport, I said, 'Well, who would we be working for?' He said Nixon. I was really taken aback, because all the actions he had talked about would have taken place in the Democratic primaries.

"The main purpose was that the Democrats not have the ability to get back together after a knock-down drag-out campaign, he said. 'What we want to do is cause enough havoc so they can't.' I said, 'Well, it sounds interesting, let me think about it.' "

The following week, Segretti had called Shipley from Fort Ord, California, to renew the offer.

"On Thursday, 1 July," Shipley continued, "I went and had an interview with a friend who had worked for Senator Albert Gore's administrative assistant and asked him what I should do. I told him I wasn't interested, but was wondering if it might help the Democrats if I played along. Or whether I should drop it immediately. He said, 'Don't stick your neck out, but don't say no; see what you can find out.'

"On the 19th of July, Segretti called and asked that I think of five names of people that I might contact [to join the operation]. I don't recall if I told him any or not. On Sunday morning, the 25th of July, he called me from Chicago and . . . said he had made a similar proposal to another Army captain there—Roger Lee Nixt, who was stationed at an Army post in Chicago, Fifth Army headquarters, I think. He said he wanted to fly to Washington to talk to me. . . . The gist of that conversation was 'Are you with me or not?'

"I asked him what he wanted me to do. He said 'Enlist people—be imaginative.'

"One thing he did stress was asking people who were fairly free to travel, and he was asking lawyers because he stressed he didn't want to do anything illegal. It wasn't represented as strictly a strong-arm operation. He stressed what fun we could have. . . ."

He said that when a rally was scheduled for 7:00 P.M. at a local coliseum "you would call up and represent that you were the field manager for the candidate and you had information that some rowdies, hippies and what-have-you were going to cause trouble. So you ask him to postpone the rally from seven o'clock, when it was actually scheduled, to nine o'clock, thereby insuring that the coliseum manager had the place padlocked when the candidate showed up."

Then again on July 28, Segretti had called Shipley, and had asked him to fly to Atlanta to help enlist another former Army captain, Kenneth Griffiths. Shipley didn't go.

The last time Shipley heard from Segretti was on October 23, 1971: "He called from California and asked me to check into Muskie's operation in Tennessee. . . . All these times he would give me these proposals, I would say, 'Sure,' but I just never did anything about it."

Did Shipley know where to get in touch with Segretti, where he lived?

"About two weeks ago, I tried to get a phone number in Los Angeles for him, but there was no listing. He told me he was going to be in a law firm by the name of Young and Segretti—he said it was a cover, that he would be doing only political work."

Shipley had finished going through his notes. Bernstein asked him to try to recall his conversations with Segretti in more detail.

"At one time, Segretti said it might be good to get a false ID to travel under, that it would be harder for anyone to catch up with us. He mentioned he might use the pseudonym Bill Mooney for himself. Just in passing, he said, 'Why don't you think up a good one and get an ID card?' I said, 'I'm not particularly good at that kind of thing.' He also told me we would be taken care of after Nixon's re-election. I would get a good job in the government. I said, 'How in hell are we going to be taken care of if no one knows what we're doing?' And Segretti said, 'Nixon knows that something is being done. It's a typical deal. Don't-tell-me-anything-and-I-won't-know.' "

How sure was Shipley that Segretti was working for the Nixon campaign?

"I don't know if he ever worked for Nixon," he said, "I don't have any proof. He could have been working for Kennedy, Muskie or Sam Yorty, for all I know." But Segretti had told Shipley that if he stayed with the operation, it would lead to a permanent job in the administration.

Bernstein asked whether Shipley knew of others Segretti had approached.

Peter Dixon, an attorney in San Francisco.

"All the people whose names I listed were in Vietnam together as Army captains in JAG in '68 and '69. Nixt is working for a law firm in Denison, Iowa, I think. Griffiths is still in Atlanta."

What other details could he remember?

"Well, Segretti said that the people who contacted him about the operation were Los Angeles people. They could have been law-school people, old friends of the family, I have no idea. He never told me any names. He said that's the way we'll operate. I was not to tell him the names of any operatives working for me. . . . He said he wanted to cover the country. Frankly, I don't think he could do it because he's not that kind of guy, he doesn't have the right personality. He's a small guy with a big smile on his face all the time—naïve."

Bernstein asked for a physical description of Segretti.

"Short, baby-faced, less than five foot eight, maybe 150 pounds."

Shipley didn't know much about Segretti's politics. "I always assumed he was fairly liberal. I don't think we ever had a political discussion."

Segretti had said that he "would more or less be the head coordinator of the operation for the whole country," but a lot of the things he proposed to do didn't seem that damaging: "He said we could get a post-office box in Massachusetts in the name of the Massachusetts Safe Driving Committee and award a medal to Teddy Kennedy.

"One thing that struck me was that he seemed to be well financed. He was always flying across the country. He said that money was no problem, that the people we would be working for wanted results for the cash that would be spent."

Shipley had pressed him on the financing, but Segretti had said, " 'Don't ask me any names because I'm not going to tell you any.' I had the feeling it was some big spender, but not a government man."

Bernstein asked Shipley not to discuss the information with anyone else, and called Woodward at home. They were on the way, Bernstein said. It would take a few days, but the story was in sight. This time, Woodward was intrigued.

Kenneth Griffiths, Roger Lee Nixt and Peter Dixon all had listed phone numbers.

Nixt didn't want to talk about it. "I had just one conversation about it with Don. He's a friend and I'm just not going to discuss it, out of consideration for him. . . . I didn't do anything. . . . Yes, he proposed some undercover work for the Nixon campaign, but I'm not going to talk about it."

At Griffiths' home in Atlanta, there was no reply. That left Dixon in San Francisco. His secretary said he was on a camping trip, but was expected to arrive that afternoon in Reno, Nevada, at the home of a friend, Paul Bible.

The Senator's son? asked Bernstein.

Yes.

That was great. Senator Alan Bible of Nevada and his family had lived next door to the Bernstein family in Silver Spring, Maryland, for more than a dozen years. Paul was a few years older than Bernstein, but they knew each other, had played street football together. He remembered when Paul had gotten his '58 Chevy Impala. It was jet black, lowered, and had dual exhausts and spinners. Bernstein had been envious.

He called Bible in Reno and told him what he was working on. He was sure Paul would help.

Bible was flabbergasted. Segretti? He couldn't imagine it. Bible, too, had served in the Army with Segretti, and Don wasn't the type of guy to get into this kind of mess. He would have Dixon call back and meanwhile gave Bernstein the names of other officers who had served in Segretti's outfit.

Dixon called from Bible's house: "Don called and asked if I'd be interested in doing some work for the re-election of the President. I said, 'Gee, Don, I'm not interested in political matters, I'm not a Republican anyway.' He didn't go into it any further."

Two acknowledgments. Bernstein reached Griffiths after two more tries. He didn't want to talk about his dealings with Segretti. They had lunched together, had talked about the campaign. Segretti had tried to recruit him to do something for the President; the word "undercover" or "underground" had come up—he didn't remember which.

"I said that, much as I'd like to do something for the President, I didn't have time to do more than send him a contribution."

Between calls, Bernstein tried to find a number for Donald Segretti. There was no such listing in Los Angeles. There was no law firm listed under Young and Segretti. There were several Segrettis, however. After several calls, Bernstein reached Mrs. A. H. Segretti in Culver City. She said she was Don's mother.

Bernstein bent the rules a bit. The *Post* had a firm policy that its reporters were never to misrepresent themselves. But he didn't tell Mrs. Segretti he worked for the *Washington Post*. When he left his name and numbers, they were for both his and Woodward's apartments. Bernstein neglected to tell Woodward about the call.

Woodward was playing Scrabble with a friend at his apartment when the phone rang that afternoon.

"Is Carl Bernstein there?"

Woodward said Bernstein wasn't there, and asked who was calling.

"Don Segretti."

Woodward froze. Why was Segretti calling Bernstein at his place? Bernstein had mentioned only the highlights of his conversation with Shipley. Woodward wasn't familiar enough with the details to put much pressure on.

After a long pause, Woodward said, "Oh."

"Who is Carl Bernstein?" Segretti asked.

Woodward sensed he was trapped and tried to recover. Both of them were reporters for the *Washington Post,* he said and—without letting Segretti get in a word—added that they wanted to ask him about some rather serious allegations involving political undercover work he had done for the Nixon campaign.

"The *Washington Post?*" Segretti asked. He said he didn't know what Woodward was talking about. Besides, he was too busy to talk, he said, and hung up.

Woodward called Bernstein at the office and asked what the hell was going on. Bernstein was furious with himself. They had lost the edge.

Bernstein and Woodward tried to figure out what to do next. One of them, or another reporter, should get on Segretti's tail right away. They called Sussman at home. He suggested using the *Post*'s West Coast correspondent or a "stringer" recommended by the national desk.

Robert Meyers, a 29-year-old former *Newsweek* stringer—the term for a reporter hired by a newspaper for special assignments on a story-by-story basis—would track down Segretti. Meyers projected an image more professorial than reporter-like—pipe-smoking, a wispy goatee, rimless eyeglasses. When Bernstein reached him at home, he was soaking in the bathtub. He had followed the *Post*'s Watergate coverage closely, and Bernstein brought him up to date on Segretti.

There were two other calls that afternoon. A woman at the Georgetown Inn was prevailed upon to search the hotel's records for the week of June 21, 1971, for a record of Donald Segretti or Bill Mooney. The other call was to Gordon Liddy's home.

Bernstein went into an unoccupied office near the newsroom. He was really going to break the rules this time, and he didn't want Bradlee or anybody else to walk by his desk and hear him doing it. Besides, there was no question about the security of that phone.

He closed the door and rehearsed his number: "Gordon . . . This is Don Segretti. I think we've got big troubles. . . ." All he wanted was some sign of recognition, something like, "What's the problem, Don?"

Unfortunately, Bernstein had not designed a scenario to deal with the possibility that Mrs. Liddy would answer the phone and ask who was calling. If Mrs. Liddy had ever heard of Donald Segretti, she gave no indication. And if her husband did know Segretti, he would probably phone him in California and find out the caller had been an impostor—probably from the *Washington Post,* whose reporters had also been in touch with Segretti and his family earlier in the day. Bernstein got off the phone in a hurry.

All the lines were out. The next call, Monday afternoon, from the Georgetown Inn, confirmed that Donald H. Segretti had registered on June 25, 1971, and checked out on the 27th. There was no record of the phone calls he had made.

Bernstein renewed a contact made in June when he had been retracing the movements of the five men arrested inside the Watergate. He had called an employee of a credit-card company who, if promised anonymity, said he could obtain selected records.

A credit card leaves a trail of hotel and restaurant charges and airplane tickets giving dates, times, places, costs, transactions. The FBI usually goes to those records first, gobbling them up with subpoenas.

Segretti, whose last name means "secrets" in Italian, had crisscrossed the country more than 10 times during the last half of 1971, according to his credit-card records, usually staying in a city for no longer than a night or two. The stops had included Miami; Houston; Manchester, New Hampshire; Knoxville; Los Angeles; Chicago; Portland; San Francisco; New York; Fresno; Tucson; Albuquerque and—repeatedly —Washington. Many of the cities were in key political states for the 1972 presidential campaign, mostly primary states. In New Hampshire, Florida, Illinois and, particularly, California, Segretti had moved from city to city, leaving his trail in territories where the Democratic primaries would be fought hardest. The travel records supported Shipley's account.

Bernstein passed the reporters' information about Segretti on to Meyers, who was staking out Segretti's apartment and talking to his neighbors. Marina del Rey, where Segretti lived, was on the water and, if you believed the ads, represented the ultimate in swinging-singles living. Lots of sailing, saunas, mixed-doubles tennis, pools, parties, candlelight, long-stemmed glasses, Caesar salads, tanned bodies, mixed double-triple-multiple kinkiness in scented sandalwood splendor.

Meyers climbed up to Segretti's balcony and looked inside. There were dirty dishes on a counter. The apartment looked comfortable— thick white wall-to-wall carpeting, a gas-jet fireplace with fake logs, a battery of stereo equipment, books, magazines and records stacked on tables. Meyers could see a 10-speed bicycle in a hallway that appeared to lead to the bedroom.

Two of Segretti's neighbors said he had left in a hurry in his white Mercedes sports coupé on Saturday afternoon and had mentioned that he might not be back for a few days. They didn't know about his work, except that he was a lawyer and traveled a lot. He didn't talk about politics much.

The garage under Segretti's building resembled something between a sports-car showroom and a racetrack pit stop. Somebody seemed to be working on a car at almost any hour of the day or night. Meyers spent a lot of time in the garage, checking there for Segretti's 280-SL, inspecting the vacant parking space for oil drippings in case he had missed a quick return. But the floor remained dry; the mail in Segretti's mailbox accumulated.

On Thursday morning, a matchstick Meyers had wedged into the interface of Segretti's front door had dropped to the floor. But there was no answer when Meyers knocked, and Segretti's car was not in the garage. Meyers waited. Segretti was back that afternoon and answered the door. Meyers introduced himself as a reporter for the *Post*. The *Post* had information about certain work Segretti had done in behalf of Teddy Kennedy, or possibly Hubert Humphrey, he said. Could they talk?

Segretti remained silent in the doorway. He looked younger than his 31 years, more as if he were in his early or mid-twenties. He had a friendly face, though it was unsmiling.

Meyers asked if he had any connection with Kennedy or Humphrey. No.

Meyers wanted to get inside. The *Post* had extensive information on Segretti, he said, about his work in the Democratic primaries. Segretti let him inside.

Did he know Alex Shipley?

"Why?"

Because the *Post* had information connecting Segretti with an attempt to recruit Shipley for undercover political work.

"I don't believe it," Segretti said.

In fact, hadn't Segretti attempted to recruit Shipley during a drive to Dulles Airport on June 27, 1971 to do work concerning the primary campaign of Humphrey or Muskie?

"I don't remember."

Did he know Alex Shipley?

"No comment."

Hadn't he called Shipley from Chicago and told him he wanted to talk to him about a job?

"I don't remember."

And later, hadn't he called Shipley and asked him to fly to Atlanta to recruit Kenneth Griffiths?

"I don't remember."

He did know Shipley, correct?

"No comment."

Had he called Shipley from California on October 23, asking him to check on Muskie's operation in Tennessee?

Segretti's demeanor remained mild, even affable. "This is ridiculous," he told Meyers. "I don't know anything about this. This all sounds like James Bond fiction."

Meyers asked him about Dixon, Nixt and whether the Treasury Department had picked up any of his tabs; about his law practice, and about his travels, and again about Shipley.

Segretti remained impassive, a faint smile on his face.

What about the name Bill Mooney, a false ID that Segretti had said he might use? Did that ring a bell?

"Ridiculous."

Segretti moved toward the door. Reaching for a 35-millimeter camera under the back of his jacket, Meyers said he wanted to take a picture before he left, and started clicking. Segretti ran outside into the hallway, yelling "No pictures!" A moment later, he came back and Meyers pointed the lens at his head. Just one more, Meyers said, aiming the camera again. Segretti tried to grab it and missed, then seized Meyers' left arm and pushed him toward the open door, the camera still clicking.

Meyers rushed to a pay phone. Bernstein was talking to Sussman in the city editor's office. Things were breaking. During a routine telephone check with a Justice Department official that morning, Bernstein had asked if the official had ever heard of Donald Segretti. It had been a throwaway question.

"I can't answer your question because that's part of the investigation," the Justice official replied.

Bernstein was startled. Woodward and he had thought they were alone in pursuing Segretti.

There could be no discussion of Segretti because he was part of the Watergate investigation, right?

That was correct, but the official would not listen to any more questions about Segretti. Bernstein went down his list of checks, crossing out each item, writing "no" or "nothing" in the margin.

Herbert W. Kalmbach?

"That's part of the investigation, too, so I can't talk about it," the official said.

Sloan had refused to say if Kalmbach was among those who could give out money from Maurice Stans' safe. But since the fund was intended for "intelligence-gathering," Segretti might have been bank-rolled that way. Shipley had the impression that Segretti had got money from a "big spender" who was not in government. That would fit Kalmbach, President Nixon's personal attorney.

Was there a connection between Segretti and Kalmbach?

The official would say nothing more.

Sussman and Bernstein were discussing all this when a copy aide rushed into the city editor's office to say Meyers was waiting on the phone, sounding all out of breath.

"Jesus, I nearly got my ass beaten trying to take pictures,"* he told Bernstein. Then he got his breath back and put the scene into better focus.

Bernstein told Meyers that the Feds knew about Segretti. Sussman came over to talk to Meyers. All agreed he should go back and contact anyone who might know Segretti, find out if his acquaintances had been contacted by the FBI, what questions had been asked, everything they might know about him. The University of Southern California and Boalt Hall law school at Berkeley, where Segretti had studied, seemed the best places. The next day, Meyers called to say that, as a USC undergraduate, Segretti had been close to several persons who were to become part of the Nixon White House. Among the USC graduates at the White House were Ron Ziegler, the President's press secretary; Dwight Chapin, the presidential appointments secretary; Bart Porter, a former White House advance man and CRP scheduling director who had received money from the fund; Tim Elbourne, who had served as a Ziegler press assistant; Mike Guhin, a member of Henry Kissinger's National Security Council staff; and Gordon Strachan, Haldeman's political aide and the White House liaison to CRP.

Bernstein and Woodward sent feelers out through the *Post* newsroom, looking for anyone who had more than superficial contact with mem-

---

* None of them came out. His camera had been incorrectly loaded.

bers of the White House staff. Their expectations weren't very high, given the relationship between the Nixon administration and the *Washington Post*. That heady era of good feeling, in which reporters had rubbed elbows and shoulders with President Kennedy's men in touch football and candlelit backyards in Georgetown and Cleveland Park, was a thing of the past.

But Karlyn Barker, a former UPI reporter who had joined the city staff on the same day as Woodward, said a friend of hers had gone to USC with the White House boys and had stayed in close touch with them. Within a few hours, Barker had given Bernstein a memo headed "Notes on USC Crowd."

Her friend had known Segretti, Chapin and Tim Elbourne since college. He referred to the "USC Mafia" in the White House and said Segretti and Elbourne had been called by their schoolmates Dwight Chapin and Ron Ziegler to help in the Nixon election business.

All belonged to a campus political party called Trojans for Representative Government. The Trojans called their brand of electioneering "ratfucking." Ballot boxes were stuffed, spies were planted in the opposition camp, and bogus campaign literature abounded. Ziegler and Chapin had hooked onto Richard Nixon's 1962 campaign for governor of California—managed by Bob Haldeman. After graduation, Ziegler and Chapin and Elbourne had joined the J. Walter Thompson advertising agency in Los Angeles, where Haldeman was a vice president. Segretti had been summoned to Washington and trained to work in a presidential election, according to Karlyn Barker's friend.

Bernstein called the Justice Department official who had originally told him that Segretti was part of the Watergate investigation. It was Saturday, October 7.

"No, I can't talk about him," the official said once more. "That's right, even though he's not directly linked to Watergate, to the break-in. . . . Obviously, I came across him through the investigation. . . . Yes, political sabotage is associated with Segretti. I've heard a term for it, 'ratfucking.' There is some very powerful information, especially if it comes out before November 7," the day of the election.

Could that powerful information involve Dwight Chapin? Had he hired Segretti? Or had Ziegler? Or . . .

"I won't say anything on either Ziegler or Chapin."

Bernstein guessed Chapin. The official said he certainly didn't want to discourage anything the *Post* might be pursuing.

In the rough code they had evolved, Bernstein interpreted the remark as confirming that there was a connection between Segretti and Chapin.

Did Segretti have anything to do with the Canuck Letter?*

The official said he couldn't talk about that letter either; it was also part of the investigation.

Bernstein groped through the paper effluvia on his desk and retrieved a manila file marked "Phones." In June he had begun jotting down phone numbers of persons contacted on the story, logging them on a sheet of copy paper. He started going through the pages, looking for people who might know about Donald Segretti, ratfucking, Dwight Chapin, the USC Mafia, the Canuck Letter.

Bernstein had been reading the clippings on the primaries for any examples of malicious dirty tricks.

* The so-called Canuck Letter had been the beginning of the end of the Muskie campaign, as far as some of the Senator's campaign aides were concerned. On February 24, two days before Muskie was scheduled to campaign in Manchester, New Hampshire, William Loeb's right-wing newspaper, the *Manchester Union Leader*, had published an anti-Muskie editorial on its front page. Titled "Senator Muskie Insults Franco-Americans," it accused Muskie of hypocrisy for supporting blacks while condoning the term "Canucks"—a derogatory name for Americans of French-Canadian ancestry, tens of thousands of whom were New Hampshire voters.

The "evidence" was a semi-literate letter ostensibly mailed to Loeb from Deerfield Beach, Florida, and published in the *Union Leader* the same day as the editorial. The signer claimed that a Muskie campaign aide at a Fort Lauderdale meeting had said that "we don't have blacks but we have Cannocks" (sic), and the Senator reportedly concurred laughingly, saying, "Come to New England and see." The Muskie campaign had contended that the letter was a fake, and had undertaken an investigation but failed to find the author.

On February 25, Loeb had reprinted a two-month-old *Newsweek* item about the Senator's wife. Titled "Big Daddy's Jane," it reported she sneak-smoked, drank and used off-color language on the press plane.

The next morning, standing in a near-blizzard on the back of a flatbed truck, Muskie had abandoned his prepared text and attacked Loeb as a "gutless coward." Then, while defending his wife, he broke down and cried. There was no dispute among Muskie's backers, his opponents and the press that the incident had a disastrous effect on his campaign. It shattered the calm, cool, reasoned image that was basic to Muskie's voter appeal, and focused the last-minute attention of New Hampshire voters on the alleged slur against the French-Canadians who would be a formidable minority of voters in the Democratic primary.

Finally he hit with one call.

"Ratfucking?" The word struck a raw nerve with a Justice Department attorney. "You can go right to the top on that one. I was shocked when I learned about it. I couldn't believe it. These are public servants? God. It's nauseating. You're talking about fellows who come from the best schools in the country. Men who run the government!"

Bernstein wondered what "right to the top" meant. But he wasn't given time to ask. The attorney had worked himself into a rage.

"If the Justice Department could find a law against it, a jury of laymen would convict them on that. It's absolutely despicable. Segretti? He's indescribable. It would be useful for you to write an article about this type of conduct. I was so shocked. I didn't understand it. It's completely immoral. All these people, unbelievable. Look at Hunt. I don't think he's involved in the ratfucking. But he's capable of anything. And he had access to the White House.

"The press hasn't brought that home. You're dealing with people who act like this was Dodge City, not the capital of the United States. Hunt bringing guns into the White House!"*

Bernstein was impressed. He had never known the man to be so outraged.

The Chapin-Segretti connection?

"Look at it more to see if your facts are straight," the attorney advised.

The secret fund—had it financed the ratfucking?

"That's a fruitful area." He was calm for a moment, then became angry again. "Why else would they have all that money lying around? It's a scandal. But it will all come out at the trial. . . ."

The Canuck Letter?

"The Muskie letter is part of it."

Kalmbach?

"I won't discuss names. There are so many things that nothing would surprise me. It'll come out at the trial, which is the best context of all because the people will know it is the truth. The prosecutors have the truth. They want an opportunity to show it. The people who did this are going to take the stand."

---

* There had been news stories reporting that the FBI had found a gun in Howard Hunt's White House office.

THE SENATOR

SAM J. ERVIN, JR.

HARRY M. ROSENFELD

HOWARD SIMONS

BARRY SUSSMAN

THE WASHINGTON POST

KATHARINE GRAHAM AND BENJAMIN C. BRADLEE

The Washington Post

THE JUDGE

JOHN J. SIRICA

THE PROSECUTION

Donald E. Campbell, Earl J. Silbert, Seymour Glanzer

THE BURGLAR

JAMES W. McCORD, JR.

MAURICE H. STANS

GORDON C. STRACHAN

RONALD L. ZIEGLER

HUGH W. SLOAN, JR., WITH HIS WIFE, DEBORAH

ROBERT C. ODLE, JR.

DONALD H. SEGRETTI

HERBERT L. PORTER

ROBERT C. MARDIAN

JOHN N. MITCHELL

G. Gordon Liddy

Joe Heiberger, The Washington Post

Charles Del Vecchio, The Washington Post

Jeb Stuart Magruder

FREDERICK C. LaRUE

HERBERT W. KALMBACH

EGIL KROGH, JR.

L. PATRICK GRAY III

H. R. HALDEMAN

E. HOWARD HUNT, JR.

CHARLES W. COLSON

JOHN W. DEAN III

JOHN D. EHRLICHMAN

THE
PRESIDENT'S
MEN

ALEXANDER P. BUTTERFIELD

DWIGHT L. CHAPIN

KENNETH W. CLAWSON

THE PRESIDENT

RICHARD M. NIXON

Official White House Photo

John Mitchell?

"Mitchell? They won't call him. But it will be there. He can't say he didn't know about it, because it was strategy—basic strategy that goes all the way to the top. Higher than him, even."

The attorney realized he had gone too far. *Higher than Mitchell?* Dwight Chapin was a functionary, an advance man and glorified valet, servant to Richard Nixon and H. R. Haldeman. At most, there were three persons who went *higher than John Mitchell:* John Ehrlichman (maybe), Haldeman and Richard M. Nixon.

Basic strategy that goes all the way to the top. The phrase unnerved Bernstein. For the first time, he considered the possibility that the President of the United States was the head ratfucker.

"When I am the candidate, I run the campaign." Richard Nixon had said that after his aides had botched the management of the 1970 mid-term elections. Sitting at his desk, Bernstein remembered the quote and wished Woodward were there, but Woodward had gone to New York for the weekend. After almost four months of working together, a kind of spiritual affinity had developed between Woodward and Bernstein. People at the paper would occasionally kid them that they were out to get the President. What if they really had to confront such a situation—not *getting the President,* but obtaining persuasive evidence that he was involved?

Bernstein tried thinking as Woodward would. What did he have? Three attorneys said they had been approached by Segretti. There was no evidence, beyond a Justice Department lawyer's angry reactions. There were the travel records—circumstantial. There was no evidence that a law had been broken.

What they had was ephemeral, but there were enough pieces to try writing *something.* The rule was: Lay it out piece by piece, write what you know is solid; the big picture can wait.

Bernstein tried a lead:

> Three attorneys have told the *Washington Post* that they were asked to conduct political espionage and sabotage on behalf of President Nixon's re-election campaign by a man who is under FBI investigation in connection with the Watergate bugging incident.

The words "espionage" and "sabotage" could not be lightly chosen. They were war terms. Bernstein and Woodward had talked about that, about the fact that the White House and CRP regarded the President's re-election campaign as a holy war.

Bernstein wrote late into the night, came in early on Sunday morning, called Sussman at home. A draft would be ready by midday for Sussman to look at. He arrived about two, read the draft, then read it over the phone to Woodward in New York.

Sussman and Bernstein wanted to run the story. Woodward argued that not enough details about the sabotage operations were known, and that their scope and purposes were unclear. Moreover, the implications should not be hinted at until there was more solid information.

Woodward prevailed. He would catch the next plane to Washington and contact Deep Throat.

He left New York on the last Eastern shuttle and, from a telephone booth at National Airport, called Deep Throat at home.

They had recently arranged a method by which Woodward could call to request a garage meeting without identifying himself. Woodward put his suitcase in a locker and got a hamburger. He took a cab to a downtown hotel, waited 10 minutes, took another, walked the final stretch and arrived at the garage at 1:30 A.M.

Deep Throat was already there, smoking a cigarette. He was glad to see Woodward, shook his hand. Woodward told him that he and Bernstein needed help, really needed help on this one. His friendship with Deep Throat was genuine, not cultivated. Long before Watergate, they had spent many evenings talking about Washington, the government, power.

On evenings such as those, Deep Throat had talked about how politics had infiltrated every corner of government—a strong-arm takeover of the agencies by the Nixon White House. Junior White House aides were giving orders on the highest levels of the bureaucracy. He had once called it the "switchblade mentality"—and had referred to the willingness of the President's men to fight dirty and for keeps, regardless of what effect the slashing might have on the government and the nation. There was little bitterness on his part. Woodward sensed the resignation of a man whose fight had been worn out in too many battles. Deep Throat never tried to inflate his knowledge or show off his importance. He always told rather less than he knew. Woodward considered him a wise teacher. He was dispassionate and seemed committed to the best version of the obtainable truth.

The Nixon White House worried him. "They are all underhanded and unknowable," he had said numerous times. He also distrusted the press. "I don't like newspapers," he had said flatly. He detested inexactitude and shallowness.

Aware of his own weaknesses, he readily conceded his flaws. He was, incongruously, an incurable gossip, careful to label rumor for what it was, but fascinated by it. He knew too much literature too well and let the allurements of the past turn him away from his instincts. He could be rowdy, drink too much, overreach. He was not good at concealing his feelings, hardly ideal for a man in his position. Of late, he had expressed fear for the future of the Executive Branch, which he was in a unique position to observe. Watergate had taken its toll. Even in the shadows of the garage, Woodward saw that he was thinner and, when he drew on his cigarette, that his eyes were bloodshot.

That night, Deep Throat seemed more talkative than usual. "There is a way to untie the Watergate knot," he began. "I can't and won't give you any new names, but everything points in the direction of what was called 'Offensive Security.' . . . Remember, you don't do those 1500 [FBI] interviews* and not have something on your hands other than a single break-in. But please be balanced and send out people to check everything, because a lot of the [CRP] intelligence-gathering was routine. They are not brilliant guys, and it got out of hand," Deep Throat said. "That is the key phrase, the feeling that it all got out of hand. . . . Much of the intelligence-gathering was on their own campaign contributors, and some to check on the Democratic contributors—to check people out and sort of semi-blackmail them if something was found . . . a very heavy-handed operation."

Deep Throat had access to information from the White House, Justice, the FBI and CRP. What he knew represented an aggregate of hard information flowing in and out of many stations. Reluctantly,

---

* The White House and the Justice Department had cited the number of interviews conducted by the FBI as evidence of the thoroughness of the Watergate investigation.

after prodding, he agreed that Woodward and Bernstein were correct about the involvement of higher-ups in the Watergate break-in and other illegal activities as well.

Mitchell?

"Mitchell was involved."

To what extent?

"Only the President and Mitchell know," he said.

"Mitchell conducted his own—he called it an investigation—for about ten days after June 17. And he was going crazy. He found all sorts of new things which astounded even him. At some point, Howard Hunt, of all the ironies, was assigned to help Mitchell get some information. Like lightning, he was pulled off and fired and told to pack up his desk and leave town forever. By no less than John Ehrlichman."

Woodward reacted with equal measures of shock and skepticism. Ehrlichman was the good guy, the resident program man in the White House who dealt with legislation, concepts, domestic crises. Politics was Haldeman's and Mitchell's turf. Woodward pointed out the gravity of Deep Throat's remark that "only the President and Mitchell know." But the man would not elaborate.

Woodward asked if the Watergate bugging and spying were isolated, or if they were parts of the same operation as the other activities Deep Throat referred to.

"Check every lead," Deep Throat advised. "It goes all over the map, and that is important. You could write stories from now until Christmas or well beyond that. . . . Not one of the games [his term for undercover operations] was free-lance. This is important. Every one was tied in."

But he would not talk specifically about Segretti's operation. Woodward could not understand why.

"Just remember what I'm saying. Everything was part of it— nothing was free-lance. I know what I'm talking about."

Ratfucking?

He had heard the term; it meant double-cross and, as used by the Nixon forces, it referred to infiltration of the Democrats.

Deep Throat returned to Mitchell on his own steam: "That guy definitely learned some things in those ten days after Watergate. He was just sick, and everyone was saying that he was ruined because of what his people did, especially Mardian and LaRue, and what happened at the White House.

"And Mitchell said, 'If this all comes out, it could ruin the administration. I mean, ruin it.' Mitchell realized he was personally ruined and would have to get out."

Woodward asked about the White House.

"There were four basic personnel groupings for undercover operations," Deep Throat said. The November Group, which handled CRP's advertising; a convention group, which handled intelligence-gathering and sabotage-planning for both the Republican and Democratic conventions; a primary group, which did the same for the primaries of both parties; and the Howard Hunt group, which was the "really heavy operations team."

"The Howard Hunt group reported to Chuck Colson, who maybe didn't know specifically about the bugging. There is no proof, but Colson was getting daily updates on the activities and the information." He shook his head. "There are stories all over town—check every one, each is good."

What about Martha Mitchell?

"She knows nothing, apparently, but that doesn't mean she won't talk." He didn't laugh.

Deep Throat had said there were "games" going on all over the map. For instance?

"I know of intelligence-gathering and games in Illinois, New York, New Hampshire, Massachusetts, California, Texas, Florida and the District of Columbia." The President's forces had been out to wreck the campaigns both of the Democrats and of Nixon's challengers within his own party—Representative Paul McCloskey of California and Representative John Ashbrook of Ohio.

Woodward asked about Howard Hunt and leak-plugging at the White House.

"That operation was not only to check leaks to the papers but often to manufacture items for the press. It was a Colson-Hunt operation. Recipients include all of you guys—Jack Anderson, Evans and Novak, the *Post* and the *New York Times,* the *Chicago Tribune.* The business of Eagleton's drunk-driving record or his health records, I understand, involves the White House and Hunt somehow. Total manipulation—that was their goal, with everyone eating at one time or another out of their hands. Even the press."

Deep Throat confirmed what the reporters' other sources had hinted. The FBI's and the grand jury's investigations had been limited to the Watergate operation—and had ignored other espionage and sabotage. "None of the outside games were checked," he said. "If it wasn't limited to Watergate proper, they would never have finished, believe me. There was also non-corroborative testimony before the grand jury, driving everyone wild, certain perjury."

Sally Harmony?

Sally and others.

Deep Throat then issued an explicit warning. "They want to single out the *Post*. They want to go to court to get at your sources."

It was 3:00 A.M. There was more general discussion about the White House, its mood, the war atmosphere. Woodward and Deep Throat sat down on the garage floor. Neither wanted to end the conversation. Their heads and backs rested against the garage wall. Exhaustion loosened them up. Woodward said that he and Bernstein couldn't go much further, what they had was too vague. Watergate would not expose what the White House had done—not without more *specific* information.

Deep Throat again told Woodward to concentrate on the other games—not the break-in at Democratic headquarters.

Still, they needed help, Woodward said. Could they say for certain that the games were White House sponsored?

"Of course, of course, don't you get my message?" Deep Throat was exasperated. He stood up.

What games? Woodward asked. One couldn't publish stories based on vague references to higher-ups, on information that might or might not have been leaked to the press by Howard Hunt; that the Eagleton records were "somehow tied into Hunt and the White House."

"There's nothing more I can say," Deep Throat replied, and began to walk off.

Woodward said that he and Bernstein needed more—something that went beyond generalities. What about the Canuck Letter?

Deep Throat stopped and turned around. "It was a White House operation—done inside the gates surrounding the White House and the Executive Office Building. Is that enough?"

It was not. They needed to know the scope of the intelligence-gathering, of the games. Were most of them carried out, or merely planned? Woodward grabbed Deep Throat's arm. The time had come to press to the limit. Woodward found himself angry. He told Deep Throat that both of them were playing a chickenshit game—Deep Throat for pretending to himself that he never fed Woodward primary information, and Woodward for chewing up tidbits like a rat under a picnic table that didn't have the guts to go after the main dish.

Deep Throat was angry, too, but not at Woodward.

"Okay," he said softly. "This is very serious. You can safely say that fifty people worked for the White House and CRP to play games and spy and sabotage and gather intelligence. Some of it is beyond belief, kicking at the opposition in every imaginable way. You already know some of it."

Deep Throat nodded confirmation as Woodward ran down items on a list of tactics that he and Bernstein had heard were used against the political opposition: bugging, following people, false press leaks, fake letters, canceling campaign rallies, investigating campaign workers' private lives, planting spies, stealing documents, planting provocateurs in political demonstrations.

"It's all in the files," Deep Throat said. "Justice and the Bureau know about it, even though it wasn't followed up."

Woodward was stunned. Fifty people directed by the White House and CRP to destroy the opposition, no holds barred?

Deep Throat nodded.

The White House had been willing to subvert—was that the right word?—the whole electoral process? Had actually gone ahead and tried to do it?

Another nod. Deep Throat looked queasy.

And hired fifty agents to do it?

"You can safely say more than fifty," Deep Throat said. Then he turned, walked up the ramp and out. It was nearly 6:00 A.M.

7

WOODWARD ARRIVED at the office four hours later and typed his notes from the meeting with Deep Throat. A carbon was in Bernstein's typewriter when he arrived half an hour later. Woodward, Bernstein, Sussman and Rosenfeld met briefly. There would be three stories: a lead by Bernstein and Woodward outlining the general program of "ratfucking," espionage and sabotage by at least 50 agents; Bernstein's story on Segretti; an account by Woodward of White House involvement in the Canuck Letter episode.

While Woodward was writing the Canuck Letter story, Bernstein was having trouble sketching a general story about the White House-directed espionage and sabotage. There were too many generalizations, and the meaty details were in the other two stories.

As he often did when he was experiencing difficulty writing, Bernstein walked across the newsroom to the water cooler. Marilyn Berger, a national-staff reporter who covers the State Department, came up to him as he scanned the bulletin board. She asked if he and Woodward knew about the Canuck Letter.

Sure, he said, they were writing it for tomorrow.

He took another sip before the peculiarity of the question struck him. Woodward had only found out about the Canuck Letter at six that morning. They were careful in the office not to talk about what they were working on. The only people Bernstein or Woodward had mentioned the letter to were Sussman, Rosenfeld, Simons, Bradlee and David Broder, the *Post's* senior political reporter.

How did Marilyn know about it?

"Dave [Broder] hasn't told you?" she asked.

Told them what?

"That Ken Clawson wrote the Canuck Letter," Marilyn said.

Bernstein's reply was loud enough to cause heads to turn in that corner of the newsroom.

Berger explained that Clawson, their former colleague on the *Post*, had told her matter-of-factly over a drink that he had written the Canuck Letter. He had said it several times.

The coincidence seemed too much. Bernstein suspected a set-up. On the same morning they learn that the White House is responsible for the Canuck Letter, Marilyn Berger waltzes into the newsroom and says Ken Clawson did it?

But Berger said Clawson had told her about it more than two weeks earlier—before Bernstein had ever heard of Segretti. Besides, he thought, Clawson was just the kind who would think nothing of pulling such a trick.

Bernstein tugged Berger by the arm and asked her to repeat to Woodward what she had said. Woodward had some doubts that Clawson would get involved in dirty tricks for the White House so soon after leaving the *Post* for the President's staff. The Canuck Letter had been printed less than three weeks after Clawson had joined the administration. Woodward raised the point; then he remembered something: a friend at the White House had once told him of an initiation rite in which new members of the President's staff were ordered to prove their mettle by screwing an enemy of the White House. Maybe the Canuck Letter had been Clawson's initiation rite, winning him a fraternity paddle with the Presidential Seal from his new brothers in the USC Mafia.

Bradlee, Simons, Rosenfeld and Sussman joined the discussion around Woodward's typewriter. All pretense of security had been abandoned and word spread through the newsroom: Clawson had written the Canuck Letter and there was a package of stories coming that would go through the White House like a rocket. It was decided that Berger should try to lunch with Clawson that afternoon and see if he would repeat himself.

Meanwhile, she filed a memo describing her conversation with Clawson.

Memo from M. Berger (Eyes Only). On the evening of September 25, 1972, at approximately 8:30 P.M., Ken Clawson telephoned me at my apartment to invite me out for a drink. I said I had already eaten dinner, was very tired, but if he wanted to come over for a drink he could. I invited him because he had called twice before with the same invitation in the course of the previous weeks, and I had said "no" each time. When Ken arrived I offered him a drink. He accepted a scotch—I forget if it was with water or soda, but I know he took ice. We sat down to talk. I had Sanka. In the course of the discussion (I would say about the first ten minutes or so) we started talking about being a reporter and being a government official. He said we reporters knew only a fraction of what goes on. I asked him if, now that he was in the White House, he would be a better reporter when he left. He said he had covered the White House before, but could *really* cover it now. He may have said something about knowing where all the bodies are buried, but I'm not absolutely sure of that.

It was then that he said, "I wrote the . . . letter." I think he said the Canuck letter, but in any case he clearly announced that he wrote that [Muskie] letter. I was so shocked I felt queasy. I asked him why. He said it was because Muskie was the candidate who would represent the strongest opposition and they wanted him out. When I said Muskie must have reacted beyond all their expectations, he indicated "yes."

I then asked him whether he had done that kind of thing when he was a reporter—i.e., that kind of dishonest thing. He said "No," that he was a straight honest reporter. I asked how he could do such a thing as write that letter, and that's when he said that's politics, that's the way things are. In the course of that conversation that evening he also spoke with enormous praise of Nixon, particularly about what a great guy he is, how warm he is, what a joker he is and how the President is always warning him and John Scali [now Ambassador to the United Nations] to behave. . . . This is the part of the conversation that evening that dealt with the Canuck letter and related matters. Naturally we spoke about a number of other things.

Berger, a 37-year-old former reporter for *Newsday,* is a diplomatic specialist. She knew that she was about to become part of the story—a situation that is congenitally distressing to reporters—but she reacted to her sudden appearance in the midst of the Watergate excitement with self-possession.

Clawson accepted her invitation for a one-o'clock lunch. Berger returned to the office about three and filed another memo.

> Lunch at Sans Souci (he bought). I told Ken that Woodward and Bernstein were on to a big story of which the Canuck letter was a part, that they had traced it to the White House and that I had said, "That's not new, Ken said he did it." Ken looked very serious, as he had throughout the lunch. Dr. Lukash [President Nixon's doctor] had just told him some days before that he has high blood pressure and he has to watch what he eats and drinks. He acted like he had determined to get off drinking altogether and to lose weight. He ordered a Caesar salad and didn't even finish it.
>
> He also mentioned that it takes a lot out of him when he has to "dress down" other officials, especially Cabinet officials. I asked him if he indeed dresses down Cabinet officials and he said he does. Concerning the Canuck letter, he said he wished I hadn't said that to the boys. I said I didn't know that was anything new. He said that Woodward and Bernstein "can't possibly have traced it to the White House" or "it can't possibly have been traced to the White House." On the statement to me, he said he would "deny it on a stack of Bibles over his mother's grave." He dropped it, then returned to it, asking what they had. I told him I wasn't entirely sure, but on the letter part they had traced some fellow from New England who went to Florida for the Muskie thing, etc. I was very vague. He said he would deny it.
>
> Later he returned to it and asked if I wanted to take down what he wanted to say about it or if I wanted to let them [Woodward and Bernstein] call. Then he said better let them call.

Bradlee, the other editors and Bernstein and Woodward studied Berger's memo. Clawson had not denied saying that he had written the letter. Woodward called Clawson at the White House. Now Clawson asserted that he had not admitted writing the letter in the first place and that the entire matter was a misunderstanding.

Woodward said that the editors believed Berger and that the *Post* was going to use what she had reported.

Clawson said: "That's your privilege. I just hope you include my denial. Marilyn misunderstood. She's a professional and did not deliberately do anything unprofessional. We were just shooting the breeze about the election. We were not in an interview situation."

Woodward asked where all this shooting the breeze had taken place. Clawson said he didn't recall.

Woodward asked if Clawson had ever known Berger to get anything wrong or misquote someone. Clawson, growing more annoyed, lashed out: "You are not going to ask a bullshit question like that. Don't give me that crap. That's straight out of Wichita, Kansas. She writes in the area of foreign affairs and I don't read very much in foreign affairs. I don't know how to answer that."

Clawson maintained that the first time he had heard of the Canuck Letter was when "I saw it on television" following Muskie's February 26 appearance. "I know nothing about it" aside from that, he insisted.

Shortly after the conversation with Clawson, Berger rushed over to Woodward's desk. "Ken Clawson is on the telephone. What should I do?"

Woodward thought perhaps Clawson was going to make some sort of personal plea to Berger. No one at the *Post* doubted that Clawson had told Berger he had written the letter; but they all tended to believe that he had been bragging and oversimplifying. It seemed likely that he had merely had a hand in the episode, and that he had taken the credit for it. Both possibilities seemed in character. When Clawson was on the national staff at the *Post,* he had a habit of leaving off the bylines of local reporters who occasionally worked with him on stories.

While Berger left Clawson on "hold," a secretary got on an extension to transcribe.

Clawson seemed much less concerned about the Canuck Letter than the circumstances in which he and Berger had discussed it. "It just occurs to me—where were we when this alleged conversation took place?" Clawson asked Berger.

"Alleged conversation? Are you denying . . . ?"

"Look, I said it was a misunderstanding. I said I thought you were a fine reporter and we probably had a misunderstanding."

Berger said something about a drink.

"Can't we have had it in a restaurant?" Clawson asked.

No, Berger said, because it had been at her apartment.

"Are you serious? No. Christ! You going to tell them that?"

"I told them already."

"You told them that?"

"Well, you did come over for a drink."

"Well, for Christ's sake."

"What's wrong with coming over for a drink?"

"Are you kidding?"

"No," she said.

"You and me in your apartment."

"Well . . ."

"You have already told them that?" Clawson said. "Jesus Christ. Well, you have just shot me down. If it appears in the paper that I am over at your house having a drink . . . do you know what that does?"

"I don't see why."

"You don't?"

"No. I have a clear conscience."

"Jesus Christ. Who did you tell?"

"I told the guys."

"That's incredible. Just incredible," he repeated.

"I don't see what's so wrong about that."

"Marilyn, I have a wife and family and a dog and a cat."

"Well, I have lots of people come over to my house for a drink."

"Oh, boy. That's the worst blow."

"There's nothing bad about it."

"Well, there sure is."

"[It] should not look bad," Berger insisted.

"Incredible. Just incredible."

"It's incredible that you [are so upset] about that when this other thing is really substantive," Berger told him.

There was a long silence. "Okay. Amazing."

"I have nothing to be embarrassed about," Berger said.

"That's the most embarrassing thing of all." He hung up.

A few minutes later, Clawson called Bradlee to ask that the *Post* not say that he'd been in Marilyn Berger's apartment during the conversation.

Bradlee was not interested in where the conversation had taken place, aside from the fact that it gave him leverage over Clawson. He had had no intention of even hinting at the context of the conversation in print.

Clawson denied to Bradlee, too, that he had claimed authorship of the letter or had anything to do with it.

At about 6:00 P.M. the editors and Bernstein and Woodward had a final meeting with Bradlee on the stories.

"What do you have and how are you saying it?" Bradlee asked.

The reporters had abandoned the earlier plan for three stories. Instead, Woodward was writing an account of the Canuck Letter, including Clawson's alleged role, and Bernstein was writing a Segretti-espionage-sabotage story. Copies of the half-finished accounts were passed to Bradlee.

He brought his chair close to his oval table-desk, held his hand in the air to request silence and began reading. Simons was reading another set of carbons. Rosenfeld nervously swiveled his orange chair in quarter-turns. Occasionally, whispered comments went back and forth. Sussman sat quietly with his legs crossed.

"Fellas"—Bradlee broke the silence—"you've got one story here. Put it into one, fit it together. It's all part of the same thing."

He turned his chair 180 degrees to his own typewriter on the ledge behind the oval table, opened a drawer and pulled out a piece of two-ply paper.

"Never mind the first several paragraphs," Bradlee said, "you work that out." He began on a section which would deal with Clawson and the letter. He banged out two long paragraphs, then flipped the page across the table to Woodward. Bernstein, meanwhile, went to his desk and wrote:

> FBI agents have established that the Watergate bugging incident stemmed from a massive campaign of political spying and sabotage conducted on behalf of President Nixon's re-election and directed by officials of the White House and the Committee for the Re-election of the President.
>
> The activities, according to information in FBI and Department of Justice files, were aimed at all the major Democratic presidential contenders and—since 1971—represented a basic strategy of the Nixon re-election effort.

Bernstein passed the draft around, first to Woodward and then to the editors who had gathered around his desk. All agreed. Not a word was changed, unusual on such a sensitive story, especially given the number of editors involved.

Woodward added the third paragraph:

During their Watergate investigation federal agents established that hundreds of thousands of dollars in Nixon campaign contributions had been set aside to pay for an extensive undercover campaign aimed at discrediting individual Democratic presidential candidates and disrupting their campaigns.

And, from suggestions made primarily by Sussman, the fourth paragraph:

"Intelligence work" is normal during a campaign and is said to be carried out by both political parties. But federal investigators said what they uncovered being done by the Nixon forces is unprecedented in scope and intensity.

Despite lack of specific examples, the crucial fifth and sixth paragraphs related that the espionage and sabotage included:

Following members of Democratic candidates' families; assembling dossiers of their personal lives; forging letters and distributing them under the candidates' letterheads; leaking false and manufactured items to the press; throwing campaign schedules into disarray; seizing confidential campaign files and investigating the lives of dozens of Democratic campaign workers.

In addition, investigators said the activities included planting provocateurs in the ranks of organizations expected to demonstrate at the Republican and Democratic conventions; and investigating potential donors to the Nixon campaign before their contributions were solicited.

Woodward called Shumway, CRP's principal spokesman, read him the first six paragraphs and outlined the Segretti business and the allegations involving Clawson and the letter.

"Now read me that again," Shumway said, apparently stunned.

Woodward repeated.

"That's one I'll have to get back to you on," Shumway said. "Now let me get it straight. You're doing that for tomorrow? . . . This never ceases to amaze me."

Shumway called back an hour later, saying: "Now, are you ready? We've got a statement: 'The *Post* story is not only fiction but a collection of absurdities.' "

Woodward waited.

"That's it," Shumway said.

Woodward asked about specific points.

"It's no use, Robert," said Shumway. "That's all we are going to say. The entire matter is in the hands of the authorities."

To Woodward and Bernstein, the latest non-denial seemed to confirm their account.

The two lead paragraphs, with their sweeping statements about massive political espionage and sabotage directed by the White House as part of a basic re-election strategy, were essentially interpretive—and risky. No source had explicitly told the reporters that the substance represented the stated conclusions of the federal investigators. But they knew that there was information in the files of the FBI and the Justice Department to support their conclusions. The story was based on strains of evidence, statements from numerous sources, deduction, a partial understanding of what the White House was doing, the reporters' familiarity with the "switchblade mentality" of the President's men, and disparate pieces of information the reporters had been accumulating for months. Those in the White House might dispute the interpretation in the lead—substituting the phrases "political intelligence-gathering" and "pranks" for "political spying and sabotage"—but the facts supported the aggressive language. Specific examples of some of the tactics listed in the fifth and sixth paragraphs were lacking, but the hard evidence was in the Canuck Letter and Segretti's activities. Hopefully, the story would push the missing examples into the open.

Shumway's statement ran as the seventh paragraph, accompanied by the refusal of the White House to comment on the story. The next 10 paragraphs dealt with the Canuck Letter. They reported that Ken Clawson had told Marilyn Berger, on September 25, that he had written the letter, and recorded his denial.

The Segretti findings were not mentioned until the 18th paragraph, the point at which the story was continued in the inside of the paper.

The involvement of "at least 50 undercover Nixon operatives [who] traveled throughout the country trying to disrupt and spy on Democratic campaigns" was not mentioned until the 19th paragraph. And the remaining text of the 65-paragraph story was a narrative of Segretti's travels, job approaches, conversation with Bob Meyers and biographical details.

The four-column, two-line head on the top half of page one read "FBI Finds Nixon Aides/Sabotaged Democrats."

The story went out over the *Washington Post–Los Angeles Times* News Service wire about 7:00 P.M. More than half of the 220 domestic subscribers used the story, several on page one, and non-subscriber coverage was broad.

In the newsroom of the *New York Times'* Washington bureau, less than five blocks from the *Post,* a night editor began making hurried phone calls to senior editors in New York and members of the staff in Washington. Within two hours, the *Times* had contacted Shipley, Dixon and Nixt, each of whom confirmed the approaches by Segretti. The *Times'* late city edition of October 10 carried a story at the bottom of page one, leading with Shipley's account, then summarizing the *Post's* allegations of a nationwide campaign of espionage and sabotage directed by the White House and CRP.

At the White House that noon, Ron Ziegler faced an increasingly skeptical press corps determined to challenge the administration's refusal to discuss Watergate substantively. During a 30-minute briefing, a clearly uncomfortable presidential press secretary declined 29 times to discuss the *Post* story. His response was that CRP and Clawson had "appropriately" responded, and that the White House had nothing further to say.

While Ziegler was fending off hostile questions in the West Wing, Bradlee came over to Woodward's desk in the *Post* newsroom and sat down in a chair. "Hey, you and Carl and I have got to have lunch this afternoon and have a little discussion," he said.

Bernstein, however, was out of town attending the funeral of a friend, the wife of his former boss.

"Then you alone," Bradlee said. "We gotta talk."

They walked across 15th Street to the Madison Hotel's Montpelier Room, an opulent French restaurant. Bradlee asked for a corner table, and began the conversation. "You'd better bring me up to date because . . ." He turned to order lunch in perfect French, and then turned back to Woodward. ". . . our cocks are on the chopping block now and I just want to know a little more about this."

Bradlee had a general idea of who the reporters' sources were, "but that's secondhand from Sussman and Rosenfeld," he said. "I'd like it firsthand now—how the stories have been put together and where they're coming from." Bradlee was a reporter by background and instinct; he understood the reluctance to discuss sources with anyone, including the editor.

"Tell me what you feel you can," he said. "Just give me their positions and tell me again that you're sure, and that Carl is sure, and that these are people who have no big ax to grind on the front page of the *Washington Post*."

Bradlee fidgeted in his chair. He and Woodward discussed how the stories had been covered, how the reporters had dealt with sources and under what circumstances they had met and communicated. The line was drawn at a point which satisfied Bradlee's reportorial instincts and responsibilities as an editor, as well as Bernstein's and Woodward's promises of anonymity to their sources.

After more than an hour, Bradlee said, "Well, okay, I'm satisfied. Now what have you guys got for tomorrow?" Bradlee liked to keep the pressure on.

The reporters were working two major areas, Woodward told him: a White House–Segretti connection and a whole catalogue of dirty tricks that had plagued the Muskie campaign. But neither story would be ready for the next day.

At 3:00 P.M., when the editors filed into Bradlee's office for the daily story conference, they considered two items as possible front-page follow-ups: the White House reaction (or lack of it) as expressed by Ron Ziegler, and a demand by Senator Muskie that President Nixon personally answer press reports of wrongdoing by White House staff members because the allegations were so serious. Muskie had insisted that any investigation of the case be done outside the Justice Department, saying it was inconceivable that the "President's lawyers" there could objectively investigate corruption of the President's staff.

Neither story generated much enthusiasm. Rosenfeld told Woodward that the editors were concerned: the lack of a strong follow-up could be interpreted as pulling back on the part of the *Post*. He urged Woodward to keep trolling for a story.

About six o'clock, Frank Mankiewicz, the crafty professional of the McGovern campaign, called Woodward. He had a list of 10 acts of alleged sabotage against the McGovern campaign, acts "so well engineered that they must have come from the Republicans," Mankiewicz said.

They ranged from the serious—an attempt by someone impersonating a top McGovern aide to set up a bogus meeting between the candidate and the AFL-CIO president, George Meany—to harassing phone calls received on the switchboard at McGovern headquarters.*

Woodward asked if there was any evidence connecting the acts to the White House or the Nixon re-election committee. No, said Mankiewicz, but it sure sounded like part of the same operation the *Post* had written about that morning.

Rosenfeld wanted a page-one story on the Mankiewicz charges. Woodward argued strongly that the *Post* lacked evidence that the incidents were part of the broad CRP campaign. He was concerned that readers might justifiably conclude that the McGovern campaign was jumping onto a sabotage bandwagon. Why hadn't McGovern's people made the charges earlier? Ziegler's reaction was a more legitimate story. But Woodward was overruled by Rosenfeld and the senior editors.

Woodward continued protesting even after he wrote a piece which stated pointedly that Mankiewicz had supplied no evidence connecting the activities with the President's campaign.

The story was headlined "Democrats Step Up Sabotage Charges." It would serve only to fuel White House charges that the *Post* and the McGovern campaign were conspiring in the last, desperate days of the Democrats' campaign.

Bernstein, who had arrived back in Washington in the midst of the argument between Woodward and the editors, was doubly chagrined. He was a few phone calls away from confirming the last act in a long list of sabotage attempts against the Muskie campaign.

The day after he had talked to Alex Shipley, Bernstein had begun calling Muskie staffers. One by one, they had told horror stories about

---

* In one instance, according to Mankiewicz, someone had impersonated him in a call to CBS-TV anchorman Walter Cronkite and had referred to a deal in which Cronkite had allegedly agreed to give 80 percent of the news coverage on the CBS Evening News to McGovern and the remaining 20 percent to Nixon. The Mankiewicz impersonator told Cronkite (who later confirmed that he had received such a call): "But everybody's getting suspicious—better give more to Nixon." Mankiewicz said that Cronkite later told him that "the guy was definitely not just a crank. It was a very good imitation."

how their campaign had been repeatedly victimized by unexplained accidents that seemed as if they could only be the results of an organized effort: stolen documents, fake campaign literature, canceled rallies, outrageous telephone calls to voters in the name of Muskie campaign workers, schedule breakdowns and—of course—the Canuck Letter.

Still, almost all agreed, the Muskie campaign had self-destructed because of the candidate's vacillation on the issues and because of what they regarded as his ineptitude. They didn't know who was responsible for the vicious things that kept occurring; but whoever had done them had been guilty of gross overkill. Some had guessed Hubert Humphrey's backers, others George Wallace's.

Bernstein had traveled with Muskie as a reporter for a week during the 1968 campaign, when the Senator was the Democratic vice-presidential nominee, and knew him slightly. He wanted to get to Muskie before anything was printed in the *Post* suggesting his bid for the Presidency had been the object of sabotage.

Woodward had been told by Roger Wilkins, a *Post* editorial writer,* that Muskie had sought legal advice during the campaign when he suspected members of his family were being followed and investigated. Wilkins, the former director of the Justice Department's Community Relations Service under Attorney General Ramsey Clark and the 40-year-old nephew of NAACP president Roy Wilkins, had said: "Muskie got a lawyer because one of his children was being followed and inquiries were being made at the child's school."

Bernstein's meeting with Muskie on Capitol Hill lasted more than an hour. With no prodding, Muskie revealed that he had long suspected that the Nixon forces were behind "a systematic campaign of sabotage" that had harmed his campaign.

"Our campaign was constantly plagued by leaks and disruptions and fabrications," Muskie said, "but we could never pinpoint who was doing it. . . . Somebody was out to ambush us. We assumed it was being done by Nixon people because that's the nature of this administration; they have no sensitivity to privacy or decency in politics. But we had no proof it was them."

Muskie described more than a dozen incidents he suspected were

---

* Wilkins wrote the *Post*'s major editorials on Watergate.

the results of sabotage, covering much the same ground as members of his staff. Since he had learned in 1970 that FBI agents had been assigned to report on a speech he made for Earth Day on April 22 of that year, the Senator said, "I have assumed I've been followed by the Republicans."

Had members of his family been followed?

"We thought we were being followed, but we never were able to establish a connection with Republican espionage." The Senator refused to be more specific or talk about what—if anything—had happened with one of his children. "Whatever happened with members of my family is private," he said.

His tone, angry and insistent, conveyed real bitterness. Bernstein kept trying to find out what might be behind it. He asked Muskie if somebody had tried to learn something specific about one of the children, like whether they smoked dope. "I'm just not going to talk about it," Muskie said.

On October 12, Bernstein wrote a story on the sabotage of the Muskie campaign, based on interviews and memoranda obtained from Muskie and his staff before the October 10 story had been published. He had been able to confirm that:

In July 1971, facsimiles of Muskie's Senate stationery were used to mail a Harris Poll reprint dealing with Senator Edward Kennedy and the incident at Chappaquiddick to Democratic members of Congress. It resulted in complaints to Muskie about unethical campaigning.

On April 17, 1972, a Muskie fund-raising dinner at the Washington Hilton Hotel had been harassed, as unordered liquor, flowers, pizzas, cakes and entertainers arrived COD.

Several days before the Florida primary, a flier on bogus Muskie stationery was distributed, accusing both Senator Humphrey and Senator Henry Jackson of illicit sexual conduct.

During the New Hampshire primary campaign, voters had been awakened in the middle of the night by phone calls from persons who identified themselves as canvassers from the Harlem for Muskie Committee, urging that New Hampshire voters cast their ballots for Muskie "because he'd been so good for the black man."

During 1971, raw polling data twice disappeared from the desk of the Muskie polling expert at campaign headquarters. This convinced Muskie that he had a middle-level spy, and members of Muskie's staff said they were subsequently warned by columnist Rowland Evans that there was a spy in their camp.

Woodward was reading over the Muskie story in the October 12 paper when Robert Meyers called from Los Angeles that morning. He had found Larry Young, a fraternity brother of Segretti's during their USC undergraduate days, who was to have been the other half of the firm Young and Segretti. Segretti had told Young a good deal about his connections with the Nixon campaign. Woodward started typing.

"Segretti told [Young] that the FBI found out about him from telephone records from the phone of E. Howard Hunt; a lot of phone calls one way, all from Hunt to Segretti. . . . Hunt would give him instructions, but Young doesn't know what events the specific instructions were connected to. . . . It wasn't the bugging. . . ."

Woodward was amazed. It had not occurred to the reporters that Segretti's operation was tied to Hunt's plans.

"Segretti said to Young, 'I'm working for a wealthy California Republican lawyer with national connections and I get paid by a special lawyer's trust fund.' "

Kalmbach. Woodward asked Meyers if he had tried the name of the President's personal lawyer on Young. Meyers said Young didn't know who Kalmbach was:

"Young is convinced that Segretti met with Dwight Chapin and with Hunt. Because Segretti talked about his going to Miami to meet with all the 'key people' he had always worked with on the phone. And he had earlier told Young that it was Hunt, and Chapin was the general organizer. Segretti would always say, 'I have to talk with DC. I have to meet with DC.' At first, Young thought he meant District of Columbia. Then he became convinced DC was Dwight Chapin. . . . Young, too, is said by others to have been a good friend of the USC Republican Mafia and kept contacts with them. . . .

"In Miami, Young thinks Segretti met with Hunt and Chapin and also was asked—don't know by whom—to recruit and organize Cubans for an assault on the Doral Beach Hotel and make it look as if they were working for McGovern. Segretti refused because he felt it would be blatantly illegal and violent."

For months the reporters had been picking up information suggesting that the Nixon forces had made routine use of provocateurs in demonstrations, and that such things had been planned for the conventions. But they had assumed that all bets were off after Watergate. Yet there had been an assault on the Doral Beach Hotel in Miami, and there was some evidence that there had been provocateurs in the crowd. Woodward remembered Deep Throat's words four nights before: *These are not very bright guys.* Somehow the bungling seemed reassuring—it tempered the frightening implications of how far the Nixon forces were willing to go to achieve their ends. Where would their efforts have ended had not the Watergate burglars been so incredibly stupid as to retape the stairwell doors on June 17, leading a security guard to call the cops? Or if Howard Hunt, the supposed master spy, had exercised the elementary caution of using pay phones?

Woodward went into Sussman's office. The city editor and Bernstein were agonizing over how tantalizingly close they were to establishing Segretti's contact with Chapin. Meyers' information from Young established the connection. But Young was not yet willing to go on the record. They went over Woodward's notes.

That afternoon, Bernstein reached Young at his office in Los Angeles. They talked for more than an hour. Young told him: "Segretti called me in a panic in August. It was about two weeks before the Republican convention. He said he had just been visited by the FBI, and wanted to talk to me very quickly. He was worried because there had been no prior warning that he would be contacted by the FBI. He had felt he would be given such a prior warning, that he would be briefed as to what to say. He wouldn't say who was to brief him, just that they were the people he was working for. He was afraid of being left out on a limb, sacrificed without any protection or coverage. He wanted some advice as to what he should do. . . .

"Don told me that he was paid from a trust account in a lawyer's name. He said the lawyer was a high-placed friend of the President and he was instructed to guard that name zealously. . . . He would never divulge any names."

Bernstein pressed for anything Young could remember about the lawyer. Young thought.

"Oh, yes, he once said the lawyer was in the Newport Beach area."

Kalmbach lived in Newport Beach and maintained his offices there.

A high-placed friend of the President; a lawyer; Newport Beach . . .

How had Segretti characterized his political activities to Young?

"Segretti said to me that he was engaged in activities that he called 'political hijinks,' that this was part of the President's re-election drive, that it was supposed to create trouble and problems for various Democratic candidates. . . .

"After he was summoned to the grand jury, he tried to get in touch with his people [who were] in Miami Beach [for the convention]. He was in an absolute panic, even more concerned than when the FBI first visited him. He felt he should have been given prior warning. He was trying to call Chapin. I said, 'Have you talked to Dwight about this?' He gave an evasive answer and said he couldn't get hold of anyone. He was very concerned with Dwight's name.

"Then I got a call around midnight from him saying he was on his way to Miami, that he had made contact—he wouldn't say with whom —and they had told him to come to Miami. He said in Miami that he was shown an FBI report of his interrogation—both of them. . . . And he was told to tell the truth [before the grand jury], not to perjure himself, not to worry about it.

"He was to stick to just what he had told the FBI, which was not any damaging material, just about the phone calls from Hunt and some small activities he was doing, some innocuous thing about being involved in some campaign activities, none of the stuff that hit the paper later. When he reported to wherever they report, the U.S. Attorney interrogated him ahead of time in an office and thoroughly went into *everything*.

"But in the grand jury, the questions went along on a very easy scale: just the innocuous stuff and some things about Hunt. Nothing about the lawyer. Nothing about whom he was working for. But then, he said, a woman member of the grand jury asked a question about who paid him and whom he knew on the White House staff. Then, he said, the names came out, especially Dwight Chapin's. He didn't mention the other names [to Young]. He said he *did* tell the grand jury the name of the lawyer on the West Coast who paid him."

Now it was definite. The Justice Department had had the information that the President's appointments secretary and his personal lawyer were involved and had done nothing to follow up. Bernstein again wondered how the prosecutors could have been manipulated to accept such a decision. "He told the prosecutors truthfully everything that he knew," Young had said. Bernstein asked Young for other specific details of what Segretti had told him.

"He mentioned a letter or pamphlet for mailing to all members of the Democratic State Central Committee in California—a scurrilous attack on Humphrey, blaming him for the war, calling him a two-time loser, giving the impression it was put out by McGovern people. He said there were some others doing the same thing. He said, 'I'm just a small fish, a cog, one of many doing the same thing.' "

And Chapin?

"My impression is that Don and Dwight are very close. As close as good friends could be. They kept contact over the years. He mentioned that he called Dwight at his home in connection with this. But he's been somewhat secretive with me."

How much had he said about Howard Hunt?

"When the FBI came to see him the first time, he learned that his phone number had turned up on a bill to an individual named Howard Hunt. He said he knew Hunt by a different name—an assumed name, a pseudonym—but that he knew he was Hunt. Hunt would always talk in a very whispery, conspiratorial voice, he said, and he thought Hunt was very odd. Hunt seemed to add even more intrigue than was already there, he said."

The conversation had been off the record, but Young said he would consider putting it on, provided he received legal advice that no violation of the attorney-client privilege was involved. Segretti had never retained him as counsel, had sought him out only as a friend, Young said. He and Bernstein and Woodward and Meyers would stay in touch daily.

On Friday, October 13, Young agreed to go on the record. Woodward went over the details with him a final time, pressing to find if there was any possibility that Young could be wrong or exaggerating Segretti's dealings with Hunt and Chapin. The answer was no.

Meyers was dispatched to get a sworn statement from Young affirming that the contents of the interviews with Meyers, Bernstein and Woodward were accurate representations of what Segretti had told him.

At last there was going to be a story based almost completely on on-the-record statements that could not be attacked by the White House as coming from anonymous sources.

For two days, Woodward had been trying to telephone Chapin at his office in the White House, a few steps from the Oval Office of the President. His calls, for the first time, were held up at the switchboard while he was asked who was calling and from what number. After about 20 seconds, the calls were put through, but when he reached Chapin's office, a secretary would say Chapin was busy and take a message. The calls were not returned.

There remained one major hurdle: Meyers had described Larry Young as a defender of "radicals and cop killers." No phrase was more likely to raise a red flag in Harry Rosenfeld's office. The metropolitan editor bluntly said he was not about to stake his reputation or that of the *Washington Post* on the word of "some hippie lawyer."

Happily, Larry Young's credentials were in order. Woodward made a dozen telephone calls to the West Coast and spent hours talking to members of the bench and bar who vouched for Young's standing as a respected and responsible representative of the legal profession. Woodward even found out what kind of clothes Young wore (modish but tasteful) and how long his hair was (shorter than Bernstein's). Rosenfeld was satisfied.

Bernstein began writing the story and Woodward left to make a round of visits at the Justice Department. After several strikeouts, he found a lawyer familiar with the case, alone in his office. Woodward was invited in and sat down. An informal late-Friday-afternoon mood prevailed. They began chatting about Tuesday's story—the espionage and sabotage in the primaries.

"Yes, we got Segretti through the records of Hunt's phone calls," the lawyer said. "The Bureau made random checks on a large portion of Hunt's calls—there were more than 700 calls altogether. One of them was to this guy Segretti. Let me emphasize that the dirty tricks were probably not illegal and here at Justice we're sticking to the Watergate bugging itself in the investigation. . . . But I'm worried about the case. The Bureau is acting funny . . . there is interest in the case at the top." He wouldn't say where the top was.

Now, more than ever, it was clear why the Watergate investigation had been so narrowly focused that the prosecutors had not pursued other crimes—no matter how obvious—unless they were directly connected to the bugging.

Woodward read aloud some notes on the Chapin-Segretti connection, and suggested they might explain high-level interest. He didn't know if the attorney would be surprised or not.

After some hesitation, the attorney said: "That's essentially what we've been told."

Woodward said that he was a little afraid of the story because it led straight into the White House—to the gatekeeper at the Oval Office, which was one of Chapin's functions.

The lawyer smiled. "I've wondered several times why you would worry so much about Chapin, who is much lower than Mitchell and Stans. What you've been told, we've been told about Segretti and Chapin. I can talk about it a little more freely because it really doesn't have anything to do with Watergate. It was part of the investigation, technically still is, but it's separate and we're not pursuing it. . . ."

About 5:00 P.M., the reporters and editors met to discuss the Chapin story. It would be too long to finish in a couple of hours; they would hold it for Sunday. The Justice Department had turned away from investigating the real conspiracy of Watergate; had focused on the narrow burglary and bugging at Democratic headquarters—the IOC (Interception of Oral Communications), as the Feds called it—and ignored the grand conspiracy directed by the President's men to subvert the electoral process.

Woodward called a casual acquaintance at the White House to get some background on Chapin. "He is one of those guys like Haldeman and Pat Buchanan [one of the President's speechwriters and the author of the White House daily news summaries] who got on the Old Man's bus very early and followed it through the ups and downs," he was told. "Chapin is the guy who made sure the Old Man's suit came back from the cleaners during the campaign. . . . He made sure everyone had coffee and made the apologies when the President was late, including calls to Mrs. Nixon and the girls. He probably gave the President a back rub if he needed one during the '68 campaign. . . . Dwight is nice to everyone, always says hello."

The decision to hold the story for Sunday had been made after Woodward had called the White House on Friday for comment. About 8:00 P.M., three hours after he'd been told the substance of the story, deputy press secretary Gerald Warren called back. "I have a statement from Dwight Chapin," he said:

As the *Washington Post* reporter has described it, the story is based entirely on hearsay and is fundamentally inaccurate. For example, I do not know, have never met, seen or talked to E. Howard Hunt. I have known Donald Segretti since college days, but I did not meet with him in Florida as the story suggests, and I certainly have never discussed with him any phase of the grand jury proceedings in the Watergate case. Beyond that, I don't propose to have any further comment.

Chapin, busily answering charges that had not been leveled against him, ignored the main point: that he was Segretti's contact. "Fundamentally inaccurate" was employed much as "collection of absurdities" had been to describe the initial Segretti-espionage-sabotage story. Along with the old "hearsay" red herring.

The "hearsay" charge rankled. The *Post* had a sworn statement from Larry Young.

At 9:00 P.M., when Bernstein sat down to write, he had three versions of the Young interviews—his own, Woodward's and Meyers'. The clutter on his desk was hopeless, so he moved to three vacant desks near his own and laid out five yards of notes. By 7:00 A.M., he had 15 pages which quoted extensively from Young. Only the biographical details on Chapin remained to be written.

He flopped down on a couch in the sports department and got less than two hours of uncomfortable sleep before being awakened by a copy aide. Bernstein wanted the story to be completed early so it could be reviewed by Rosenfeld, Simons and Bradlee without any last-minute hassles. He had looked through the library at the *Post* for more background on Chapin. There was only one half-page handout, issued by the 1968 Nixon campaign organization. It said that Chapin had been graduated from USC, and had worked for the J. Walter Thompson advertising agency under Bob Haldeman. Bernstein added details from Meyers' notes.

At about 9:30 A.M., he called the former administration official he had talked to the week after the Watergate arrests. The man knew Chapin well. "If Dwight has anything to do with this, it means Haldeman," he said. Chapin was no self-starter. "He does what two people tell him to do: Haldeman and Nixon."

Woodward and Sussman arrived at the office that Saturday at about 10:00 A.M. and began going over Bernstein's draft. There was no problem with the lead; it was the same as read to the White House:

> President Nixon's appointments secretary and an ex-White House aide indicted in the Watergate bugging case both served as "contacts" in a spying and sabotage operation against the Democrats, a California attorney has said in a sworn statement.

Sussman was concerned that the top section of the draft did not adequately stress Chapin's position in the White House, that it conveyed the impression that he was merely some flunkey calendar-keeper who worked out of a closet. He typed out a new second paragraph:

> The appointments secretary, Dwight L. Chapin, 31, meets almost daily with the President. As the person in charge of Mr. Nixon's schedule and appointments, including overall coordination of trips, Chapin is one of a handful of White House staff members with easy access to the President.

Bernstein was pleased with the addition. But he protested when the next paragraph, describing Chapin as a functionary who responded to orders from Haldeman, was struck from the draft.

Anger turned to anguish when the following paragraph was struck —an observation that Larry Young's description of the Newport Beach lawyer who allegedly paid Segretti "appears to fit Herbert W. Kalmbach, the President's personal attorney and former deputy finance chairman of the Nixon campaign."

Woodward had tried to reach Kalmbach on Friday and been told by Kalmbach's secretary that no member of the firm would comment to reporters on anything. Now Bernstein was prepared to argue strenuously, but Woodward joined the editors and said he preferred to kill the paragraph until Kalmbach was contacted, or until another source specifically identified Kalmbach as Segretti's paymaster. Bernstein conceded that they should be able to confirm Kalmbach's tie to

Segretti within a few days, as well as to identify the President's lawyer as one of five persons with overall control of the secret funds that had financed the campaign of espionage and sabotage.

A new paragraph was added, quoting Young as saying that the money for Segretti's activities, including a $20,000 annual salary, was paid from a "trust account in a lawyer's name . . . a highly-placed friend of the President, and [that Segretti] was instructed to guard that name zealously."

Despite the deletions, the story—headlined "Key Nixon Aide Named as 'Sabotage' Contact"—broke new ground. Almost four months after the break-in at Democratic headquarters, the spreading stain of Watergate had finally seeped into the White House.

8

BERNSTEIN HAD LEFT Washington Saturday night to spend the rest of the weekend in the Virginia countryside, horseback riding. When Woodward awoke Sunday, the radio news was quoting the *Post* story, as well as a press release from *Time* magazine dealing with the Segretti-Chapin connection: *Time*'s story was better than the *Post*'s in some respects. Though it was based on anonymous government sources and lacked any personal account such as Young's, it had several additional details: Chapin had hired Segretti—not merely served as his "contact." Another USC alumnus, Gordon Strachan, the political aide to Haldeman, also had a hand in hiring his old classmate. Segretti had been paid more than $35,000 by Herbert W. Kalmbach, the President's lawyer.

Woodward, his Sunday shot to hell by *Time* magazine—not for the first nor the last time, he was sure—went to the office and started working the telephone.

Late in the afternoon, he reached a Justice Department attorney whose overriding interest seemed to be getting back to the television set to watch a football game. He hurriedly confirmed that Kalmbach was indeed the paymaster for Segretti's secret activities. Woodward didn't even have time to ask him about Gordon Strachan.

Woodward called Hugh Sloan. Working around the edges, the two talked for a few minutes about Kalmbach's role in the campaign. Kalmbach had resigned as deputy finance chairman on April 7, the date the new campaign finance disclosure law took effect. Until

Maurice Stans resigned as Secretary of Commerce, Kalmbach had been in charge of fund-raising for the President's re-election, although Stans was doing political work while still at Commerce. There was very little about the financial side of the Nixon campaign that Kalmbach did not know, Sloan said, even after he resigned his position.

Then Kalmbach had to be one of the five persons with authority to approve disbursements from the secret stash in Stans' safe, Woodward suggested.

"Well, yes," Sloan said. "But he had some of the money in California."

The money from Stans' safe?

It was all really one cash fund, whether it was in California or Washington, Sloan said; it had all showed up on the same burned books. It was a Special Projects fund.

For espionage and political sabotage?

"That's what it was, but I didn't know it at the time," said Sloan. He responded with resignation, off-handedly, like a patient recounting a bad dream to a psychiatrist for the fourth time.

Kalmbach had distributed other money from the fund, far in excess of the amount received by Segretti, Sloan said. But he would not disclose how much or to whom. "The cash fund seems to be at the center of this," he understated.

Woodward called Bernstein in the country and filled him in. Bernstein agreed that Kalmbach's control over the fund was more important than the payments to Segretti and should lead the story Woodward would write. It would also include the *Time* material on Strachan, which Woodward had been unable to confirm.

This time, the White House did not trouble to comment, and the next day's front page of the *Washington Post* carried a two-column head above Herbert Kalmbach's picture: "Lawyer for Nixon Said to Have Used GOP's Spy Fund."

Woodward had taken time out to watch John D. Ehrlichman's appearance on ABC-TV's *Issues and Answers.* On TV, Ehrlichman resembled a snarling prune, he thought, one eyebrow cocked high, the other low. He was saying that everything in the papers about the Nixon campaign's program of political espionage and sabotage involved "a lot of charges, not much proof, not any proof. . . ." He suggested that the McGovern campaign was somehow responsible for the allegations which people were reading in their newspapers and hearing on television.

Reminding the audience that the election was only three weeks away, Ehrlichman said this was the "mud month," when political charges would be thrown around. He was not personally aware of any campaign of political espionage mounted by Republicans in or out of the administration, he said; certainly nobody in the White House had known anything about Watergate in advance. He couldn't "affirm or deny" the charge that Chapin was involved with Segretti. But, he added, it was important to distinguish between the Watergate bugging, which "involves a crime," and such activities as "finding out what the other fellow's schedule is." Political pranks, said Ehrlichman, that kind of thing, "has been in American politics as long as I can remember."

Woodward and Bernstein concluded that Ehrlichman was perhaps the only high White House aide clean enough on Watergate to be safely trotted out before the TV cameras. Haldeman sure as hell couldn't be sent out—not after the Chapin story. Both felt certain that Ehrlichman's appearance signaled that he was clear. Maybe Deep Throat had been wrong when he said Ehrlichman had ordered Howard Hunt out of town.

Ehrlichman's remarks on television were a mild prelude. The Chapin connection had brought Watergate to the doors of the Oval Office. Now the White House was ready to fight back. Although *Time* had developed information as damaging as the *Washington Post*'s, the paper had been selected as the target.

It began with Ron Ziegler's White House briefing the next morning, October 16.

"Mr. Chapin has made a comment on that, and I don't have anything to add to it," Ziegler responded to the first question concerning the Segretti connection.

QUESTION: "Is the President concerned about the report?"

ZIEGLER: "The President is concerned about the technique being applied by the opposition in the stories themselves. I would say his concern goes to the fact that stories are being run that are based on hearsay, innuendo, guilt by association."

QUESTION: "Who is the opposition?"

ZIEGLER: "Well, I think the opposition is clear. You know, since the Watergate case broke, people have been trying to link the case with the White House . . . and no link has been established . . . because no link exists. Since that time the opposition has been making charges which are not substantiated, stories have been written which are not substantiated, stories have been written that are based upon hearsay and on sources that will not reveal themselves, and all of this is being intermingled into an allegation that this administration, as the opposition points out, is corrupt. . . . That is what I am referring to and I am not going to comment on that type of story."

QUESTION: "Why don't you deny the charges?"

ZIEGLER: "I am not going to dignify these types of stories with a comment . . . it goes without saying that this administration does not condone sabotage or espionage or surveillance of individuals, but it also does not condone innuendo or source stories that make broad sweeping charges about the character of individuals."

The White House had decided that the conduct of the press, not the conduct of the President's men, was the issue.

"The President has confidence in Mr. Chapin," Ziegler concluded.

Speaking to an assembly of black Republicans at a downtown Washington hotel that afternoon, Senator Bob Dole, the Republican national chairman, delivered three pages of prepared remarks designed to link the *Post*'s investigative reporting with the failing fortunes of Senator McGovern's campaign. Less restrained than Ziegler, Dole got right to the point:

> For the last week, the Republican Party has been the victim of a barrage of unfounded and unsubstantiated allegations by George McGovern and his partner-in-mud-slinging, the *Washington Post.* Given the present straits in which the McGovern campaign finds itself, Mr. McGovern appears to have turned over the franchise for his media attack campaign to the editors of the *Washington Post,* who have shown themselves every bit as sure-footed along the low road of this campaign as their candidate.

While wire service stories on Dole's and Ziegler's statements piled up, the reporters were told that Clark MacGregor, Mitchell's successor as director of the Nixon campaign, had scheduled a 5:00 P.M. press conference to discuss the latest charges of political espionage and sabotage. Both reporters hated press conferences and rarely attended them, but Bernstein decided to go to this one. He had never seen MacGregor and wanted to find out if his reputation of being open with reporters was deserved. When Bernstein arrived in the large conference room at CRP headquarters shortly before five, an unusually large crowd of about 100 reporters was waiting.

MacGregor entered the room from the rear and walked up the middle aisle. He is a big man, six foot three inches, about 210 pounds. Arriving at the lectern, he grabbed both sides of it and gave a half-hearted smile. Because of the "unusual developments of the past few days," MacGregor said, he would be unable to answer any questions.

Clark Mollenhoff, six foot four inches and 230 pounds, Washington bureau chief of the Des Moines Register and Tribune Syndicate, rose, his face contorted in anger. Mollenhoff, a Pulitzer Prize-winning investigative reporter, had briefly served at the White House as resident ombudsman charged with keeping things honest. MacGregor and Mollenhoff looked like two giants getting ready to lay clubs on each other.

"What credibility do you have?" Mollenhoff shouted. His voice was booming, and the other reporters fell silent. "What documents have you seen?" Mollenhoff demanded. "Because if you can't tell us, you have no right to stand there."

When MacGregor had entered the room, copies of his prepared statement had been handed out, so the reporters knew what was coming. Others were shouting at him now, though none as vigorously as Mollenhoff. "Why should we sit here and listen to you, why should we print a word you say?" he insisted.

"That will be a matter you will have to determine in consultation with your editors," MacGregor replied. Then, looking into the television cameras, he began reading:

> According to the Gallup, Harris, Sindlinger and Yankelovich polls, the political elitist movement known as McGovernism is about to be repudiated overwhelmingly by the American people. As it should be. But frustrated, 26 points behind in the polls, with three weeks to go, George McGovern and his confederates are now engaging in the "politics of desperation." We are witnessing some of the dirtiest tactics

and hearing some of the most offensive language ever to appear in an American presidential campaign.

Lashing out wildly, George McGovern has compared the President of the United States to Adolf Hitler, the Republican Party to the Ku Klux Klan, and the United States Government to the Third Reich of Nazi Germany. . . .

And the *Washington Post*'s credibility has today sunk lower than that of George McGovern.

Using innuendo, third-person hearsay, unsubstantiated charges, anonymous sources and huge scare headlines, the *Post* has maliciously sought to give the appearance of a direct connection between the White House and the Watergate—a charge which the *Post* knows and half a dozen investigations have found to be false.

The hallmark of the *Post*'s campaign is hypocrisy—and its celebrated "double standard" is today visible for all to see.

Unproven charges by McGovern aides, or Senator Muskie, about alleged campaign disruptions that occurred more than six months ago are invariably given treatment normally accorded to declarations of war—while proven facts of opposition-incited disruptions of the President's campaign are buried deep inside the paper. When McGovern headquarters in California was used as a boiler room to rally hard-core, anti-war militants to confront the President—that was apparently of no significance to a newspaper which has dispatched a platoon of reporters to investigate charges that somebody sent two hundred pizzas to a Muskie rally last spring.

Bernstein groaned. It was the second time that day that the President's surrogates had mentioned the "pizzas." He and Woodward had considered leaving it out of the story they had written on the harassment of Muskie's campaign because it might appear trivial. But they had listed it as among the tricks that had been intended to disrupt a Muskie fund-raising dinner—like sending a number of items COD, timed to arrive during the affair.

Implying that the McGovern campaign was responsible, now MacGregor was demanding to know why the *Washington Post* hadn't investigated . . .

The Molotov cocktail discovered on October 8 at the door of the Newhall, California, Nixon headquarters?

The extensive fire damage suffered September 17th by the Nixon headquarters in Hollywood, California?

The arson of September 25th which caused more than $100,000 in damage to the Nixon headquarters in Phoenix, Arizona?

The extensive window breaking and other trashing this fall at Nixon storefronts in New York City; Arlington, Massachusetts; and Los Angeles County?*

MacGregor went angrily on for several more minutes about Mc-Govern's encouragement of "Daniel Ellsberg to commit a deed for which he faces a possible 115 years in a Federal Penitentiary," and about the *Washington Post*'s hypocrisy. By the time he had finished, he was flushed and shaking. He mentioned again the "unusual circumstances" that prevented him from entertaining questions, and strode from the room. A number of incensed reporters yelled their questions, and, less calm than when he'd arrived, Bernstein joined the shouting match. As MacGregor passed, Bernstein shouted, "Are you willing to deny the Chapin story?" But MacGregor merely looked at him blankly as he passed.

When Bernstein returned to the office, Ben Bradlee was examining the statements by Ziegler, Dole and MacGregor, noting that all had emphasized the same things and had used similar language. At the *Post*, there was little doubt that the attacks were orchestrated and, if not ordered by the President, made with his knowledge and approval.

Reporters from other news organizations were calling Bradlee for a response. He put a sheet of his two-ply paper in his typewriter and banged out a statement:

> Time will judge between Clark MacGregor's press release and the *Washington Post*'s reporting of the various activities of CRP. For now it is enough to say that not a single fact contained in the investigative reporting by this newspaper about these activities has been successfully challenged. MacGregor and other high administration officials have called these stories "a collection of absurdities" and the *Post* "malicious," but the facts are on the record, unchallenged by contrary evidence.

* A *Post* reporter spent two days investigating the charges. He found there was no evidence known to the local police or the FBI of any connection between these incidents and the McGovern campaign.

Bradlee was primed for a fight. He sensed that "the denials were not holding water." Weeks earlier, he had told Bernstein and Woodward that he was not about to go on the defensive, and had urged them to use extra caution.

Now, in his office, he showed them his statement and offered some further advice. "I understated it before," he said. "This is the hardest hardball that's ever been played in this town. We all have to be very careful, in the office and out. I don't want to know anything about your personal lives, that's your business." But if the reporters were doing anything that they didn't want known, "cut it out," Bradlee advised Watch who you talk to, who you hang around with; be careful on the telephones; start saving receipts for income taxes and get a lawyer to handle any future tax matters; make sure nobody brings any dope into your house; be restrained in what you say to others about the President and the administration.

Bradlee was saying nothing that the reporters hadn't discussed between themselves, and they had taken those precautions.

"Okay, fellas?" Bradlee asked rhetorically, then tightened his fist and delivered a lightning-fast uppercut to the air. He grasped his biceps with his opposite hand as he followed through the punch.

Outside Bradlee's office, Harry Rosenfeld was pacing around the newsroom, getting nervous. Bernstein and Woodward were budgeted to do a page-one story on the attacks. Few stories cause editors so much anxiety as those in which their newspapers and reporters are protagonists. Rosenfeld wanted to ensure that the story was absolutely fair to the administration. So did Bernstein and Woodward, but they were also insisting that it be fair to their reporting.

They described the attacks on the paper as having failed to answer the allegations. Rosenfeld struck the paragraph—it was "argumentative." It was one thing to be fair to the White House, the reporters said, but Rosenfeld was being unfair to their work and to the paper. Rosenfeld insisted, maintaining that the offending paragraph gave the appearance of bias. He was getting angry.

The first-edition story was very short because of the dispute. Writing for the second edition, Bernstein and Woodward renewed the debate, insisting that Dole, Ziegler and MacGregor had not addressed the substance of the *Post*'s allegations.

Compounding the problem was Bernstein's deadline-pushing. Both

Woodward and Rosenfeld were hollering at him. Bernstein kept making language changes in what Woodward had written and Rosenfeld had approved, putting everyone's nerves on edge. It took four hours to get a barely satisfactory story—a 52-inch monster that quoted endlessly and offered the reader little help in understanding the charges and countercharges. It had been a disastrous night.

Newspapers across the country reported the next day on the ire of the President's men. The White House was pitting its credibility against the *Washington Post*'s, and in the process was giving the paper's allegations more currency.

On October 18, the *New York Times* published a story that severely undermined the White House position. The *Times* had obtained telephone records which showed that Donald Segretti's telephone or credit card had been used for at least half a dozen calls to the White House and to Dwight Chapin's home in Bethesda, Maryland. In addition, Segretti's phone or credit card had been used for at least 21 calls to Howard Hunt's home and office.

The White House would have a rough time brushing aside that documentation as hearsay, innuendo, or geyser of misinformation. Bernstein and Woodward were in the *Post*'s newsroom about 11:00 P.M. on the night of the 17th when the *Times* front-page facsimile came over the UPI.* They were ecstatic, their competitive instincts abandoned in gratitude.

At the White House the next noonday, October 18, Ron Ziegler faced a hostile and aggressive press corps. Asked repeatedly to deny specifically the allegations and evidence cited by the *Post*, the *Times,* and *Time* magazine since October 10, he dodged and darted, retreating each time to the break-in at the Watergate.

"My observation on it [the *New York Times* story] is, in reading it, that it links Mr. Chapin by suggestion to the Watergate case. . . . I will repeat again today that no one presently employed at the White House had any involvement, awareness or association with the Watergate case."

* The *Post* receives a telephoto of the next day's *New York Times* front page each night at about 11:00.

What about political spying and sabotage aside from the June 17 break-in at the Watergate?

"In the briefing yesterday and the day before yesterday, I made it clear that no one in the White House at any time directed activities of sabotage, spying, espionage, or activities that related to following people around and compiling dossiers on them or anything such as that."

Reporters tried to refine their questions to draw a direct response. Each time, Ziegler gave the same answer, carefully using the word "directed" and avoiding "involved."

An insistent reporter tried to nail the secretary: "Three times you've used the word 'directed.' Were they aware of what was going on?"

"I think 'directed' is quite clear. As I said before, anyone who would have been involved in any such activity wouldn't be around here any more."

"But are you asserting that nobody in the White House was involved in this?"

"I am saying that if anyone was involved in that type of activity which I referred to, they would not be working here."

Involved in what? Some of the reporters recalled that Ziegler's talent for communication had first been tested as a Disneyland barker during summer vacations from college, taking tourists on the Jungle Ride. "Welcome aboard, folks. My name's Ron. I'm your skipper and guide down the River of Adventure. . . . Note the alligators. Please keep your hands inside the boat. They're always looking for a hand out. Look back at the dock; it may be the last time you ever see it. Note the natives on the bank; they're always trying to get a head."

Now Ziegler was running the President's Jungle Ride.

Was Mr. Nixon concerned about the allegations raised about his aides?

"His concern goes to the fact that stories are being run that are based on hearsay, innuendo, guilt by association." Etc., etc.

Ziegler's response and the *Times'* findings on Segretti's phone records were on the front page of next day's *Washington Post*.

Spared the brunt of the attack, the *New York Times* provided, in addition, an analysis of the White House behavior by Robert B. Semple, Jr., then the *Times'* White House correspondent:

The essence of the Administration's recent counterattack to the charges that some of President Nixon's assistants created or at least condoned a network of political espionage and disruption has been to denounce the newspapers that print them without explicitly discussing them. Behind the strategy lie two assumptions that tell much about the Administration's perceptions of the voters and newspapers that serve them. Judging by recent interviews with Mr. Nixon's aides, these assumptions seem to be widely shared in his inner circle. First, at the moment, the White House feels, the alleged conspiracy is perceived by most of the public as a distant and even amateurish intrigue far removed from the Oval Office, and thus a denial or even discussion of the charges by the White House would give those charges undeserved visibility and currency.

The second is that the public—softened up by three years of speeches from Vice President Agnew—has less than total confidence that what it reads and hears—particularly in the so-called Eastern Establishment media—is true and undistorted by political prejudice. Hence the recent Administration attacks on the *Washington Post,* which has been giving the corruption allegations front-page treatment. . . . Repeated requests to senior White House aides to get the full story, as they see it, have gone unanswered. This leaves the field to Mr. Ziegler, who appears increasingly uncomfortable with questions about Mr. Chapin and Mr. Segretti.

"Do you know why we're not uptight about the press and the espionage business?" one White House aide—not Mr. Ziegler—asked rhetorically the other day. "Because we believe that the public believes that the Eastern press really is what Agnew said it was—elitist, anti-Nixon and ultimately pro-McGovern."

9

FROM HUGH SLOAN, the reporters knew that the fifth person who controlled the secret fund was a White House official. There were many reasons for believing that it was H. R. Haldeman, the White House chief of staff. Indeed, there was some cause to suspect that behind Watergate stood Harry Robbins Haldeman.

Trim, crew-cut and powerful, Haldeman, at the age of 46, had gone from managing the Los Angeles offices of the J. Walter Thompson advertising agency to managing the business of the President of the United States.

Though John Mitchell had been the manager of the 1972 Nixon campaign, CRP was very much the creation of Bob Haldeman, and he was its executive officer at the White House. When CRP was formed in March 1971, Haldeman chose Jeb Magruder and Hugh Sloan to take charge of its day-to-day political and financial operations. Both had been members of the "Beaver Patrol," composed of bright, fiercely loyal young men brought to the White House from the advertising and marketing worlds by Haldeman.

Dwight Chapin was the most trusted of Haldeman's eager beavers. Gordon Strachan, who had also played a role in the hiring of Donald Segretti, was the beaver who served as Haldeman's liaison to CRP. Bart Porter, another Beaver Patrol member, had left his position as an advance man at the White House to become chief of advance for CRP.

With the exception of John Mitchell and his two lieutenants, Fred

LaRue and Robert Mardian, the senior Nixon men who had figured thus far in the Watergate disclosures owed their loyalty only to the President and to Haldeman. (Maurice Stans ordinarily was responsible only to the President, but he had worked closely with Haldeman in previous Nixon campaigns.)

Herbert W. Kalmbach had been introduced to Vice President Richard Nixon in the mid-fifties by Haldeman. In handling the President's personal legal matters and fund-raising, Kalmbach dealt mostly through Haldeman.

Charles W. Colson began his White House career in 1969 at the age of 37. He reported to Haldeman and the President as the administration's liaison to outside political and special-interest groups—and as the resident White House practitioner of underhanded political crafts.

Several middle-level White House aides had assured Bernstein and Woodward that in the Executive Mansion there was little doubt that the Segretti-Chapin operation had been approved by Haldeman.

For weeks, Sloan had been adamant in refusing to identify the fifth person who controlled the secret fund, repeating at each mention of the matter that it was part of his reason for "suspecting the worst."

Haldeman was held in awe throughout the administration. At the mention of his name, Cabinet officials would become silent and fearful. The few who would talk knowledgeably about him said they might lose their jobs if he ever found out. Tough . . . pragmatic . . . ruthless . . . devoted only to Richard Nixon . . . would stop at nothing . . . The descriptions were often similar and many quoted Haldeman's celebrated self-description: "I'm the President's son-of-a-bitch." But Haldeman was far more complicated than such descriptions indicated.

The reactions to Haldeman reminded Woodward of the military and of his Navy background. Haldeman was like the executive officer on a ship, the number two in command, always the ambitious, hard-charging zealot who would do anything for the captain.

One of Haldeman's methods of operation, the reporters knew, was "deniability." This was the device of insulating himself from controversial decisions by implementing them through others so that, later, he could deny involvement. Thus, the reporters were certain that Haldeman would never hire a Howard Hunt as a White House consultant.

He would make someone else—Colson or Ehrlichman—the employer of record. If Haldeman were behind Segretti's operation, he would not have come in direct contact with him.

The reporters knew from Sloan and others that Haldeman seldom dealt directly with CRP. That was Gordon Strachan's job. Deniability was the rule in the White House staff system; the bosses stood behind an impenetrable beaver dam. If Haldeman stood behind Watergate, it was unlikely he had left tracks. It would have been out of character for him to maintain direct control over funds for clandestine operations. Indeed, if he had, no one was telling the reporters. Still, sources in Justice and the FBI were not denying it. Guided by past experience, Bernstein and Woodward were interpreting this reticence as a sign that their suspicions were correct.

On October 19, Woodward dragged his balcony flower pot back into position to signal Deep Throat. At about one the next morning, he left his apartment for the long journey to the underground garage. He arrived at about 2:30 A.M. Deep Throat was not there. Fifteen minutes passed, then half an hour. An hour. Woodward was becoming worried.

Deep Throat rarely missed an appointment. In the dark, cold garage, Woodward began thinking the unthinkable. It would not have been difficult for Haldeman to learn that the reporters were making inquiries about him. Maybe Deep Throat had been spotted? Woodward followed? People crazy enough to hire Gordon Liddy and Howard Hunt were crazy enough to do other things. Woodward got mad at himself for becoming irrational, tried to put out of his head the vision of some goon squad terrorizing Deep Throat. Would it leave a black glove with a knife stuck through the palm in Deep Throat's car? What did a 1972 goon squad do, especially if it worked for the White House? Woodward went outside to look around, and then walked back down the ramp into the black. He spent another half-hour becoming more and more terrified—of exactly what he wasn't sure—and then ran from the garage and most of the way home. He told Bernstein later that day that Deep Throat had failed to show. There were a hundred possible explanations, but they both worried.

The following day, Woodward's copy of the *New York Times* arrived with a circle on page 20, and a clock face indicating a 3:00 A.M.

meeting. He took the familiar route, arrived about 15 minutes early, descended to the level of their meeting place, and there, smoking a cigarette, was Deep Throat. Woodward was both relieved and angry, saying that he hadn't appreciated the anxiety of the other night. Deep Throat said that he hadn't had a chance to check the balcony that day and hadn't called because things were getting hotter. Woodward moaned slightly more than necessary, hoping that it might help elicit some information on Haldeman.

Though it wasn't true, Woodward told Deep Throat that he and Bernstein had a story for the following week saying that Haldeman was the fifth person in control of disbursements from the secret fund.

"You'll have to do it on your own," Deep Throat said.

Woodward tried another angle. He asked if Deep Throat would feel compelled to warn him if his information was wrong.

Deep Throat said he would.

Then you're confirming Haldeman on the fund? Woodward asked.

"I'm not. You've got to do it on your own."

The distinction seemed too subtle.

"You cannot use me as a source," Deep Throat said. "I won't be a source on a Haldeman story." As always, the stakes seemed to quadruple when Haldeman's name was mentioned.

"Chapin took it close in and there's a lot of tension," Deep Throat explained. "That's to put it mildly—there's tension about Haldeman. Be careful."

He was tired and in a hurry. He said that he would try to keep the reporters out of trouble.

Woodward asked if they were in trouble on Haldeman.

"I'll keep you out," Deep Throat said.

Since he had not cautioned them on Haldeman, he was effectively confirming the story. Woodward made it clear that he expected some sign from Deep Throat if there was any reason to hold back.

Deep Throat replied that failing to warn Woodward off a bad story "would be a misconception of our friendship." He would not name Haldeman himself. He shook hands with Woodward and left. Woodward was now more certain of two things: Haldeman was the correct name, and Haldeman had accumulated frightening power. Deep Throat did not scare easily.

On Monday, October 23, Woodward reconstructed the meeting for Bernstein. Bernstein was uncomfortable with the "confirmation." Was it really absolute confirmation? Yes and no, Woodward said.

That night, the reporters visited Hugh Sloan. A light rain was falling when they arrived. Woodward banged the outsize brass doorknocker two or three times. Sloan came to the door and stepped outside. "I just can't talk tonight," he said. His tone was soft, friendly.

The reporters explained that they had only a few questions, about information they had received that Sloan might be able to confirm. They realized they were playing on his good manners; Hugh Sloan would never shut the door on anyone. But Haldeman was important.

They went over the secret fund and Sloan's repeated unwillingness to discuss the amounts of money spent. There were five people who had authority to approve the disbursements, right? Bernstein asked.

"Yes, I'd say five," Sloan said.

Magruder, Stans, Mitchell, Kalmbach and someone in the White House, Woodward reiterated.

"That's right," said Sloan, who was leaning against the door frame.

Did you mention the names before the grand jury? Woodward asked.

Sloan thought for several seconds. "Yes," he said.

We know that it's Haldeman, Bernstein said. The way he said it was meant to convey both urgency and inevitability. He wanted Sloan to think he would be giving nothing away by confirming. Haldeman, right? he repeated.

Sloan shrugged. "That may be, but I'm not your source on that."

All they needed was confirmation, Bernstein said. No need to say the name. Just yes.

"Not here," Sloan responded.

Woodward then asked if it was John Ehrlichman.

"No," Sloan said. "I can tell you it wasn't Ehrlichman."

Colson? asked Bernstein.

"No," said Sloan.

Unless they were way off base, that left only Haldeman and the President, Bernstein said. Certainly it wasn't the President.

"No, not the President," said Sloan.

Then it had to be Haldeman, Bernstein repeated. Look, he said, we're going to write it and we need your help if there's anything wrong about it.

Sloan paused. "Let me put it this way, then. I have no problems if you write a story like that."

Then it's correct? Woodward asked.

"Yes," Sloan said.

The reporters were trying to restrain their excitement. They asked a few more questions for form, and scarcely listened to the answers. Then they shook hands with Sloan and walked down the path to Woodward's car.

That was almost enough, Bernstein said. He was still uneasy. Woodward was more confident but he agreed they should try for one more confirmation.

The reporters arrived back at the office at about 10:00 P.M. They made a list of persons who were in a position to confirm or deny that Haldeman was the final name. There were only two people they hadn't contacted.

One was an FBI agent Bernstein had talked to during the first week of October. It had been an odd encounter. Bernstein had called the agent at his office. The agent had hung up on him and said he had nothing to say to any reporters. About 10 minutes later, the agent had called back and told Bernstein to meet him in a drugstore about eight blocks from the *Post*. He would be sitting at the counter reading a newspaper.

Bernstein had slipped onto a seat beside him. The agent made some small talk about the stock market, then finished his coffee. "Time to go," he said. The two left the drugstore and began walking west.

"You guys are causing big trouble," the agent said. "Our reports are showing up in the paper almost verbatim."

Bernstein was encouraged. He and Woodward were not always sure their information was the same as the Bureau's, despite the general opinion that it was their source.

"You've been right on the mark—except for Mitchell. We didn't have that, that he controlled the funds. But it might have come out in grand jury. If it did, we didn't follow it up. . . . We're going back now to see if we missed anything."

Bernstein was confused. He and Woodward had been all but certain that the FBI knew. They thought the Mitchell information was in the files, he said.

"That's what has some of us bothered," he said. "We're not sure we're getting all the files. The agents have been busting ass, but they might not be getting everything to follow up."

The FBI man kept asking questions about Mitchell. Bernstein was unsure of his purposes. The agent was alternately interrogating him, expressing doubts about the Bureau's investigation ("Nobody believes the case stops with the seven who were indicted. The question is why did it stop there") and then acting angry at the reporters. They were walking toward the White House.

"Look," the agent said, "the only person who knows I'm with you is my boss. We like our jobs. We don't want to get transferred. It's not fair when we come into the office in the morning and there's our whole report showing up in your paper."

He confirmed that the Bureau had run into information on political espionage and sabotage and done nothing with it. "You'll have to talk to Justice about that," he said. "It went through channels to Justice and never came back."

They turned north on East Executive Avenue, walking on the Treasury Department side of the street, directly across from the East Wing of the White House. The agent paused to tie his shoe, raising his foot onto the Treasury fence to balance himself. Bernstein looked around. There was a long line of tourists, many of them with cameras, waiting to enter the White House. The agent retied his other shoe. Maybe Bernstein was getting paranoid, but he was beginning to think the stop was intended to get his picture taken. It was the perfect place, all those tourists with their cameras; but why bother? Anybody could get his picture from the *Post* files. The agent's behavior hardly dissipated the paranoia. The G-man paused for another 30 seconds or so to ask additional questions about Mitchell, casually holding on to the fence with one hand. Finally, they resumed their walk toward Lafayette Square and sat chatting on a bench for a few minutes before parting.

Now, Woodward picked up a telephone extension while Bernstein called the agent at his home in the suburbs to ask him about Haldeman.

Bernstein knew he would never get the information merely by asking.

He had decided to try to anger the agent by telling him they were work-ing on a story about what a lousy job the FBI had done. Maybe there was an explanation for it, that's why he was calling, Bernstein said.

Woodward, listening on the extension, took notes.

AGENT: "We did not miss much."

BERNSTEIN: "Then you got Haldeman's name in connection with his control over the secret fund?"

AGENT: "Yeah."

BERNSTEIN: "But it also came out in the grand jury?"

AGENT: "Of course."

BERNSTEIN: "So it came out then in both the FBI interview with Sloan and when he was before the grand jury?"

AGENT: "Yes."

BERNSTEIN: "We just wanted to be sure of that because we've been told that it came out only in grand jury, that you guys fucked it up."

AGENT: "We got it, too. We went to everybody involved in the money . . . we know that 90 percent of your information comes from Bureau files. You either see them or someone reads them to you over the phone."

Bernstein said he would not talk about their sources. He returned to the question of Haldeman and asked again if Haldeman was named as the fifth person to control the secret fund.

"Yeah, Haldeman, John Haldeman," he said.

Bernstein ended the conversation and gave a thumbs-up signal to Woodward. Then it came to him that the agent had said *John,* not *Bob,* Haldeman. At times, it seemed that everyone in Washington mixed up Bob Haldeman and John Ehrlichman—"the German shep-herds," "the Prussians," "the Berlin Wall," as they were called. The reporters could not let the confusion persist, however. Bernstein called the agent back.

"Yeah, Haldeman, Bob Haldeman," he replied. "I can never re-member first names."

Deep Throat, Sloan, the FBI agent. The reporters concluded they had the story firmly in hand, finally. They left for home before mid-night feeling secure.

Next morning, they told Sussman what they had, and did not hide their jubilation. This story would be different from all the preceding ones about the secret fund. Instead of unnamed sources, it could be attributed to secret grand-jury testimony by Hugh Sloan, former treasurer of the CRP, former White House aide of H. R. Haldeman.

For months, the ante in Watergate had been steadily upped; with Haldeman, the stakes had become awesome. H. R. Haldeman was the principal surrogate of the President of the United States. When he acted, it was in the President's name. Given the nature of his relationship to Richard Nixon, it seemed unlikely that Haldeman would become involved in arrangements for funding clandestine operations without either the implicit or the explicit approval of the President. Especially if those operations had represented the basic re-election strategy of the Nixon campaign.

Bernstein had spent most of the previous night unable to sleep, thinking about the implications of what they had written and what they were about to write. What if they were being unfair to the President of the United States, damaging not just the man but the institution? And, by extension, the country? Suppose the reporters' assumptions were wrong. That somehow they had been horribly misled. What happened to a couple of punk reporters who took the country on a roller-coaster ride? Could it be that the wads of cash in Stans' safe had been merely discretionary funds that had been misspent by a few overzealous underlings? Or that the reporters and their sources had fed on one another's suspicions and speculations? No less awful, suppose the reporters were being set up. What if the White House had seen its chance to finish off the *Washington Post* and further undermine the credibility of the press? What if Haldeman had never asked for authority over the money, or had never exercised his authority?

Maybe all the fears were inflated and irrational. Maybe Nixon never read the damn paper anyway. Maybe nobody paid any attention (sometimes it was almost a relief when the polls showed that Watergate wasn't having much impact).

Bernstein was a shambles when he arrived at the office the next morning—sleep-starved, full of doubts, timorous. He confided in Woodward. It was not the first time one of them had gotten the shakes. They often reversed roles. Woodward had the reputation of being the more cautious, more conservative of the two—at the outset of Watergate, he probably had been. But over the months, each had worked as a brake on the other. If either of them had any doubts, they told the editors they were in agreement on holding off, no matter how much they might disagree privately. Or they told the editors nothing and held off.

Woodward, too, had gone through periods of apprehension about whether the foundation of their reporting—largely invisible to the reader—was strong enough to support the visible implications. Before informing Sussman that they had established the Haldeman connection solidly, the reporters reviewed their bases again. The exercise was reassuring—something like what astronauts must experience when they check their systems prior to lift-off and watch the green lights flash on one by one.

The afternoon of October 24, they wrote the Haldeman story. Essentially, it contained only one new fact—that the fifth person who had been in control of the campaign's funds for political espionage and sabotage was the President's chief of staff.

"The numbers," Ben Bradlee noted, were "getting terribly, terribly heavy." Bradlee was calling it a major escalation. He summoned Simons, Rosenfeld, Sussman, Bernstein and Woodward to his office.

"I was absolutely convinced in my mind that there was no way that any of this could have happened without Haldeman," he told the reporters later. "But I was going to do everything in my power to be sure that we didn't clip him before we had him. I felt that we were aiming higher and I suspected that you guys . . . had him in your targets maybe even before you should have. That maybe you knew it but you couldn't prove it. I was determined to keep it out of the paper until you could prove it."

During that 7:00 P.M. meeting, just before the deadline, Bradlee served as prosecutor, demanding to know exactly what each source had said.

"What did the FBI guy say?" Bradlee asked.

The reporters gave a brief summary.

"No," Bradlee said, "I want to hear exactly what you asked him and what his exact reply was."

He did the same with Deep Throat, and the doorstep interview with Sloan.

"I recommend going," Rosenfeld said.

Sussman agreed.

Simons nodded his approval.

"Go," Bradlee said.

On the way out, Simons told the reporters he would feel more comfortable if they had a fourth source. It was past 7:30; the story could not hold beyond 7:50. Bernstein said there was one other possibility, a lawyer in the Justice Department who might be willing to confirm. He went to a phone near Rosenfeld's office and called him. Woodward, Simons and Sussman were going over the story a final time.

Bernstein asked the lawyer point-blank if Haldeman was the fifth person in control of the secret fund, the name missing from Hugh Sloan's list.

He would not say.

Bernstein told him that they were going with the story. They already had it from three sources, he said; they knew Sloan had told the grand jury. All we're asking of you is to warn us if there is any reason to hold off on the story.

"I'd like to help you, I really would," said the lawyer. "But I just can't say anything."

Bernstein thought for a moment and told the man they understood why he couldn't say anything. So they would do it another way: Bernstein would count to 10. If there was any reason for the reporters to hold back on the story, the lawyer should hang up before 10. If he was on the line after 10, it would mean the story was okay.

"Hang up, right?" the lawyer asked.

That was right, Bernstein instructed, and he started counting. He got to 10. Okay, Bernstein said, and thanked him effusively.

"You've got it straight now?" the lawyer asked.

Right. Bernstein thanked him again and hung up.

He told the editors and Woodward that they now had a fourth confirmation, and thought himself quite clever.

Simons was still nervous. Smoking a cigarette, he walked across the newsroom and sat down opposite Woodward's typewriter.

"What do you think?" he asked. "We can always hold it for one more day if there is any reason. . . ."

Woodward told Simons that he was sure the story was solid.

Next Rosenfeld trooped over to Woodward's desk and asked if he had any doubts. None, said Woodward.

Rosenfeld suggested a change in the lead paragraph. He wanted Haldeman's control of the fund attributed not only to "accounts of sworn testimony before the Watergate grand jury," but to federal investigators as well. Woodward said fine; the FBI agent had confirmed it and Deep Throat had also made clear that the investigators knew it. The change was made.

The same two sources were the basis of another addition that said all five who controlled the fund had been questioned by the FBI.

With the deadline only minutes off, the story dropped down to the composing room to be set. There would be an insert for the ritual White House denial.

Woodward called the White House press office and read the story to deputy press secretary Gerald Warren, asking that it be confirmed or denied.

An hour later, Warren called back. "Your inquiry is based on misinformation because the reference to Bob Haldeman is untrue."

What the hell does that mean? Woodward asked.

"That's all we have to say," Warren replied.

Woodward and Bernstein picked over the statement for some time. They decided that it was halfhearted and weak. They inserted it into the story.

Shortly before nine o'clock, Woodward got a call from Kirby Jones, press secretary for the McGovern campaign. "I hear you've got a good one for tomorrow," Jones said. "How about sending a copy over?"

Woodward blew up and said *Post* stories on Watergate were not written for Democrats or McGovern or anyone else in particular, and that he resented the request. Jones seemed stunned. He didn't see anything unreasonable about it, especially since the paper would be out in a few hours.

Woodward said that he and Bernstein were having enough trouble already with accusations of collusion. He told Jones to get his own copy of the paper at a newsstand, like everyone else, and slammed down the phone.

Before they left that night, the night suburban editor showed them a long item off the Maryland AP wire. Senator Robert Dole had delivered a 20-minute attack on the *Post* before members of the

Maryland State Central Committee in Baltimore. The speech contained 57 references to the *Post*.*

The reporters finally left the paper, forgetting to give Hugh Sloan a courtesy call to alert him that the story was coming. He would be besieged by other reporters, and they should have warned him what to expect. But they had to finish putting together their outline for a book on Watergate. The outline had to be submitted at lunch the next day.

They were up almost until dawn writing, and met the next morning at nine in the coffee shop of the Madison Hotel. At breakfast, they quickly read through the Haldeman story in the *Post*'s final edition, and at about 10:30, Bernstein and Woodward strolled across 15th Street to the *Post* and went into Sussman's office for a general discussion of how they would follow the Haldeman story. It was a lighthearted session. This time they really had the White House. The attribution to Sloan's grand-jury testimony was something Ziegler would not be able to duck. That was not hearsay. Hugh Sloan was the guy who'd handled the money, and he had sworn an oath.

At their desks, Bernstein and Woodward were going through their notes to decide whom they should see that afternoon. Eric Wentworth, an education reporter, came over to Woodward.

---

* They included: "The greatest political scandal of this campaign is the brazen manner in which, without benefit of clergy, the *Washington Post* has set up housekeeping with the McGovern campaign. With his campaign collapsing around his ears, Mr. McGovern some weeks back became the beneficiary of the most extensive journalistic rescue-and-salvage operation in American politics.

"The *Post*'s reputation for objectivity and credibility have sunk so low they have almost disappeared from the Big Board altogether.

"There is a cultural and social affinity between the McGovernites and the *Post* executives and editors. They belong to the same elite; they can be found living cheek-by-jowl in the same exclusive chic neighborhoods, and hob-nobbing at the same Georgetown parties.

"There is the historic *Post* hostility to the person and political fortunes of the President of the United States—dating from the days of Alger Hiss when the President was proven right, and the *Post* and its friends exposed as gullible and naïve.

"It is only the *Washington Post* which deliberately mixes together illegal and unethical episodes, like the Watergate Caper, with shenanigans which have been the stock-in-trade of political pranksters from the day I came into politics.

"Now Mr. Bradlee, an old Kennedy coat-holder, is entitled to his views. But when he allows his paper to be used as a political instrument of the McGovernite campaign; when he himself travels the country as a small-bore McGovern surrogate— then he and his publication should expect appropriate treatment—which they will with regularity receive."

"Hey," said Wentworth, "have you heard about what Sloan's attorney said?"

Woodward hadn't.

"Sloan's attorney said that Sloan didn't name Haldeman before the grand jury. He said it unequivocally."

Woodward was stunned.

Wentworth repeated his words, then went to his desk and typed out what he could recall from a CBS radio account he had heard on his way to work. Woodward followed him. Wentworth handed the piece of paper to Woodward, who returned to his desk because he had to sit down.

He called Sloan. No answer. Then he tried Sloan's attorney, James Stoner. Stoner was not in his office. He asked Stoner's secretary urgently to have him return the call the minute she heard from him.

Woodward went over to Bernstein's desk and tapped him on the shoulder. We may have a problem, he said softly, and handed Wentworth's note to Bernstein. Bernstein suddenly felt sick and thought he might throw up. Flushed, he sat in his chair until it passed over.

Then he and Woodward walked into Sussman's office and passed him the note. All three went into Rosenfeld's office and turned on the television. What they were to see on the screen was something they would never forget. Sloan and his attorney, Stoner, were walking into a law office where Sloan was to give a deposition. Daniel Schorr, the veteran CBS correspondent, was waiting there with a camera crew. Schorr approached Sloan and asked him about the *Post*'s report of Sloan's testimony before the grand jury. Sloan said his attorney would have a comment. Schorr moved the microphone to Stoner.

"Our answer to that is an unequivocal no," he said. "We did not— Mr. Sloan did not implicate Mr. Haldeman in that testimony at all."

Sussman, Woodward and Bernstein looked at one another. What had gone wrong? They had been so sure.

A few minutes later, Bernstein, Woodward, Sussman, Rosenfeld and Simons met in Bradlee's office. Bradlee had seen the CBS interview.

He would later recall: "You all want to know my lowest moment in Watergate? It was watching Dan Schorr shove a mike in front of Sloan and then his attorney the next morning and say the *Washington Post* said you told the grand jury that Haldeman had control of this fund, is that true and all that, and Sloan's attorney said no. . . . Those bastards on the television, walking down the street, turning right into the courtyard and there's Dan, big, dangerous Dan Schorr, whom I've only known for thirty years, really tucking it to them and winding up tucking it to us."

Bernstein and Woodward decided not to cancel their noon lunch with Dick Snyder, their publisher, but to hurry through it instead. As they walked to the Hay-Adams Hotel, the magnitude of what was involved began to sink in. They had made a grievous error—Hugh Sloan would never lie. But how? And what was the mistake? There was no question that Sloan had confirmed Haldeman as the fifth controller of the fund. So had the FBI agent. And Deep Throat. It had something to do with the attribution itself, about Sloan's testimony before the grand jury. There, they had gotten something horribly wrong. They considered the possibilities as they walked the four blocks to the historic hotel on the site of the old Hay-Adams House, directly across Lafayette Square from the White House.

While they walked, Ron Ziegler was beginning his regular daily press briefing in the Executive Mansion. It began at 11:48 A.M. After 10 minutes or so of discussion and announcements about the President's campaign and speech schedule, a reporter asked: "Ron, has the FBI talked to Bob Haldeman about his part in allegedly managing a secret slush fund for political sabotage?"

That began 30 minutes of denunciation of the *Post*.

ZIEGLER: "The answer to your question is no, they have not. . . . I personally feel that this is shabby journalism by the *Washington Post*. . . . I think this effort on the part of the *Post* is getting to the point, really, of absurdity. . . .

"The story and headline ["Testimony Ties Top Nixon Aide to Secret Fund"] refers to a secret fund, a term developed exclusively, virtually exclusively, by the *Washington Post,* based again on hearsay and based again on information obtained from an individual that they again refuse to identify, anonymous sources. I am told [by John W. Dean III] that there is no such secret fund. . . . this story was denied, and yet they ran it as their lead story this morning, with a distorted headline that was based totally on hearsay and innuendo. . . .

". . . it is a blatant effort at character assassination that I do not think has been witnessed in the political process in some time. . . .

". . . I am not attacking the press at all. I have never done that in this position, but I am making some very direct observations about the *Washington Post* and suggesting that this is a political—and saying that this is a political effort by the *Washington Post,* well conceived and coordinated, to discredit this Administration and individuals in it.

". . . Now, we have had a long run of these types of stories presented by this particular newspaper, a newspaper once referred to as a great newspaper, but I would, as I said before, suggest that the journalistic tactic being used here is shoddy and shabby and is a vicious abuse of the journalistic process.

". . . I do not intend to in any way respond to these types of stories other than the way I have responded up to this point, and that is an unequivocal denial of the allegations put forth. . . ."

Ziegler had never previously issued any such unequivocal denial of a *Post* Watergate story, a reporter there said, and added, "I think you have just issued what must be the longest comment by a White House news secretary on a story."

QUESTION: "If all of these men—Haldeman, Chapin and Colson— are clean and innocent of this, why are they not made available for questions? When we ask you questions to ask them specifically, we do not get direct answers."

ZIEGLER: ". . . We are not going to play into the hands of the *Washington Post* that way or play that particular game with them. . . ."

QUESTION: "Some of the denials are rather broad, and in the case of Mr. Chapin it was 'basically, fundamentally, incorrect,' but if there is something that should be said which clears it up from your standpoint, why don't you do it?"

ZIEGLER: "I think we have this morning."

QUESTION: "As long as we are on the subject, was Mr. Donald Segretti recruited to conduct political espionage by the White House or the committee, and was his contact man Dwight Chapin?"

ZIEGLER: "I think I anticipated that question this morning."

QUESTION: "But you didn't answer it."

ZIEGLER: ". . . If I began to go back over all of the sources, all of the hearsay stories, and began to address each of these specifically, it would not only be a futile attempt, because it is difficult to track what has become a distorted, confused event, but it wouldn't be worth while, because [of the] . . . type of journalistic technique that has been used. . . ."

QUESTION: "Ron, *Time* magazine and the *New York Times* have also carried various articles about the incidents that allegedly have taken place. Do you include those in your general condemnation as being shabby journalism?"

ZIEGLER: "Quite frankly, I wouldn't lump those publications with the *Washington Post*. I don't think I would. . . ."

Ziegler was then asked about the *Post*'s reason for running the stories.

ZIEGLER: "I don't know what their motivation is. I have personal observations about what their motivation may be. You have a man who is the editor over at the *Washington Post* by the name of Ben Bradlee. I think anyone who would honestly want to assess what his political persuasions are would come quickly to the conclusion that he is not a supporter of President Nixon.

"I read the other day where Mr. Bradlee was giving a speech and he said the Nixon Administration is committed to our destruction— referring to the press—that this Administration is committed to the destruction of the free press.

"There has been nothing as long as I have been press secretary where we have ever involved ourselves in a program of destruction of the free press. We respect the free press. I respect the free press. I don't respect the type of shabby journalism that is being practiced by the *Washington Post*, and I have stated that view to you."

Lunch was nerve-racking and strained. Woodward and Bernstein were too preoccupied to discuss anything coherently, much less writing a book. If the situation was deteriorating as badly as they feared, they would probably offer their resignations to the paper. There is little demand in journalism or book publishing for discredited reporters. They hardly touched their food, and instead gulped down cup after cup of coffee.

When the meeting ended, they stepped into the hotel's old, oak-paneled elevator. Herbert Klein, the White House director of communications, was inside. All three stared at the floor in silence as the elevator descended. At the lobby level, Klein stepped out hurriedly and strode to a White House car waiting in the driveway.

Bernstein and Woodward held copies of the *Post* over their heads as they walked back to the office in the rain.

Wire-service summaries of Ziegler's briefing were in their typewriter carriages when they returned. The self-confidence and ferocity of Ziegler's attack and his flat denial of the Haldeman story were more signs that something had gone terribly wrong.

Physically and mentally, the reporters were in no condition to deal effectively with the crisis. They were tired, frightened and confused.

Soaked and shivering, Woodward called Sloan's attorney again. This time he reached him and asked him to explain the meaning of his denial.

"Your story is wrong," Stoner said icily. "Wrong on the grand jury."

Woodward was at a disadvantage: he couldn't betray Sloan's confidence and tell Stoner that his own client had been one of the sources.

Was Stoner certain that Sloan hadn't named Haldeman before the grand jury? Woodward tried to say it suggestively.

"Yes," said Stoner. "Absolutely certain." He anticipated the next question: "The denial is specifically addressed to your story. No, he has not said it to the FBI. No, he has not said it to any federal investigators."

Woodward was breaking into a cold sweat. Had the entire thing been a set-up? He had not expected antagonism from Hugh Sloan's attorney.

He tried another approach. Leaving aside the question of whom Sloan might have divulged it to, was the story's essential fact correct? Did Haldeman indeed have control of the fund?

"No comment."

Wasn't that the important question?

"No comment. I'm just not going to talk about information my client may or may not have."

Squirming in his chair, Woodward considered their plight. Christ, what were they going to do? He asked Stoner if he could offer any guidance that might help resolve the impasse. But Stoner wasn't giving anything.

Woodward directed Stoner's attention to the *Post*'s repeated recognition that Sloan was not criminally involved in Watergate. It had been the first newspaper to say so. It had said explicitly that Sloan had quit his job because he was honest.

Stoner said he appreciated that fact but Woodward sensed that the lawyer was getting impatient. Woodward needed time to think. He stalled.

Did the *Post* owe Stoner's client an apology for misrepresenting what he had told the grand jury?

Stoner said that no apology was necessary.

Woodward paused. Maybe he should ask if Haldeman deserved an apology. But suppose Stoner said yes. A printed apology would probably have to appear. The thought was horrible.

Painful as the answer could turn out to be, Woodward asked if an apology to Haldeman was in order. He couldn't think of anything else to ask.

"No comment."

Woodward told Stoner that the *Post* had a responsibility to correct an error.

No comment.

If an apology was called for, it would be given.

No comment.

Woodward raised his voice to impress on Stoner how serious it was when a newspaper made a mistake.

Finally, Stoner said he wouldn't recommend making any apology to Bob Haldeman.

For the first time since the radio report of the denial by Sloan's lawyer, Woodward relaxed a little.

He asked whether Sloan had been asked by the grand jury or investigators whether Haldeman controlled the fund.

No comment.

Could the FBI's investigation have been so bad, he wondered aloud, and the grand jury's investigation so inadequate that Sloan was never asked about Haldeman?

No comment.

That left them dangling, Woodward said.

Stoner said he sympathized with their precarious position.

Woodward couldn't argue with that. There was nothing left to say. Both reporters were losing their composure. Woodward couldn't contact Deep Throat until that night at the earliest. Bernstein couldn't reach Sloan. The whole office was in limbo; a pall had descended over the newsroom. Other reporters watched silently as the tension built. Bradlee and Simons occasionally came out of their offices to tell the reporters to stay cool, touch all bases. Sussman looked agonized. Rosenfeld kept shuttling between his office and the reporters' desks, demanding to be kept informed of every nuance as they backtracked their conversations with the sources.

At 3:00 P.M., Bernstein and Woodward left the office to find the FBI agent who had confirmed the Haldeman story two nights before. They found him in a corridor outside his office. Bernstein approached him and attempted to ask if the reporters had misunderstood.

"I'm not talking to you," the agent said, backing away.

Bernstein moved toward him as the agent backpedaled in the corridor. Inexplicably, the agent seemed to be smiling. This was no fucking joke, Bernstein told him. The agent turned and walked quickly to the end of the corridor, then turned down another.

Bernstein and Woodward had already determined their course of action. If the agent didn't stand by his remarks, they were going to talk to his boss and demand an explanation. It now seemed clear that Sloan had not told either the FBI or the grand jury about Haldeman.

Bernstein waited a moment, then ran after the agent and cornered him in the hallway. This was a deadly serious business, he told him, not some G-man version of hide and seek. They wanted some answers—immediately. Woodward walked up and joined the discussion. He was holding a folded copy of notes typed from Bernstein's conversation with the agent. It was time for some straight answers or the matter would be taken up with his boss, Woodward told the agent.

The agent was no longer smiling. He looked panicked. "What the hell are you talking about?" he said. "I'll deny everything. I'll deny everything."

Woodward unfolded his copy of the notes and showed them to the agent. They didn't want to get anyone in trouble, he said. They just needed to know what, if any, error they had made. And they needed to know that minute.

"I'm not talking to you about Haldeman or anything else," the agent said. "I can't even be seen talking to you two bastards."

Bernstein tried to calm him. Something had gotten screwed up, and they needed to know what; there was no reason to suspect each other of being devious or acting in bad faith.

The agent was sweating, his hands were trembling. "Fuck you," he said and walked into his office.

The reporters spotted one of the agent's superiors in the hallway. Their next move represented the most difficult professional—unprofessional, really—decision either had ever made. They were going to blow a confidential source. Neither had ever done it before; both knew instinctively that they were wrong. But they justified it. They suspected they had been set up; their anger was reasonable, their self-preservation was at stake, they told each other.

Bernstein and Woodward walked over to the agent's superior and shook hands. The three of them needed to go somewhere and talk, Woodward said.

What was the problem?

The reporters told him about Bernstein's telephone conversation with the agent concerning Haldeman. Both had been on the line. Woodward showed him the typed notes.

The man read them hurriedly. They could see his anger building. "You realize that it's against the law for one person to monitor a call that goes across a state line," he told them.

The reporters said they would readily accept the consequences if they had violated the law. But the immediate issue was Haldeman and whether they had been wrong.

The superior marched off without saying another word.

In a few minutes, the agent came rushing down the hall toward the reporters. "I'm ordering you two to stay in this building," he said, pointing and waving a finger in the air. "You're not to leave."

As he went racing off, Bernstein and Woodward agreed that the agent had no authority to order them to stay in the building unless he arrested them. They decided they had better call Sussman and get some advice. Woodward thought it might be a good idea to get a lawyer to join them.

They walked out of the building to a pay phone across the street and called Sussman. He suggested that they return to the *Post*, observing that it was absurd that the agent should order them around. "Did he arrest you?" Sussman asked. Bernstein said no. Rosenfeld was on the line too, calling the agent various names and saying they would teach him not to dick around with the *Washington Post*.

The reporters decided to ignore the advice and went back to the agent's boss. Maybe there was a way to straighten it out. He was in his office. A secretary admitted them at once. The boss sat behind a large desk; the agent stood next to him. His superior ordered the agent to leave. "Now, exactly what is this all about?" he asked as the door closed.

Unless they could determine the accuracy or inaccuracy of the Haldeman story, they might have to use the name of any source who had knowingly misled them. They were obliged to defend themselves. They wanted to know if the agent had purposely given them false information.

More important, Bernstein said, they had to know *how* they had made such a mistake. They still did not understand. Was Haldeman one of the five, or wasn't he? Had Sloan said he was, or hadn't he? They thought that their problem was not the substance of the report, but the mention of Sloan's grand-jury testimony.

"We're not discussing the case," the boss said.

The reporters tried again. If they were wrong, a correction and an apology were required. Whom should they apologize to? What should they say?

"You're getting no answers from here," the man said.

Half an hour later, the reporters were in Bradlee's office again, with Sussman, Rosenfeld and Simons.

"What happened?" Bradlee asked, leaning over his desk and extending upturned hands toward Bernstein and Woodward. They explained that they still did not know.

Woodward observed that they had the option of naming their sources because any agreement with a source was broken if he had given bad information. Rosenfeld was unsure. Bernstein was against it.

Bradlee signaled for quiet. "You're not even sure whether you've got it right or wrong." He was agitated, but displayed no anger. "Suppose you name sources—they'll just deny it and then where are you? Look, fellas, we don't name our sources. We're not going to start doing that."

Bernstein felt relieved. Rosenfeld looked dispirited, but stayed calm. He suggested going back to each one, talking with Deep Throat and Sloan and anyone else they could find. Then, in a day or two, they could see where they were.

The reporters said they were virtually certain that Sloan must not have given testimony about Haldeman before the grand jury. Woodward suggested writing that much, at least, and acknowledging their error.

Bradlee grimaced. "You don't know where you are. You haven't got the facts. Hold your water for a while. I don't know whether we should believe Sloan's attorney even now. We're going to wait to see how this shakes out."

Bradlee then turned to his typewriter to write a statement for all the news organizations that had been calling that afternoon for a comment. The two-ply paper flew through his typewriter and onto the floor like a scene from a Marx Brothers movie. After a number of false starts, he issued the following statement: "We stand by our story."*

Bernstein and Woodward sat tight and didn't do a story for the next day. But others did. Many papers which had not carried the Haldeman story gave prominent notice to the White House's denial. Ben Bagdikian later wrote in the *Columbia Journalism Review* that "the first information readers of the *Chicago Tribune* received of the *Post*'s Haldeman story was not the morning it broke . . . but the next day on page 7, under the headline 'Ziegler Denounces Post Spy Stories, Denies Link.' "

Peter Osnos, who had recently returned to Washington from a tour as the *Post*'s Vietnam correspondent, put together a front-page story on the statement by Sloan's attorney and the White House denial.

At 8:45 P.M., Bernstein finally reached Hugh Sloan by telephone. Bernstein explained their dilemma: they realized they were in error, but they weren't sure where.

Sloan was sympathetic. "The problem is that I do not agree with your conclusions as you wrote them."

---

* He was later to recall: "I issued two statements in that one year—both on Watergate. . . . Geez, what options did I really have? By this time I was up the river with these two reporters. I can remember sitting down at the typewriter and writing about thirty statements and then sort of saying, 'Fuck it, let's go stand by our boys.' "

Haldeman had indeed controlled the fund, but the matter had not come up in the grand jury, right?

"Bob Haldeman's name has never come up in my interviews with the grand jury. Our denial is strictly limited to your story. It just isn't factually true. I never said it before the grand jury. I was never asked. I'm not trying to influence your pursuit of the story. The denial was strictly low-key, purposely low-key."

Sloan's message seemed clear, though not explicit. Haldeman had controlled the fund; the matter had not come up during his grand-jury testimony. Either the reporters had misunderstood what Sloan had told them about the grand jury earlier that week or Sloan had misinterpreted their question.

The telephone conversation with Sloan was at least a hopeful sign; if the reporters could re-establish beyond any doubt that Haldeman controlled the fund, and could explain the error, their credibility might not be totally destroyed. Bernstein and Woodward were exhausted. They tried to analyze the steps that had led them to such a monumental blunder.

They had assumed too much. Persuaded by their sources, and by their own deductions, that Haldeman loomed behind "Watergate," they had grasped a slim reed—the secret fund. The decision had some justification. The Nixon campaign's cash had been the tangible key that had unlocked the secret activities. But they had taken shortcuts once they had themselves come to be convinced that Haldeman controlled the fund. They had heard what they wanted to hear. The night Sloan confirmed that Haldeman was one of the five, they had not even asked whether Haldeman had exercised his authority, whether he had actually approved any payments. They had not asked Sloan specifically what he had been asked before the grand jury, or what his response had been. Once Sloan mentioned the magic words, they had left and not called back. They had not asked him to say it again, to be sure they understood each other. In dealing with the FBI agent, they had compounded their mistakes. Bernstein's questioning had been perfunctory. He should have attempted to get the agent to mention the name himself, in his own context. If the agent had failed to do so, then the confirmation route might have been acceptable. The Haldeman-Ehrlichman mix-up should have served as a warning that the agent might have been saying more than he knew. Bernstein's ruse of accusing the FBI of ineptitude in order to provoke the agent had been bad judgment. Bernstein had not dealt with the agent enough to know how reliable he was, or how he would react.

They had realized that confronting the agent's boss was unethical as soon as they had done it. They had endangered the agent's career, betrayed his trust and risked their credibility with other sources.

There were other miscalculations. Bernstein should not have used the silent confirm-or-hang-up method with the Justice Department lawyer. The instructions were too complicated. (Indeed, they learned, the attorney had gotten the instructions backward and had meant to warn them off the story.) With Deep Throat, Woodward had placed too much faith in a code for confirmation, instead of accepting only a clear statement.

The next afternoon, October 26, several hours after Henry Kissinger met with the press in the White House to declare that "peace is at hand" in Southeast Asia, Clark MacGregor entered the Washington studios of the National Public Affairs Center for Television to be interviewed. From the administration's point of view, it was a perfect opportunity to adjust its public posture to hard realities and correct some of the misstatements that might haunt the White House later, particularly since anything MacGregor said would be overshadowed by Kissinger's announcement.

MacGregor confirmed the existence of a CRP cash fund for clandestine activities, though he quarreled with the term "secret" and insisted that disbursements from the fund had not knowingly been spent for illegal activities. He maintained that the money in Stans' safe had been used to determine if there were organized efforts to sabotage Nixon's primary campaign. He named five persons who had authorized or received payments: Mitchell, Stans, Magruder, Porter and Liddy.

MacGregor's remarks seemed to salvage some of the credibility the reporters had lost in the Haldeman debacle. The day before, Ziegler had denied the fund's existence.

Bradlee ruled it off page one, which already had another Watergate story. "That would look like we're grinding it in on their day of peace-at-hand," Bradlee told Woodward, who had been lobbying for the front page.

The *New York Times* put the MacGregor story on page one, adding a significant fact. Sworn testimony by individuals connected with the Nixon committee, the *Times* reported, showed that cash disbursements of $900,000 had been made from the fund.

That morning, Woodward had moved the red-flagged flower pot on his balcony. He knew this would be the grimmest meeting ever with Deep Throat.

When he got home at about 9:00 P.M., Woodward made himself an Ovaltine milk shake and fell asleep reading. He did not awaken until 1:30 A.M. Angry at being late, he considered driving, then rejected the idea as too risky. He and Bernstein had already been incautious once too often.

Woodward put on warm clothes and dashed down the back stairs and into the alley. He walked 15 blocks, found a cab and made it to the parking garage shortly before 3:00 A.M. Deep Throat was waiting in a dark corner, huddled against the wall.

The reporters needed help badly, Woodward told him, then spilled out all of his feelings of uncertainty, confusion, regret and anger. He talked for 15 or 20 minutes.

Deep Throat asked an occasional question, and appeared to be deeply concerned—more sad than remorseful. Woodward wanted him to know how desperate their situation was. The mistake had jeopardized all of their earlier reporting, he believed. The stories had been building. Eventually the White House would have had to yield. Now the pressure was off the White House because the burden of proof had shifted back to the *Post*.

"Well, Haldeman slipped away from you," Deep Throat stated. He kicked his heel at the garage wall, making no attempt to hide his disappointment. The entire story would never become known now; the Haldeman error had sealed the lid.

Deep Throat moved closed to Woodward. "Let me explain something," he said. "When you move on somebody like Haldeman, you've got to be sure you're on the most solid ground. Shit, what a royal screw-up!"

He stepped even closer, speaking in a whisper. "I'm probably not telling you anything you don't know, but your essential facts are right. From top to bottom, this whole business is a Haldeman operation. He ran the money. Insulated himself through those functionaries around him. Now, how do you get at it?"

Deep Throat described the Haldeman operation. "This guy is bright and can be smooth when necessary . . . but most of the time he is not smooth. He is Assistant President and everyone has access to him if they want to take it. He sends out the orders; he can be very nasty about it."

Haldeman had four principal assistants to whom he delegated orders but not responsibility: Lawrence Higby—"a young-punk nobody who does what he is told"; Chapin—"smarter and more urbane than Higby, also a dedicated yes-man"; Strachan—"soldierly and capable"; and Alexander Butterfield—"an ex-Air Force colonel who knows how to push paper and people."

"Everybody goes chicken after you make a mistake like you guys made," Deep Throat continued. "It contributes to the myth of Haldeman invincibility, adds to the fortress. It looks like he really stuck it in your eye, secretly pulling the strings to get even the *Washington Post* to fuck it up."

The story had been "the worst possible setback. You've got people feeling sorry for Haldeman. I didn't think that was possible."

Deep Throat stamped his foot. "A conspiracy like this . . . a conspiracy investigation . . . the rope has to tighten slowly around everyone's neck. You build convincingly from the outer edges in, you get ten times the evidence you need against the Hunts and Liddys. They feel hopelessly finished—they may not talk right away, but the grip is on them. Then you move up and do the same thing at the next level. If you shoot too high and miss, then everybody feels more secure. Lawyers work this way. I'm sure smart reporters must, too. You've put the investigation back months. It puts everyone on the defensive—editors, FBI agents, everybody has to go into a crouch after this."

Woodward swallowed hard. He deserved the lecture.

That afternoon, Woodward told Bernstein what Deep Throat had said. They agreed they should write a story saying that Haldeman had not been named by Sloan before the grand jury, but reasserting that reliable sources had again confirmed Haldeman's authority over the secret fund.

Bradlee and the other editors didn't want the story. The fires were cooling; they didn't want to fan them.

Sunday, Senator McGovern appeared on NBC's *Meet the Press* and welcomed the opportunity to drive home his Watergate message. It was all true, McGovern said, because two respected reporters from the *Washington Post* had said so.*

The same afternoon, Spiro Agnew, on ABC's *Issues and Answers,* offered a different opinion: "Journalistically reprehensible," he said of the *Post*'s coverage in general, and described the Haldeman account as "a contrived story constructed out of two untruths attempting to tie this to the President."

Minutes after the shows, Simons was on the phone to Rosenfeld. The paper now had no choice but to correct the Haldeman story. It was intolerable to have the Democratic presidential candidate running around the country quoting inaccurate information from the *Washington Post.*

Bernstein and Woodward were told to write an account clarifying the controversy. They were sitting by Bernstein's desk when a wire-room attendant brought them a press release from *Time* magazine.

The release stated that *Time* had obtained information from FBI files showing that Dwight Chapin had "admitted to FBI agents that he had hired" Donald Segretti to disrupt the Democratic campaign; that "Chapin had also told the FBI that Segretti's payment was set by Nixon's personal attorney, California lawyer Herbert Kalmbach." And that the President's personal lawyer had also admitted making the payments to Segretti.

But, *Time*'s account continued, "no hard evidence could be developed to support a charge by the *Washington Post* that H. R. Haldeman,

---

* McGovern said: "We have the written reports of respected reporters citing sworn testimony before the grand jury by the treasurer of the Committee to Re-elect the President, that a $700,000 fund was set up that was controlled, first, by Mr. Mitchell and, later, by Mr. Ehrlichman—Mr. Haldeman, the President's Chief of Staff, and that that money was set aside for the purposes of political espionage, political sabotage, and all these dirty tricks that have been played to disrupt the democratic process."

the White House chief of staff, was one of those with control over a fund that paid for spying and disruption."

Woodward and Bernstein were aware that *Time*'s access to FBI files was unquestioned. They wrote a routine account that led with *Time*'s Chapin-Kalmbach information and the magazine's conclusion on Haldeman. Then the story said that Sloan had been asked by the *Post* if Haldeman was one of those authorized to approve payments from the fund—even if Sloan had not imparted such information to the grand jury. The story quoted Sloan as saying, "Our denial was strictly limited," and added:

> The *Post* reporters then went back to their federal sources and were told that the *Post* story was incorrect in identifying Sloan's grand jury testimony as a source of information on Haldeman's link to the fund.
>
> However, these same sources, who have provided detailed information on the Watergate investigation, confirmed once more that Haldeman was authorized to make payments from the fund.
>
> One source went so far as to say "this is a Haldeman operation," and that Haldeman had "insulated" himself, dealing with the fund through an intermediary.

10

FOR SOME WEEKS, Bernstein and Woodward had been looking forward to Election Day. The final stretch of the campaign was the most frustrating period they had encountered since June 17. In addition to the Haldeman debacle, they had begun to run into one stone wall after another. After the self-congratulations and enthusiasms generated by the initial accounts of Segretti's operations and the Chapin-Kalmbach connections, the *Post* had mounted a huge investigation under Sussman's command. More than a dozen reporters were intermittently involved—investigating, analyzing the political fallout, writing profiles of the central figures, following the action in the courts, on Capitol Hill, at the White House. Little new information was developed: a few more Segretti contacts, isolated incidents of sabotage by the Nixon forces, additional examples of the narrowness of the course pursued by the FBI and federal prosecutors.

Bernstein and Woodward had resumed their evening visits. Nothing. The election was too near. Several people suggested they might be more talkative after Nixon's victory.

The promise of easier access to information after November 7 was not the only reason the reporters wanted the election behind them. With Nixon's re-election, the White House would be forced to abandon the line that the *Post* was working for the election of McGovern.

Woodward spent Election Day idly at the office, sometimes watching Sussman indulge his fascination with polling. Puffing his pipe, Sussman was trying to see if there were any way the polls could be wrong—

199

calculating that if George McGovern were to win, it would entail a shift of so many million votes. The latest surveys were strewn around—scrap-paper remnants of long division, multiplication, additions and symbols understandable only to Sussman. He concluded that it was mathematically impossible for Richard Nixon to lose.

Woodward, a registered Republican, did not vote. He couldn't decide whether he was more uneasy with the disorganization and naïve idealism of McGovern's campaign or with Richard Nixon's conduct. And he believed that not voting enabled him to be more objective in reporting on Watergate—a view Bernstein regarded as silly. Bernstein voted for McGovern, unenthusiastically and unhesitatingly, then bet in the office pool that Nixon would win with 54 percent.*

The day after the election, Bradlee and Simons asked Sussman for a memo advising how Bernstein and Woodward intended to pursue their investigation and listing areas on which they intended to concentrate. Sussman told the reporters he detected a lot of pressure for a story—any story, as long as it was good; something that would take the heat off the *Post* and put away the notion that the paper had been promoting George McGovern's campaign.

Woodward was demonstrably angered at the request. Not without a touch of arrogance, Bernstein and he advised Sussman to write a memo for the editors saying any damn thing that came into his head.

Sussman wrote a one-page memo which concluded: "Woodward and Bernstein are going back to virtually every old source and some new ones who have shown an interest in talking now that the election is over. Some of our best stories to date were pretty much unexpected and did not come from particular lines of inquiry, and quite possibly the same will be true now."

At five on the morning of November 11, a *Post* switchboard operator tracked down Bernstein at the home of a friend. She said she had been calling all over town for him since midnight.

Great, said Bernstein, and wondered loudly how the operator had found him and whom else she had called to do so.

---

* Nixon won the election with 61 percent of the vote.

"We don't disclose our sources of information, dear," she replied.

He was to call Sussman at home immediately. Bernstein had received middle-of-the-night calls from the office before. Usually, they signaled calamity or tragedy—Robert Kennedy's assassination, bombings at the Pentagon, the Capitol.

Sussman answered the phone, "Segretti's back home. Bob Meyers spoke with him very briefly."

Sussman wanted Bernstein to get the next plane to Los Angeles and talk to Segretti—if he would talk. Segretti had disappeared immediately after the October 10 story.

Bernstein reached Dulles Airport five minutes before the flight, with less than $20 in his wallet.

Meyers met Bernstein at the Los Angeles airport and they drove immediately to Segretti's apartment in Marina del Rey, about 20 minutes away. He was not at home, so Meyers stuck one more matchstick in the door.

Bernstein reached Segretti by phone late that afternoon. "Hi, Carl," he answered. "I wondered when we'd meet up with each other." His tone was cheerful and chipper, but not flip. He agreed to let Bernstein and Meyers come over. "I won't discuss any specifics, and everything has to be off the record."

Segretti was dressed in corduroy jeans and Scandinavian sweater and had a grin on his face when they arrived. He shook hands with Bernstein warmly. "How've you been?" he asked. Bernstein was struck by the fact that he was only about five foot four. This was the master spy? Secret agent with a White House badge? Segretti had a baby face, a slightly toothy smile and traces of a cowlick.

Segretti invited Bernstein and Meyers to sit down on the living-room couch and chatted about his hi-fi equipment.

"The fact is that I'm about broke," he said after a while, "out of a job and I still have payments on the car—and there will be legal fees."

Segretti was, by his own account, confused, scared, angry, and without friends. Bernstein found him likable, and his situation pathetic.

"I really want to tell the whole story and get this thing over with," Segretti said. "I don't understand how I got in over my head. I didn't know what it was all about. They never told me anything except my own role. I had to read the papers to find out."

They?

"The White House."

Segretti was agitated about the inquiries made to his family, friends and acquaintances by the press, and by the investigators from Senator Edward Kennedy's subcommittee.*

"Kennedy is out for blood and I'm the one treading water and bleeding," Segretti said. "Kennedy will tear me to shreds. Some people even asked my friends if I knew Arthur Bremer."† Segretti's eyes filled with tears. "How could anybody even ask something like that? It's terrible. It's horrible. I didn't do anything to deserve that. What do people think I am? If that's the kind of thing Kennedy gets into, that might just be the point where I say 'Fuck the whole thing' and get up and walk out and let them put me in jail. . . . I've been dragged through the mud, maligned—you'd think I was making bombs or something. I haven't done anything illegal, or even that bad. My friends have been harassed, my parents, my girlfriends; my privacy has been invaded; my phone is tapped, it clicks all the time; people have been following me; everybody I ever telephoned has been bothered."

Segretti's naïveté was compelling. He traced most of his difficulties to the press. He was particularly angry with the *New York Times* and *Newsweek* for getting his phone records and badgering his family. So Meyers and Bernstein calculatedly dumped on the opposition.

The process was excruciatingly slow. Segretti wouldn't volunteer any information without prodding and refused to discuss his activities except in general terms.

"What I did was mostly nickel-dime stuff," he said. "Maybe fifteen cents or a quarter every once in a while."

Finally, Segretti admitted he had been hired by Chapin. Strachan also had discussed the job with him. Kalmbach had paid him. The first approach had been from Dwight Chapin to Segretti, not vice versa.

"I didn't go looking for the job," Segretti said bitterly. "What would you do if you were just getting out of the Army, if you had been away from the real world for four years, you didn't know what kind of law you wanted to practice, and you got a call to go to work for the Presi-

* Two days after the *Post*'s October 10 story, Senator Kennedy directed his Subcommittee on Administrative Practice and Procedure to open an investigation into the allegations of White House-sponsored sabotage and spying.

† Arthur Bremer was the man who had attempted to assassinate Governor George Wallace of Alabama.

dent of the United States? If the really sinister things actually happened, I don't think Dwight knew about them," Segretti said. "Dwight just did what he was told."

Told by whom?

"Well, I'd sure like to meet Haldeman," he suggested.

Did Segretti have any hard evidence that it was Haldeman? Had Chapin ever said so?

"No, but I understand that Dwight generally takes his orders on everything from Haldeman."

Segretti confirmed meeting Howard Hunt and a man he thought was Gordon Liddy in Miami; Hunt had asked him to organize an anti-Nixon demonstration to embarrass McGovern. He would not say what the plan was, "but it sounded illegal to me, and I didn't want anything to do with being violent or breaking the law."

After each visit from the FBI, Segretti acknowledged, he had called Chapin for advice, but he would not say who had counseled him just before his grand-jury appearance. He denied that his testimony had been prompted or rehearsed, or that he had been shown FBI reports. "That's an example of some of the lies and bullshit that have been written," he said. "That would be as bad as the Watergate bugging." He had "discussed" his upcoming testimony with someone from the White House; they had agreed that every question asked by the grand jury would be answered truthfully. Bernstein got the impression that the discussion had been with John Dean. Segretti said he had been interviewed for what he presumed was the "Dean investigation." But he wouldn't say whether the interview had been conducted by Dean himself or a member of his staff, or whether it had occurred immediately prior to the grand-jury appearance. "I won't discuss John Dean," he said, and he would not say whether he had ever met him.

Segretti said he was through being a pawn of the White House. "They're going to have to break down my door and drag me to get me out of here again. All I want is to get my life back in order. I think the lowest point was when the mother of an old girlfriend told me she didn't want her daughter to see me any more. People can really be cruel."

Again Segretti's eyes glazed over and filled with tears. "Everyone is out to rip me apart and crucify me—Kennedy, the White House, the press. I just want to stay here and enjoy myself for a while—sail, swim, sit in the sun, see some girls."

During the visit, which lasted several hours, Segretti seemed as interested in finding out what Bernstein knew as Bernstein was interested in what he knew. There would be more to come, Bernstein said. None too subtly, he warned Segretti that he could expect to get swallowed up if he didn't get his story on the record soon. Unlike his superiors, he had no cloak of high office for protection. Segretti agreed, but he wanted more time. They would talk again the next day.

Bernstein called the office from his motel. Woodward, Sussman, Rosenfeld and Bradlee were all hanging on extensions. "Get it on the record, for Chrissakes," Bradlee said. There was enough in the scant information Segretti had offered to seriously challenge White House claims of innocence.

Bernstein spent five more days in Marina del Rey, persuading his colleagues at the *Post,* and himself, that Segretti was going to "convert" and go on the record. But it was no go.

"Well, kid, we struck out on that one," was Bradlee's reply when Bernstein returned to the office. Bernstein had typed a 12-page, single-spaced memo detailing every aspect of his dealings with Segretti.

Bradlee had scanned the memo and made an open-fisted gesture, jerking his arm. "Quit beating yourself off, kid," he told Bernstein, "and get some information."

Bradlee's frustration was understandable. The election had not stilled the White House guns. The self-confidence that flowed from the electoral triumph had emboldened the President's men. The post-election offensive was led by Charles Wendell Colson, the 41-year-old former Marine Corps captain and a White House commandant on political warfare.

About a week after the election, Colson traveled to Kennebunkport, Maine—very near Edmund Muskie's summer home—to address the New England Society of Newspaper Editors. He opened the speech by noting that his home state, Massachusetts, was the only one that had gone for George McGovern. The President, he joked, had decided to mend some fences and locate a new federal installation in Massachusetts—a nuclear-waste disposal center in Harvard Square.

Assuring his audience that "the First Amendment is alive and well in Washington," he accused the *Post* of McCarthyism, and called Bradlee "the self-appointed leader of what Boston's Teddy White* once described as 'that tiny little fringe of arrogant elitists who affect the healthy mainstream of American journalism with their own peculiar view of the world.' . . .

"If Bradlee ever left the Georgetown cocktail circuit, where he and his pals dine on third-hand information and gossip and rumor, he might discover out here the real America. And he might learn that all truth and all knowledge and all superior wisdom just doesn't emanate *exclusively* from that small little clique in Georgetown and that the rest of the country isn't just sitting out here waiting to be told what they're supposed to think."

Bradlee read Colson's speech in his office and walked over to Woodward's desk. "They're really kicking it at me," he said. "That's some pretty personal shit."

Woodward thought he was ruffled.

"I know it's there," Bradlee said.

Woodward recognized an admonition to dig harder.

"I know it's there," Bradlee repeated.

Later, Bradlee told an interviewer that he'd been "ready to hold both Woodward's and Bernstein's heads in a pail of water until they came up with another story. That dry spell was anguish. Anguish."

In the four weeks following the election, the reporters went chasing around as if their heads *were* in a pail of water. They were learning things, but were unable to make any meaningful stories out of what information they got. . . . Magruder's secretary told Bernstein she did not understand why she had not been interviewed by the FBI. . . . John Dean had sat in on all the FBI interviews with White House personnel, a Justice Department attorney said, and the prosecutors were upset about it. Dean had also received copies of the FBI reports for the Watergate investigation. . . . A secretary at the Mullen firm told Woodward that Dorothy Hunt, wife of Howard Hunt, was saying that "Howard is being made a scapegoat." . . . A middle-echelon White House aide said: "Dwight Chapin walks around as if he's just packed his bags" . . . and the big election victory seemed muted,

* Theodore H. White, author of *The Making of the President* series.

other White House aides were saying, and Watergate was number-one priority with the President, Haldeman, Ehrlichman and Colson. . . . Some presidential aides who were normally insiders were saying they didn't know what was going on. . . .

There were discussions in the White House of releasing a report on Watergate, a "White Paper" to lay out the facts, but it had been discarded as too risky. . . . A prominent Washington lawyer who had high political connections told Woodward: "I understand that someone is taking care of Hunt and McCord either through CRP or the White House; someone from the White House got to Judge Richey through the back door and got him to help the administration; a Republican governor said he could get to Richey and word came back that there was no need, it had already been done."* . . . A close friend of John Mitchell's described the former Attorney General as "essentially a very decent man who didn't have any use for the kind of Mickey Mouse stuff that Haldeman and Colson and the others were dreaming up." . . . One of the President's former top aides argued that Haldeman "would have been delinquent" if he had not set up a procedure to gather political intelligence for the President. . . . A ranking Justice Department official observed: "From what I hear, some of my best friends should be in jail.". . . At least a dozen people said that Jeb Magruder was finished and would not get an administration job that required Senate confirmation. . . . An Assistant Attorney General was convinced that the Dean investigation was "a fraud, a pipeline to Haldeman.". . . Mrs. Graham was told by a close friend who had ties to the administration that the phones of several *Post* reporters and news executives were tapped. A sweep which was conducted by electronics experts for a fee of $5000 turned up nothing. . . . The government had inexplicably failed to execute search warrants for the homes of the five arrested burglars. . . . A former Internal Revenue Service official related keen White House interest in some tax investigations of

---

* Dean, Mitchell and Haldeman all later testified that a Washington lawyer, Roemer McPhee, had engaged in private discussions about the civil case with Judge Richey. Dean testified that McPhee initiated private discussions with the judge to seek favorable treatment for the administration in the civil suit. Mitchell acknowledged that he had had at least nine meetings during the summer of 1972 with McPhee, who has been a personal friend of Richey's for many years. However, Mitchell said it was "inconceivable" that McPhee had approached the judge improperly. Judge Richey flatly denied any improper conduct and said that he and McPhee had never discussed any substantive aspects of the case.

the President's friends: "Nothing I could put my finger on fully, but the message was coming over." . . . Disillusioned campaign workers at CRP referred to a "cover story" that had been told to the prosecutors. . . . Hunt and Liddy had been members of the "Plumbers," a secret White House team investigating leaks to the news media. (The White House had no comment in the summer when *Time* magazine said there was such a group.)

One late November Saturday night, a *Post* editor asked for a word with Woodward in a deserted section of the newsroom. One of his neighbors had told him that his aunt was on a grand jury. His neighbor thought it was the jury on Watergate; she'd made some remark about knowing all about it. "She's a Republican, but she says she really hates Nixon now. My neighbor thinks she wants to talk."

A few days later, the editor handed Woodward a slip of paper with the woman's name and address. Bernstein and Woodward went to Rosenfeld, who seemed to like the idea of a visit but suspended final judgment until he had checked with Bradlee for a policy decision. Bradlee asked the *Post*'s lawyers.

Bernstein and Woodward consulted the *Post*'s library copy of the Federal Rules of Criminal Procedure. Grand jurors took an oath to keep secret their deliberations and the testimony before them; but the burden of secrecy, it appeared, was on the juror. There seemed to be nothing in the law that forbade anyone to ask questions. The lawyers agreed, but urged extreme caution in making any approaches. They recommended that the reporters simply ask the woman if she wanted to talk.

Bradlee was nervous. "No beating anyone over the head, no pressure, none of that cajoling," he instructed Woodward and Bernstein. He got up from behind his desk and pointed his finger. "I'm serious about that. Particularly you, Bernstein, be subtle for once in your life."

He instructed them to get in touch with him the moment the visit was over. "Get to a phone booth and call me—no matter what happens."

They drove to her house. She wasn't there. Woodward called Sussman at the office and asked him to pass the word to Bradlee.

The next morning, the reporters drove across town, knocked at the woman's door and identified themselves. She invited them inside. They did not mention the grand jury, and said simply that they had heard she knew something about Watergate.

"It's a mess, I know that," the woman said. "But how would I know anything about it except for what I read in the papers?"

It took 10 minutes to figure out that the woman was indeed on a grand jury at the courthouse, but not the Watergate one. They thanked her and left.

The episode had whetted their interest. They knew the outlines of the information they needed. They lacked the details a cooperative grand juror could probably supply. That afternoon, Bernstein called the chief prosecutor, Earl Silbert, and asked for a list of the 23 grand jurors. Silbert refused flatly, rejecting Bernstein's contention that the membership of the jury was a matter of public record.

Woodward asked a friend in the clerk's office if it was possible to get a roster of the Watergate grand jury. "No way whatsoever," he was told. "The records are secret."

Next morning, Woodward took a cab to the courthouse.

The clerk's office employed about 90 people. Woodward started at one end of the large complex of file rooms and after half an hour had found someone willing to direct him to a remote corner of the main file area where lists of trial and grand juries were kept. He identified himself to another clerk as a *Post* reporter and said he wanted to look through the file. The clerk looked at Woodward suspiciously. "Okay," he said, "but you aren't allowed to copy anything. You can't take names. No notes. I'll be watching."

Woodward started going through the file drawers and finally found the master list of 1972 grand juries. Two grand juries had been sworn in on June 5. He remembered that the foreman of the Watergate grand jury had an Eastern European name and worked for the government as an economist or something like that. He found the right name on Grand Jury Number One, sworn in on June 5, 1972.

Each of the grand jurors had filled out a small orange card listing name, age, occupation, address, home and work telephones. Woodward began sifting through the cards, then glanced over his shoulder. The clerk was sitting at his desk, about 15 feet away, staring at him. Woodward took the first four cards, set them face up in the bottom of the file drawer and began studying the names, ages, addresses, phone numbers and occupations. It took about 10 minutes to memorize the information. He asked the clerk where the men's room was.

Inside the washroom, Woodward went into a stall, took a notebook from his jacket pocket and wrote out what he had memorized. *Priscilla L. Woodruff, age 28, unemployed.* Trying to visualize what each of the grand jurors looked like helped him keep track of the information. *Naomi R. Williams, 56, retired teacher and elevator operator. Julian L. White, 37, janitor at George Washington University.*

Woodward drew a mental picture of a coat of arms and the name of Haldeman etched beneath a pair of crossed daggers guarding a throne: *George W. Stockton,* he wrote in his notebook, *Institute of Heraldry, Department of the Army, technician, age 53.* He hitched up his trousers. Four down, 19 to go.

Woodward memorized the next five cards. Straining not to look guilty, he asked the clerk where the chief judge's chambers were.

The man frowned. "You're sure spending a lot of time with those files. I'm not so sure that you're allowed to even look in there."

Woodward said he would be back—as soon as he had checked something with the chief judge. Upstairs, in a third-floor washroom, he wrote down the five names and the other information. That left 14. At the rate he was going, the job would take all morning.

On the third try, he was able to memorize six cards. Returning from the lavatory to the file room, he asked the clerk when he went to lunch. "I don't go out for lunch," the man said curtly. The perfect clerk, Woodward thought ruefully: even eats at his desk. He needed to get the rest this time because the clerk was getting impatient. It took nearly 45 minutes to memorize the last eight names and accompanying details.

At the office, he typed a list of the jury members and the accompanying data. In Bradlee's office, the editors and Bernstein and Woodward eliminated nearly half the members of the grand jury as too risky. Low-grade civil servants—especially older ones, for instance—were accustomed to doing things by the bureaucratic book, checking with their superiors, rarely relying on their own judgment. Military officers the same. They were looking for the few least likely to inform the prosecutors of a visit. The candidate would have to be bright enough to suspect that the grand-jury system had broken down in the Watergate case and be in command of the nuances of the evidence.

Ideally, the juror would be capable of outrage at the White House or the prosecutors or both; a person who was accustomed to bending rules, the type of person who valued practicality more than procedure. The exercise continued with Bernstein, Woodward and their bosses trying to psych out strangers on the basis of name, address, age, occupation, ethnic background, religion, income level. The final choices were left to the reporters.

Everyone in the room had private doubts about such a seedy venture. Bradlee, desperate for a story, and reassured by the lawyers, overcame his own. Simons doubted out loud the rightness of the exercise and worried about the paper. Rosenfeld was concerned most about the mechanics of the reporters not getting caught. Sussman was afraid that one of them, probably Bernstein, would push too hard and find a way to violate the law. Woodward wondered whether there was ever justification for a reporter to entice someone across the line of legality while standing safely on the right side himself. Bernstein, who vaguely approved of selective civil disobedience, was not concerned about breaking the law in the abstract. It was a question of *which* law, and he believed that grand-jury proceedings should be inviolate. The misgivings, however, went unstated, for the most part. The reporters' procedure would be to identify themselves, tell the juror that they had learned from an anonymous mutual acquaintance that he or she knew something about Watergate and ask if he or she was willing to discuss the matter. They would leave unless the juror, without prodding, volunteered something. Nothing would be said about the grand jury unless the juror mentioned it.

Bradlee, addressing them in a final briefing before bivouac, repeated the marching orders: "No strong-arm tactics, fellas. Right?"

Working separately over the first weekend of December, Woodward and Bernstein attempted the clumsy charade with about half a dozen members of the grand jury. They returned with no information and a clear impression that the prosecutors had warned the jurors to beware of jokers bearing press cards. Only one person volunteered that he was on the grand jury, and he explained to Woodward that he had taken two oaths of secrecy in his life, the Elks' and the grand juror's, and that both were sacred trusts. The others said they didn't know anything about Watergate except what they had learned from the media. One told Bernstein: "Watergate? Oh yeah, that fancy apartment down in Foggy Bottom. . . . I heard about it on the television, all that break-in business and stuff; there's no place safe in this city."

Until he heard about the Elk, Bernstein had feared that his partner with the fantastic memory had wasted it on the wrong list.

On Monday, Bradlee called the reporters into his office for an urgent meeting. He shut the door, a gesture often reserved for such delicate matters of state as firings. "The balloon is up," he said. At least one of the grand jurors had told the prosecutors he'd been visited by a *Washington Post* reporter. One of the prosecutors had called Edward Bennett Williams, the *Post*'s principal attorney. The prosecutors had gone to Judge Sirica with the juror's complaint and Williams had advised Bradlee to have his reporters sit tight.

They asked Bradlee how much trouble Williams thought they were in.

"You're not going to get an award," said Bradlee. "Williams said that it's up to the Judge." But he was worried. John Sirica, the chief judge of the United States District Court for the District of Columbia, was known as "Maximum John" because of the stiff punishments he imposed.

Late in the afternoon, Bradlee told the reporters to be in Williams' office at nine the next morning. "Things look a little better," he said. "Williams talked to Sirica and to the prosecutors; he thinks he can keep you out of the slam."

The next morning, Williams was pacing around his handsome office. "John Sirica is some kind of pissed at you fellas," he said. "We had to do a lot of convincing to keep your asses out of jail." Williams had pledged there would be no more *Post* contact with grand-jury members. The prosecutors, too, had interceded in the reporters' behalf, recommending to Sirica that no action be taken because none of the grand jurors had imparted any information. But Sirica was still fuming, Williams said, and would probably lecture them, at a minimum. "Stay in touch and keep your noses clean," he warned. The Judge could be very unpredictable.

The reporters returned to more conventional sources. A few nights later, Bernstein signed a *Post* car out of the office garage and drove to an apartment several miles away. It was about eight o'clock when he knocked on the door. The woman he was looking for answered, but when he told her his name, she did not open the door. She slipped a piece of paper underneath it with her unlisted telephone number written on it. "Call me later this evening," she said, adding, "Your articles have been excellent."

The woman was in a position to have considerable knowledge of the secret activities of the White House and CRP. Bernstein had attempted to contact her before, but she had rejected every approach. He drove back to the office and dialed the number. Her voice was unsteady, nervous. "At this point, I don't trust a soul," she said. "But I respect your position." She asked if Bernstein was calling from a safe phone. He was at the desk of a reporter on the Maryland staff; he thought so.

"I'm forced to agree 100 percent with Ben Bradlee; the truth hasn't been told," she said.

Bernstein printed the letter Z on the top sheet of a blue memo pad; X had been retired with the Bookkeeper. "My boss calls it a whitewash," said Z. "Two years ago, I never would have believed any of this, but the facts are overwhelming." She advised him to reread carefully the reporters' own stories. "There is more truth in there than you must have realized—many clues. You're doing very well, but you could do a lot better. It's a question of putting on more pressure."

She refused to be interrogated, and laid down the ground rules: She would point the reporters in the right direction to help them fill in some of the right names in the right places—certain hints, key avenues to pursue. She would answer questions only in the most general way, if at all. Much of what she called her "message" might seem vague, partly because even she didn't understand things completely, and because the information would be difficult to sort out.

"Your perseverance has been admirable," she said. "Apply it to what I say."

Bernstein, who had no idea what to expect, thought she sounded like some kind of mystic.

She began with Haldeman: "Someone had to pull the strings. You have a lot of company in thinking it's Haldeman. . . . John Dean is very interesting. It would be really interesting to know what Dean's investigation really was. His involvement went way beyond that. . . .

Magruder and Mitchell are very definitely involved. . . . Mitchell requires more perseverance."

Bernstein had already interrupted her several times, but she would not be more specific. Involved in what? Dirty tricks? Wiretapping?

She advised him to consider Haldeman, Ehrlichman, Colson and Mardian as a group. "Disclosure is the common thread," she said. ". . . Yes, of wiretap information."

Meaning they had received information from the Watergate tap?

"Disclosure," she repeated, "is the common thread. When people have jobs to lose in high places, they will go to any extent to protect them. The general theme is 'Don't blow the lid,' even now. They are better organized now than before June 17. They are good organizers but, to a certain extent, very sloppy. Financing is the most important way to learn who is involved. Pursue other Segrettis. Kalmbach was the paymaster. A lot of activities grew out of Plumbing. It goes back a lot farther than the Pentagon Papers. The Plumbers are quite relevant; two of them were indicted. I'd like to know how many more Plumbers there were."

Bernstein tried to learn more.

Z said there would be no further messages; he was forbidden to call her.

The next night, Woodward and Bernstein drove the familiar route to Hugh Sloan's house. Perhaps he could help decipher Z's message. Knowing that Sloan was always less than anxious to see them, they did not telephone ahead. As usual, he was too polite to close the door in their faces. He looked pale and defeated. He had lost weight. He invited them into the front hallway. The job-hunting was going badly, he said—the taint of Watergate. Equally awful, there was no end in sight to the trials and civil suits and depositions that were making him a professional witness at about $20 a day. They did not know how to respond. Visiting Sloan always made them feel like vultures.

The reporters outlined what they had learned from Z, but Sloan said he could make no more sense of it than they. Then he was apologetic about the Haldeman debacle, and finally it became painfully clear what had happened that night in the rain. Sloan had misunderstood Woodward's question, thinking that Woodward had inquired if Sloan *would have* named Haldeman before the grand jury had he been asked.

Now he was more enlightening than before on Haldeman's relationship to the fund and to CRP:

"Bob ran the committee through Magruder until Mitchell and Secretary Stans came over in the first part of '72. Jeb authorized the first payments to Liddy. I think Liddy was still working at the White House at the time, in the summer of '71. Actually, Haldeman stood behind all four who got bulk payments from the fund: Kalmbach, Liddy, Magruder and Porter."

Haldeman was insulated from the fund. Magruder, Kalmbach, Stans and even Mitchell had effectively acted on his behalf, Sloan explained. Haldeman had never personally ordered Sloan to hand out any payments. But spending money was the province of the White House chief. "Maury [Stans] frequently complained that too much money was being given out [from the fund]," he said.

Woodward asked more about the structure of Haldeman's office. Chapin was the presidential appointments secretary; Strachan, the political lieutenant; Larry Higby, the office manager and majordomo; and Alexander Butterfield supervised "internal security and the paper flow to the President." Typing his notes that night, Woodward underlined the words "internal security." That was the name of the Justice Department division in charge of government wiretapping, formerly headed by Robert Mardian.

While Woodward typed his notes, Bernstein pulled out a three-inch-thick file folder marked "To Be Checked." Several days earlier, Lawrence Meyer, a city-staff reporter whose beat was the federal courthouse, had obtained a confidential copy of a routine legal agreement between the prosecutors and attorneys for the seven Watergate defendants—whose trial was to begin on January 8. Bernstein read the 12-page "stipulation." It described telephone, travel and bank records that the prosecution and defense had agreed were accurate. Most of the information was already known to the reporters. Two matters intrigued them, however. There was evidence that Gordon Liddy and Howard Hunt had traveled to Los Angeles together under false names on September 4, 1971, and also on January 7, 1972, and February 17, 1972. That included the period when both were working at the White House, months before the Watergate break-in. They also found a note that a telephone had been installed "on August 16, 1971, in room 16 of the Executive Office Building located at 17th Street and Pennsylvania Avenue N.W., Washington, D.C., and . . . disconnected on March 15, 1972." It had been listed in the name and home address of Kathleen Chenow, of Alexandria, Virginia.

There was no Kathleen Chenow in the phone book, but, using a crisscross directory, Bernstein found a former roommate who said Miss Chenow had moved to Milwaukee. He reached her there. It took only a few minutes to establish that Kathleen Chenow had been the "Plumbers' " secretary. She did not seem hesitant about talking. Bernstein, who could hardly remember the last time he had encountered a willing source, did not know quite where to start. He finally asked her just who and what the Plumbers were. Her answer was straightforward: The Plumbers were Howard Hunt, Gordon Liddy, David Young and Egil (Bud) Krogh. They investigated "leaks" to the news media and reported to John Ehrlichman. Their office was in the Executive Office Building basement, across from the White House. Technically, she had been David Young's secretary; he was on loan to Ehrlichman's staff from Dr. Henry Kissinger's office. Young had made regular reports to Ehrlichman on the progress of the Plumbers' investigations. Krogh was one of Ehrlichman's principal deputies.

"Originally the administration had wanted a study of how close the *New York Times* version of the Pentagon Papers was to the actual documents," she explained. "Then they tried to determine how the Pentagon Papers got out. That started it all, the business of looking for leaks. For a while, they were studying State Department leaks. They checked embassy cables and tried to put two and two together about whose desks the cables went across. Most of Mr. Hunt's work that I saw was State Department cables he had reviewed dealing with the substance of the Pentagon Papers."

Bernstein asked if she could remember what specific leaks had been investigated.

"The Pentagon Papers, of course. Then there was a time when Jack Anderson was running columns on the administration, in December. They were checking those for leaks, too. Mr. Mardian from the Justice Department came down to the basement two or three times during that period.

"There was another occasion when Mr. Mardian was at a big meeting in Mr. Krogh's office with Liddy, Hunt and three or four people I didn't recognize," Chenow said. "And David [Young] used to talk to John Mitchell . . . I don't know what about; I don't know how often."

He asked about the telephone listed in the "stipulation."

"That was Mr. Hunt's phone. It was put in for me to answer and take messages for him. Mr. Barker always called on that phone; he was about the only one who ever called. It rang an average of once a week, sometimes two or three times a week." Hunt and Bernard Barker "were always chummy on the phone: Mr. Hunt would usually say 'How are you? What you been up to?' . . . Sometimes when he talked to Mr. Barker he spoke Spanish; he apparently liked to speak Spanish for some reason. . . . No, I don't speak Spanish. . . . I remember Mr. Hunt calling Mr. Barker and his [Barker's] wife— nobody else. Sometimes Mr. Liddy might have used the phone to talk to somebody Mr. Hunt had placed a call to. I guess it was Mr. Barker. Most of the phone calls were from August to November. The phone was taken out March 15; by then it hadn't been used in ages."

Bernstein asked the obvious. Why would a telephone in the White House complex, which had the benefit of the most sophisticated communications system in the world, be listed in the name and address of an individual in Alexandria?

"That's a good question," she replied. "They apparently wanted it in my name because they didn't want any ties with the White House —for what reason I don't know."

Bills for the phone service had been mailed to her home and she had sent them to another Ehrlichman deputy, John Campbell—"so the White House would pay them. Apparently it had been arranged —by Mr. Hunt, Mr. Young and Mr. Liddy. They had talked to Mr. Campbell and he would take care of it."

Chenow had left the White House staff on March 30, 1972 and was traveling in Europe at the time of the Watergate arrests. About two weeks later, she was located in Birmingham, England, by John Dean's assistant, Fred Fielding.

"He had flown to Europe to pick me up," she said. "He said the White House was talking to the FBI and that they—the White House and the FBI—were going to have an investigation. Apparently, the FBI had asked Mr. Dean to find me. Mr. Fielding requested that I come back and said that I should just recall my work and that they would ask me questions about the telephone and to try and recall. . . . On the flight back, Mr. Fielding gave me a *Time* magazine and tried to bring me up to date. He asked, 'Do you know anybody in the articles [on the break-in]?' and I said, 'Of course—Mr. Hunt.' "

She had reported to John Dean's office at 8:45 A.M. the day after her return, the first week of July. Fielding and David Young were also there. "Mr. Dean said I'd be interviewed by the FBI at nine, that I would be asked what my role was, whether I knew about the bugging, and to give perfectly straightforward answers to the best of my ability." The interview had lasted about 40 minutes as Dean, Fielding and Young sat by silently. "There were no questions asked by Mr. Dean and he didn't take any notes."

Afterward, she had talked briefly with Young. "He seemed kind of surprised that something like that [the bugging] could happen. He knew the telephone was in. I think after the whole thing came out he put two and two together." The same week, Chenow had met with the Watergate prosecutors and testified before the Watergate grand jury. "Silbert never asked about Ehrlichman," she said—"just Colson, besides Hunt and Liddy and Young." Bernstein's conversation with Chenow had lasted more than an hour and a half.

The next morning, Pearl Harbor Day, Woodward called Jack Harrington, the Chesapeake & Potomac Telephone Company official in charge of White House service, who confirmed that Ehrlichman's office had ordered the phone and had arranged the unusual billing system—the first of its kind he'd seen in 25 years.

Both reporters, meanwhile, had been told by White House sources that John Campbell had been Ehrlichman's office manager. There was no chance that the phone would have been installed without Ehrlichman's approval, the sources said.

By late afternoon, Bernstein had completed a 2000-word story on the secret phone installation, on Chenow's report about the Plumbers, and on her interview with John Dean. Gerald Warren, the deputy presidential press secretary, told Woodward there would be no White House comment—because it might affect the upcoming trial. "By not commenting," Bernstein wrote in the fifth paragraph, "the White House left unanswered the questions of how Hunt's official duties could require a camouflaged telephone listing and why Ehrlichman's office would approve the arrangements for such phone service."

To his chagrin, Bernstein was alone in his enthusiasm for the story. For the first time, someone had said for the record that the Plumbers existed, that Ehrlichman's office was involved in their activities, and that Hunt and other presidential aides had investigated "leaks."

Rosenfeld didn't seem much interested in the story and left it to Sussman. Sussman and Woodward were lukewarm and thought it "didn't prove anything." Bradlee expressed relief more than anything else: regardless of its shortcomings, it was the *Post*'s first strong Watergate story since the Haldeman report. He was inclined to give it a B-minus, but assigned extra points because its primary source was mentioned by name. The White House could argue its meaning, but not the facts. He wanted the story on the front page—if for no other reason than to demonstrate that, five weeks after George McGovern's defeat, the *Post* was still in the Watergate business.

That night, Bernstein and Woodward left aboard a 747 for Los Angeles, hoping that, if they got lucky, Donald Segretti would be more forthcoming than during Bernstein's last trip. Copies of Hunt's and Liddy's travel records were in their suitcases, and Woodward had talked by telephone to a secretary in Herbert Kalmbach's law firm who had seemed friendly.

On the flight out, Bernstein got into a high-stakes poker game in the lounge of the 747. He was about $30 ahead when Woodward wandered back and asked to join, arousing Bernstein's protective instincts. Sometimes, Bernstein worried that his partner didn't have enough street savvy to keep himself out of trouble. (Woodward, conversly, frequently worried that Bernstein would be all too comfortable in fast company.) But Woodward held his own against the high rollers and broke even. Bernstein won $35 in the $5-ante game.

(Woodward, Bernstein did not know, had spent a lot of weekends in Las Vegas while stationed at the Navy base in San Diego.) That night, they stayed in a $9-a-night tourist home in Marina del Rey; all the hotels in Donald Segretti's swinging harbor village were filled. And Segretti was not home.

The next day, they drove to the Beverly Wilshire Hotel—a Beverly Hills elephant of marble and red-velvet plush where Hunt and Liddy had stayed in September 1971. The reporters talked to the security chief there, an elderly former police captain who had no idea where the hotel's telephone records were kept. The hotel's chief accountant, who might have received his CPA and green eyeshades from Central Casting on the other side of Santa Monica Boulevard, was only slightly more helpful. Surrounded by stacks of bills and financial statements in his disheveled backroom office, he resolutely informed the reporters that he had given the FBI his word never to discuss Hunt's and Liddy's visit. In a corridor, Bernstein asked the accountant's secretary if she would care for a drink in the bar, then or later. "You're kidding," she said, and walked off slowly.

Bernstein said he wasn't kidding.

"You should be," she said.

Woodward later reached one of Segretti's alleged contacts on the telephone and proposed a visit. "I'll shoot you if you come out here," he replied.

Woodward drove south to Kalmbach's law offices at Newport Beach. The President's personal lawyer was out of town. The secretary to whom Woodward had spoken on the phone gave him a cup of coffee and offered her opinion: "Mr. Kalmbach is one of the finest men I know. He is an honest man, and when all of this is over, you will understand that." She would say no more.

At Kalmbach's home, a woman came to the door and said, "Absolutely not," when he asked for a moment of her time. She escorted Woodward out the inner courtyard gate and slammed it behind him.

They ate lunch with Larry Young, Segretti's ex-friend who had been so helpful in October; he knew nothing new. After four days, they finally reached Segretti by phone, and he agreed to meet them in a nearby Howard Johnson's. Over milkshakes and banana splits, they talked for about an hour. Segretti was unyielding about talking for the record in the foreseeable future.

The reporters returned to Washington on the night of December 11. At the White House press briefing the next noonday, Ron Ziegler, pressed again on the matter of Howard Hunt's secret telephone and the Plumbers, gave the first White House acknowledgment that the Plumbers had been in the business of investigating leaks to the news media. But he seemed to deny that either Howard Hunt or Gordon Liddy had been a Plumber. "To the best of my knowledge," said Ziegler, Liddy was never assigned to the team. Hunt? "I don't believe so, no."

Neither Bernstein nor Woodward had attended Ziegler's briefing. Convinced that they could learn more elsewhere, and concerned that their presence might further personalize Ziegler's responses, they customarily avoided the White House press room.*

Around this time, the White House began excluding the *Post* from covering social events at the Executive Mansion—first, a large Republican dinner; then, a dinner for past, present and newly designated Cabinet officers; then, a Sunday worship service; finally, a Christmas party for the children of foreign diplomats. The immediate target was *Post* reporter Dorothy McCardle, a gentle, 68-year-old grandmotherly fixture of the *Washington* press corps, who had covered White House social events for five administrations.

On the same day Mrs. McCardle was barred from the prayer meeting at the White House, Bernstein had dinner with friends, among them a reporter from the *Washington Star*.

The *Star* reporter told him an interesting story about a conversation he'd had with Colson a few days before November 7:

"As soon as the election is behind us, we're going to really shove

---

* That afternoon, Bernstein and Woodward wrote the story of Ziegler's remarks from notes taken at the briefing by Carroll Kilpatrick, the *Post*'s veteran White House correspondent. The reporters had a special fondness for Kilpatrick, who had been a Washington reporter for more than half of his 60 years and had covered the White House since the Kennedy administration. If anyone at the *Post* had suffered as a result of the paper's Watergate coverage, it was Kilpatrick. Many of his old sources on the Nixon staff refused to talk to him after November 7, when it no longer served their purposes. Of those few who were still talking to him after the election, Kilpatrick did not know which, if any, to trust—a disillusioning experience for any reporter who had dealt in good faith with those he covered. Kilpatrick, like most of his colleagues in the White House press corps, was skeptical of much of what Bernstein and Woodward had written. But he had never imposed his own judgment on their stories. The story on Kathleen Chenow and the Plumbers seemed to dull Kilpatrick's previous skepticism. "There has to be a lot more meaning in that story than meets the eye," he said.

it to the *Post*," he quoted Colson as saying. "All the details haven't been worked out yet, but the basic decisions have been made—at a meeting with the President." Colson advised the *Star* reporter to "start coming around with a breadbasket" because "we're going to fill it up with news" that would make reading the *Star* indispensable, while freezing out the *Post*. "And that's only the beginning. After that, we're really going to get rough. They're going to wish on L Street [location of the *Post*] that they'd never heard of Watergate."

Soon, challenges against the *Post*'s ownership of two television stations in Florida were filed with the Federal Communications Commission. The price of *Post* stock on the American Exchange dropped by almost 50 percent. Among the challengers—forming the organizations of "citizens" who proposed to become the new FCC licensees —were several persons long associated with the President.

11

JUDGE SIRICA wanted Bernstein and Woodward in his courtroom at 10:00 A.M. on December 19. A hearing before the Judge on another matter involving the press—a defense motion to force the *Los Angeles Times* to turn over tapes and notes of its interview with Alfred C. Baldwin—was already scheduled for that hour.

The reporters dressed neatly for their day in court. Woodward got his hair trimmed. The courtroom was packed, mostly with media people who were there for the confrontation over the tapes. Bernstein and Woodward took seats in the second row.

Sirica, they learned at precisely 10 o'clock, was capable of expressing his displeasure with a frown so deep as to leave no doubt about his reputation for toughness. He had decided to make the reporters the first order of business. The grand jurors had entered the courtroom. The audience obeyed the command of "All rise." The Judge's frown deepened. "Oh boy," Woodward whispered to Bernstein, bouncing on his toes and sucking in his breath so the words sounded as if he were ordering a horse to stop. Bernstein was contemplating which fate he preferred—the ignominy of being stripped naked in front of his colleagues for his half-assed conduct, or the mitigating honor of being dispatched by "Maximum John."

"It has recently come to my attention . . ." Sirica began recounting the unfortunate facts: grand jurors had been approached over the first weekend of December in an attempt to get information; but, judging from a transcript of the prosecutors' subsequent discussion of

222

the matter with the grand jury, no information had been disclosed; thus, the investigation had not been compromised. The jurors were to be commended for their silence. Their resolve could only be strengthened if once more they were reminded of the oath which had bound their deliberations "sacred and secret."

The Judge peered out into the audience. "Now I want it understood by the person who approached members of this grand jury that the court regards the matter as extremely serious."

The reporters were hanging on the Judge's every word now, less confident than before that Ed Williams and the prosecutors had been convincing in their arguments.

Sirica was scowling. He noted thoughtfully that the person who had attempted to subvert the sanctity of the grand-jury proceedings was neither defendant nor counsel but . . . "a news media representative." A buzz in the assembled press corps. Who among them? Bernstein and Woodward waited for the Judge to unmask them and, maybe, to ask if they wished to throw themselves on the mercy of the court.

First, however, Sirica desired to point out the legal ramifications and to remind the assembly that attempting to gain information from a grand juror is, "at least potentially," a contemptuous offense. Then he excused the grand jury and strode from the court. The clerk declared a recess.

It took the reporters several moments to understand what had happened, that that was the end of it. They had gone free.

Bernstein and Woodward tried to look nonchalant as their colleagues asked who they thought was guilty. They declined to speculate. Dan Schorr of CBS, who knew a sham when he spotted one, was the first to suggest, privately, that Bernstein and Woodward were the offenders. Hearsay, innuendo and character assassination, protested Bernstein. Schorr responded with a knowing smile. The reporters had reluctantly agreed during a rush to the halls that only as a last resort would they deny the allegation outright; maybe they could get by with indignation and artful footwork.

The confused scene in the hallway did not lend itself to careful thought. Two dozen of their colleagues were shouting private theories or polling one another in search of the guilty party. Accused again, Woodward said the first thing that came into his head: the grand-jury contact had taken place over the first weekend in December. That was six weeks after he and Bernstein had written a major story. Somehow, the compelling illogic of the syllogism got by. Bernstein, feeling grubby, listened raptly to another newsman explain why the offender was probably a radio or television reporter, not someone from a newspaper. "Sirica specifically used the phrase 'news media representative.' That's the term he always uses when he's talking about radio and television reporters. When he means newspaper reporters, he says 'the press.' " Yeah, said Bernstein, he thought he had noticed that, too.

Woodward and Bernstein were trying to avoid a colleague who was interviewing reporters in the hallway about the session in Sirica's courtroom. He caught up with Woodward near the elevator and asked point-blank if the Judge had been referring to him or Bernstein.

Come off it, what do you think? Woodward answered angrily.

The man persisted. Well, was it one of them or wasn't it? Yes or no.

Listen, Woodward snapped. Do you want a quote? Are we talking for the record? I mean, are you serious? Because if you are, I'll give you something, all right.

The reporter seemed stunned. "Sorry, Bob, I didn't think you'd take me seriously," he told Woodward.

The danger passed. The nightmare vision that had haunted them all day—Ron Ziegler at the podium demanding that they be the object of a full federal investigation, or some such thing—disappeared. They tried to imagine what choice phrases he might use ("jury tampering"?), and they realized that they didn't have the stomach for it. They felt lousy. They had not broken the law when they visited the grand jurors, that much seemed certain. But they had sailed around it and exposed others to danger. They had chosen expediency over principle and, caught in the act, their role had been covered up. They had dodged, evaded, misrepresented, suggested and intimidated, even if they had not lied outright.

That afternoon, Woodward returned to Judge Sirica's courtroom for the hearing on the *Los Angeles Times'* Baldwin material. The notes, tapes and related documents of reporters Jack Nelson and Ronald

Ostrow had been subpoenaed by lawyers for the Watergate defendants.

The *Times'* interview with Baldwin had been the most vivid piece of journalism in the whole Watergate saga, definitively portraying the difference between a "third-rate burglary attempt" and the brand of political gang warfare practiced by the President's men. Woodward, remembering his own dealings with Alfred Baldwin's lawyers, doubted there would have been any interview without assurances that the tapes and notes would remain in the *Times'* possession. Certainly, the stories Bernstein and he had done could not have been written without such guarantees.

The Judge ordered John F. Lawrence, the *Los Angeles Times'* bureau chief in Washington, to turn over the tapes, which the paper had placed in his custody.

"I must respectfully decline," Lawrence, a thin man in his late thirties, said mildly.

Sirica held him in contempt and ordered him jailed.

Lawrence's lawyer argued strenuously that jailing him while the First Amendment issue was being considered on appeal would serve no purpose. He also pointed out that it was Christmastime and that Mr. Lawrence had a wife and small children. But Sirica would not be swayed, and the marshals led Lawrence off to jail, not even permitting him to say goodbye to his wife.*

Bernstein had rarely seen Woodward so shaken. They were both painfully aware of the contrast. Lawrence, whose only offense had been to act professionally and to follow his conscience, was in jail. They had gotten off with a lecture and with their secret intact.

The grand-jury adventure was not the reporters' last encounter with Judge Sirica or the prosecutors.

Several days after their court appearance, Woodward phoned a former secretary in the office of Morton B. Jackson, a Los Angeles lawyer with whom Hunt had stayed during the week following the

---

* Lawrence spent several hours in a basement cell before the U.S. Court of Appeals released him pending appeal. Three days later, attorneys for Alfred Baldwin announced that he was voluntarily releasing the *Los Angeles Times* from its agreement to keep the tapes confidential. The tapes were handed over to the court.

Watergate break-in. Woodward identified himself and explained that he knew she had been interviewed by the FBI.

"Leave me alone," she said. "I have my life to live. I can't stand it. Why do you want to bother me?"

Woodward said that he was checking information which indicated that she knew something about the purpose of Howard Hunt's and Gordon Liddy's travels to the West Coast.

"I'm nobody. Nobody at all. . . . Leave me alone." She was crying. Woodward ended the conversation.

The next day, Bradlee called Woodward and Bernstein to his office. "Williams got another call from the prosecutors. . . . Some woman from California complained that one of you phoned her and said you were an FBI agent."

Bernstein broke up laughing at the thought of Woodward as an FBI agent. But Bradlee was serious. During the hearing on the Baldwin tapes, Sirica had directed all potential witnesses in the case not to talk to reporters until after the trial.

"Now we're back with Sirica," Bradlee said. "The prosecutors had to go to the Judge. They don't think you posed as an FBI agent. But they think you might have violated the witness rule."

Bradlee said that Ed Williams would visit Sirica again. Bernstein complained that it would be impossible to continue the investigation if he and Woodward couldn't talk to witnesses. Bradlee agreed. "Until we get it settled," he said, "you're going to have to stay away from witnesses completely."

The reporters asked how they were supposed to know whether someone was a witness.

No way, Bradlee said, so you'll have to stop your reporting—that is, stop digging new ground—until this is settled.

For the first time in six months, Bernstein and Woodward were called off.

Two days later, Bradlee put new ground rules in writing. Copies went to Rosenfeld, Sussman, Woodward and Bernstein: "Williams talked to Sirica this morning. It is OK for us to talk to witnesses . . . PROVIDED that the minute a witness tells us he or she has been forbidden by the court to talk to us, we call off the dogs. And that means *the minute* they tell us that. In other words, we can *not* try to talk a witness into talking if that witness has expressed an understanding that he or she is not supposed to talk. We *must* live up to the spirit and the letter of this ground rule."

Later that week, they stopped by the office of Earl Silbert to discuss the guidelines. It was about 9:00 P.M. and the courthouse was almost deserted. Silbert seemed in a good mood. As usual in such sessions, he refused to discuss the case substantively, and they all chatted about the election. The chief prosecutor was a registered Democrat and his wife, an artist, had been a volunteer in the McGovern campaign. She had used her maiden name so that there would be no unfair connections made between her political activities and the prosecution of the Watergate case.

Like almost everything about Silbert, his office was meticulous. (His mother had once told an interviewer that Earl was so fastidious that he lined up the heels of his shoes in the closet.) The stacks of file folders and papers that covered almost every available inch of surface space in the room were arranged in perfect piles. Woodward noticed a letter on Silbert's desk, and recognized the letterhead—The Watkins-Johnson Company of Rockville, Maryland. Woodward knew it was the company where McCord had bought some of the equipment used to bug the Watergate.

He mentioned it to Bernstein as they took a cab back to the *Post*. So what? Bernstein said. Woodward didn't know, but he got on the phone to the company the next morning, and learned that McCord had left his CRP calling card when he bought the equipment, and had paid with $100 bills—35 of them.

Woodward wrote a brief story about the transaction which ran December 23 on the inside of the paper.

The next Monday, Bernstein got a call from Silbert saying that he wanted to see the two of them in his office at once. Bernstein had no idea what Silbert wanted. Woodward figured that Silbert had put together the information on the $3500 radio and their having seen the letter on his desk. Bernstein thought it was inconceivable that Silbert would be calling them down for such a trivial matter, especially since they already had some documents on McCord's purchase.

When they arrived, Silbert and his associate, Seymour Glanzer, were wearing very stern expressions. Silbert demanded to know the source of the radio story. The letter was in the same position on his desk, at the far lefthand corner, clearly in sight from where Woodward sat. Woodward said he had seen the letter and decided to call Watkins-Johnson to learn if anything new had come up about the equipment since the reporters had last checked.

"For me to believe that," Silbert said, "you're going to have to tell me your original source of information."

They refused.

Silbert was persuaded that their information had come from the letter, and only the letter. He threatened to circulate a memorandum in the U.S. Attorney's office, telling everyone about the incident and recommending that no one there ever again talk with Woodward or Bernstein. He was considering taking legal action. If he let something slip in conversation, Silbert added, it was perfectly proper for the reporters to use it. But to get information off someone's desk was "sneaky and outrageous." Glanzer said it was dishonest.

Bernstein had learned years before that the ability to read upside down could be a useful reportorial skill, but he did not disagree strongly with the prosecutors, and he apologized profusely. Woodward also apologized, but he thought Silbert and Glanzer were being irrational, and said so.

Silbert said he didn't know if he could ever trust the two reporters again.

If the prosecutors took any action on the matter, Woodward and Bernstein did not hear of it.

In December, a few weeks before the trial of the Watergate Seven was to begin, Woodward went to lunch with Sussman and Rosenfeld at the Jefferson Hotel. The editors—fraternally but insistently—wanted to know more about where the *Post*'s Watergate investigation was going.

Woodward had his fantasies about the future of Watergate: one was that Gordon Liddy invites Bernstein and Woodward out to his home, gives them drinks and spends the evening telling them the whole story while they get it on tape.

The editors were not interested in his fantasies; they wanted more legwork. Woodward inquired who was going to cover the trial for the *Post*. Rosenfeld said he had not decided. Woodward felt that he and Bernstein should cover it. Rosenfeld disagreed. More than ever, he said, it was important that the *Post* have irreproachably objective coverage. Other reporters more removed from the story should be assigned. Woodward insisted that they had earned the chance. Rosenfeld glared at Woodward and said no decision had been made.

Several days later, Rosenfeld informed the reporters that he had chosen Lawrence Meyer, the regular federal-court reporter. Woodward and Bernstein were to continue their investigation. One of them would attend the trial each day, looking for leads in the testimony.

Rosenfeld was right, but the reporters didn't realize it at the time. They were resentful. The case was moving into a new phase; they were afraid the *Post* might write off the earlier Watergate stories as the excesses of the young.

Their fears increased when, just before the trial, Bernstein and Woodward drafted a long "news analysis." Based on days of research, including long interviews with Justice Department officials, the burden of their story was that the government's case would leave most questions about the financing and sponsorship of the Watergate operation unanswered, and ignore the extensive campaign of political espionage and sabotage. Rosenfeld rejected the piece: "Let's wait and see what happens, then report."

Two days before the opening of the trial, Bernstein heard that the Miami men were staying in a high-rise apartment house in Arlington, Virginia, with their families and lawyers. That night, he visited one of the men and was told of the defense with which they all hoped to support their not-guilty pleas. They would contend that they had been assured the Watergate raid was approved by high government officials and, therefore, that they had been working, clandestinely, on an authorized mission. There was one snag, Bernstein was told. Howard Hunt, though he wanted a unified defense, was vehemently opposed to any courtroom strategy that might suggest the conspiracy extended beyond the seven defendants.

On the morning of January 8, the opening day of the trial, a gray and gaunt Hunt arrived at the courthouse wearing a black topcoat with a small, aristocratic, though slightly frayed fur collar. He puffed on his pipe and paced the corridors, whispering frequently to his partner, Gordon Liddy. The two walked down the hall talking. Hunt, whose wife had died in a plane crash a few weeks before, held his arm high on Liddy's neck, as if seeking support.

Liddy had arrived smoking a large cigar, smiling, waving and strutting confidently. Later in the day, when he was introduced to the prospective jurors, he bounded to his feet and waved his right hand triumphantly, like a politician greeting a crowd. The four Miami men, looking tense, appeared with their attorney, Henry B. Rothblatt, who wore a toupee and had a small mustache that appeared to be accented with eyebrow pencil. McCord, looking serious, came in a few minutes later. He warded off reporters' questions with a "No comment."

The members of the prosecution team—Earl Silbert, 36, Seymour Glanzer, 46, and Donald E. Campbell, 35—were spruce and well groomed. Each carried a foot-thick stack of files. As they got off the elevator, reporters swarmed on them. "All your questions will be answered," Glanzer said. "Just wait."

U.S. District Court Chief Judge John J. Sirica, who had assigned the case to himself, sat high on the bench, his wavy black hair making him look much younger than his 68 years. At a pre-trial hearing in December, he had expressed his intentions: "This jury is going to want to know: What did these men go into that headquarters for? Was their sole purpose political espionage? Were they paid? Was there financial gain? Who hired them? Who started this?"

Sirica's critics—and he had many in knowledgeable legal circles, including the prosecutors—contended that a trial was not the place to conduct an investigation; that task properly belonged to the grand jury.

Woodward and Bernstein both attended the first day of the trial and listened as Silbert presented a two-hour opening statement. The chief prosecutor seemed rather exasperated when he said that he would be able to account for only $50,000 of $235,000 in presidential campaign funds that had been handed to Gordon Liddy in $100 bills. Basing his theory primarily on the statements of Jeb Magruder and Herbert L. Porter, Silbert contended that Liddy had been given the funds to conduct legitimate intelligence-gathering activities. Liddy, Silbert said, had gone off on his own, and planned and executed the illegal Watergate operation. It was the CRP "cover story" that had been described to the reporters months earlier, during their evening visits.

As Silbert spun out his tale of low-level conspiracy, Woodward sat among other reporters furiously taking notes. He did not have to write a story, so he could just think about what Silbert was saying.

He recalled a lesson he had learned in his freshman year at Yale.

The instructor had assigned the students to read some medieval documents that gave somewhat conflicting accounts of Henry IV's famous visit to Canossa in 1077 to seek Pope Gregory's forgiveness. According to all of them, the King had waited barefoot in the snow outside the Vatican for days. Woodward had pored over the documents, made notes and based his paper on the facts on which most accounts agreed. All the witnesses had Henry IV out there in the snow for days with his feet bare. The instructor had failed Woodward because he had not used common sense. No human being could stand for days barefoot in the snow and not have his feet freeze off, the instructor said. "The divine right of kings did not extend to overturning the laws of nature and common sense."

As Silbert worked himself up into a state of indignation against Gordon Liddy—the boss of the whole operation, he said—Woodward wondered if Silbert had taken a good freshman history course at Harvard. Silbert, a Phi Beta Kappa graduate, had all this evidence. Sixty witnesses. An airtight case. There was only one thing wrong: it didn't make sense. CRP would not have paid $235,000 for inconsequential intelligence which was readily available from the FBI and local police. CRP's managers would have wanted to know the exact purposes of the expenditures and the precise results.

Silbert had told Bernstein and Woodward that he expected to please no one with his Watergate investigation. He was going to succeed, that seemed clear. He had repeatedly stressed that there was no evidence to indict any more than the seven men who had been caught. "There is an unwritten rule in the Justice Department—the higher up you go, the more you have to have them by the balls. And I think it's a good rule."

After the opening statement, Howard Hunt changed his plea to guilty. He told reporters outside the courtroom that no higher-ups were involved in the conspiracy, "to my personal knowledge."

Bernstein had been told the day before by a member of the Miami contingent that the four Florida men might also plead guilty if Hunt did. The rumors persisted. On Friday afternoon, after the session ended, Bernstein and Woodward were standing outside the courthouse with *Post* columnist Nicholas von Hoffman and *Post* editorial writer Roger Wilkins. Henry Rothblatt, the Miami men's lawyer, was standing on a corner with his clients trying to hail a taxi.

We'll lose them, Bernstein said, unless one of us goes. Woodward agreed. Bernstein said that he wanted to go. Woodward gave him $20. Rothblatt and his clients found a cab as Bernstein raced toward them. The lawyer, the stocky Frank Sturgis, and the three other men filled the cab, but Bernstein, uninvited, got in anyway, piling in on top of them as the door slammed. Von Hoffman and Wilkins nearly fell off the curb laughing. Woodward wrote a note to himself that Bernstein owed him $20.

Bernstein arrived back in the office late Saturday, mole-eyed and wrinkled. He had gone to the airport with Rothblatt and his clients, bought a ticket on a flight one of them was taking, edged his way in by offering to carry a suitcase and engaging in friendly banter, and slipped into the adjoining seat. Bernstein did not really have to press the man too hard to turn the conversation around to the trial. The story came out in a restful flow of conversation as the jet engines surged peacefully in the background. The interview was costing the *Post* more than a dollar a minute, Bernstein thought.

According to the man on the plane, Hunt had been visiting the four men from Miami for a week, urging them to change their pleas to guilty; their families would be cared for financially, and they could count on executive clemency after a few months in jail. In the enduring CIA fraternity, Hunt, the seasoned case officer, was again passing out the orders to his lower-level operatives. For more than a decade, the men had had unquestioned trust in Hunt, even after he had supervised their participation in the Bay of Pigs operation. He was their leader, the tie between their own projects and the cause of American patriotism. Rothblatt, Bernstein learned, was furious, and had instructed his clients "to stay away from that son-of-a-bitch Hunt," but it was too late. The guilty pleas would be entered the next week.

On the phone to Woodward, Hunt's attorney, William Bittman, denied that his client was pressuring the Miami men. "I would think that the suggestion is absurd . . . I can't conceive of it," he said.

The reporters and *Post* managing editor Howard Simons discussed the story. They were nervous about running it. Judge Sirica might haul the reporters into court again, this time to find out their source, and begin an investigation of what appeared to be an obstruction of justice. Simons asked some of the *Post* lawyers about the prospects of Sirica ordering such disclosure. Opinion was divided as the deadline neared.

Excessive caution prevailed, and the story on Hunt was held for more consideration the next day. One thing was certain: if it ran, it would carry only one reporter's byline. If Sirica demanded disclosure, only one of them would probably have to go to jail for refusing to name their sources.

That night, both Bernstein and Woodward were called at home. A *New York Times* story said that the four Miami men were still being paid by persons as yet unnamed. The story, by Seymour M. Hersh, also said that Watergate burglar Sturgis had acknowledged that he had been told that John Mitchell had been aware of the Watergate operation and had in fact encouraged the team. The next day *Time* magazine sent out a press release of a forthcoming story that said that the four Miami man had been promised up to $1000 for each month they spent in jail. An account by Jack Anderson pushed the matter further: "Most of the money for the defendants has been funneled through Hunt [who] delivered part of the cash to Bernard Barker," the columnist said.

The stories eased Simons' qualms. "Sirica will have to throw the reporters from *Time,* the *New York Times,* and Jack Anderson in jail, along with you guys," he said.

The next day, Monday morning, the story on Hunt's maneuvers ran in the *Post*. In court that morning, the four Miami men fired Rothblatt and were assigned a new attorney, who immediately entered guilty pleas for them.

Sirica was seething. After accepting the new pleas, he called the four men from Miami before him. They walked up and stood before the bench. Defendant Barker bounced up and down on his toes, wringing his hands behind his back. Apparently torn by the anxiety of the moment, he went into a deep-knee bend. As he answered the Judge's questions, his head wagged up and down and sideways in short jerks as if his neck had turned to rubber.

Judge Sirica asked about "these $100 bills that were floating around like coupons."

Barker replied that he didn't know where they had come from. The others nodded. "I got the money in the mail in a blank envelope," he said.

"Well, I'm sorry," replied Sirica, "I don't believe you."

Sirica questioned the men for about an hour. The heads of all four defendants seemed to be attached to the same strings; they bobbed up and down in unison. Yes, they said, the decisions to plead guilty were made free from any pressure. No, Your Honor, they said, when asked if anyone had mentioned executive clemency.

The Judge's frown deepened. Had any of the men ever worked for the CIA?

"Not that I know of," answered defendant Martinez, who had been on a CIA retainer of $100 a month until the day after his Watergate arrest. Among those who laughed out loud was Gordon Liddy, who had finished a brief nap at the defense table when Sirica began questioning the men.

Why did you break into the Watergate? Sirica asked.

"It pertained towards the Cuban situation," Martinez said. "When it comes to Cuba and when it comes to Communist conspiracies involving the United States, I will do anything to protect this country against any Communist conspiracy."

Sirica rolled his eyes in disbelief. What, he asked, did the Democratic headquarters have to do with Cuba or the Communist conspiracy?

"I don't know," Martinez said, and added that that was what Barker and Hunt had told him.

All four denied that they had received any money. "These are not men that sell themselves for money," Barker said proudly.

"Were you working under the direction of Mr. Hunt or other people in this job that was pulled off?" Sirica asked Barker.

"I was working with Mr. Hunt and I wish to state that I was completely identified with Mr. Hunt. . . . I have the greatest honor and distinguish him," Barker said.

As Sirica interrogated them, chief prosecutor Silbert shook his head in disgust and stared at the yellow legal pad in front of him. Glanzer leaned back in his chair and rubbed one side of his face. The prosecutors' assurances that everything would come out at the trial were fading into nothingness, as the defendants ducked into the haze of their guilty pleas.

Sirica asked Barker about the $114,000 in Nixon campaign checks that had been deposited in his Miami bank account. Barker said he just didn't know where the money had come from.

Now wasn't that strange? Sirica asked.

"I don't think it is strange, Your Honor," replied Barker. "I have previously before this been involved in other operations which took the strangeness out of that, as far as I was concerned."

The Miami four were led off to jail.

That noon, Woodward took a cab back to the *Post* for a lunch with Katharine Graham and Howard Simons. "Katharine wants to go over some of the stories and ask about the sources," Simons said.

Mrs. Graham, the publisher, was the daughter of Eugene Meyer, who bought the paper in 1933. When her husband, Philip Graham, who was publisher of the *Post,* committed suicide in 1963, she assumed control.

Woodward was glad that Mrs. Graham had waited until after the intense period of major investigative stories and the attack by the White House in the fall before asking for a meeting. He took the elevator to the eighth floor and walked through the double glass doors onto the thick white carpet that led to her office. Simons was already there, a drink in hand, and the three of them sat down in a corner.

"What's happening in the trial today?" Mrs. Graham asked.

Woodward told her about the guilty pleas by the four Miami men and Sirica's interrogation. The trial was getting increasingly ridiculous, Woodward said, and described the scene of the four men talking and nodding as if on cue.

Mrs. Graham asked several questions about what it all might mean and what would happen. "Is it all going to come out?" she asked, somewhat apprehensively. "I mean, are we ever going to know about all of this?"

Woodward thought it was the nicest way possible of asking, What have you boys been doing with my newspaper? He said that he and Bernstein weren't sure it ever would come out.

Depression seemed to register on her face, and she shook her head. "Never?" she asked. "Don't tell me never." She laughed, throwing her head back with a bright smile. "Well, let's eat," she said, rising and leading them to the dining room directly behind her office.

A woman in a traditional maid's uniform of black and white served eggs benedict. Howard Simons outlined the purpose of the lunch, a confidential discussion of the sources for the Watergate stories.* Woodward had finished two bites of his eggs benedict and now he was going to have to give a monologue. He told her about Martin Dardis in Florida, several Justice Department attorneys, an FBI agent, a White House aide, the Bookkeeper, Hugh Sloan. Mrs. Graham said she was less interested in the names than in the positions they held.

Woodward said that he had told no one the name of Deep Throat. Mrs. Graham paused. "Tell *me*," she said.

Woodward froze. He said he would give her the name if she wanted. He was praying she wouldn't press it. Mrs. Graham laughed, touched his arm and said she was only kidding, she didn't really want to carry that burden around with her. Woodward took a bite of his eggs, which were cold.

"Now, about the Haldeman business," Mrs. Graham said, looking as if she were not sure she wanted to hear it.

Woodward put down his fork and told the story of the mistake he and Bernstein had made about Sloan's grand-jury testimony.

"But are you absolutely sure we're right?" The question carried an intensity absent from the previous conversation. "I remember talking with Henry Kissinger," she continued, "and he came up and said, 'What's the matter, don't you think we're going to be re-elected? You were wrong on Haldeman.' And he seemed upset and said something about it being terribly, terribly unfair."

If there's anyone who has not been wronged, Woodward said, it is Bob Haldeman. It was the most definite statement Woodward made during lunch.

"Oh really," said Mrs. Graham. "I'm glad to hear you say that, be-

---

* Months later, Howard Simons summarized his private feelings about the *Post's* position during the trial. "I had this nagging feeling that the Watergate might turn out like the Reichstag fire. You know, forty years from now will people still be asking did the guy set it and was he a German or was he just a crazy Dutchman? . . . I'll tell you, it's like being in a bathtub, where scientifically, you know, you turn the water a little bit hotter at a time and burn yourself to death without realizing it because the increments are so small that the body doesn't understand or feel. . . . That's the difference between Watergate and the Pentagon Papers. In the Pentagon Papers, damn, you had the lawyers involved the first day . . . getting advice, and Katharine actually making the decision to publish. Nothing like that happened with Watergate. We never called the lawyers and said, Are we okay, what's the legal view of this? I do think we did slip into it. It was incremental."

cause I was worried." She paused. "You've reassured me. You really have." She looked at Woodward. Her face said, Do better.

The trial lasted another two weeks. Woodward and Bernstein continued to attend, sifting through exhibits and papers filed with the court. Woodward copied down the phone numbers in the defendants' address books, which were entered into evidence, and one evening he called some of the numbers. "The FBI?" one man asked. "They never, never contacted me. I never talked to them."

Woodward slammed down the phone. In the biggest, most wide-ranging investigation since the assassination of President Kennedy, the FBI didn't even call the numbers in the address books?

While going through the list of witnesses, Woodward found one who knew Hunt quite well. He called the witness at his office and asked what he was going to testify about. The witness said: "I'll tell you what I *could* testify to, but Silbert won't ask. If the Judge does or any of the attorneys, I'll say it."

Woodward sat up straight in the large blue chair at his desk and asked what that testimony might include.

"Howard always used 'they' or 'the White House' when he was talking about his activities. But one day I remember he was complaining about Ehrlichman and saying what an amateur Ehrlichman was, because Ehrlichman put a hold on a lot of things Howard was doing, various secret, intelligence-type things. The operation was delayed for two to three weeks because Ehrlichman was holding up the budget."

Ehrlichman. Woodward snapped a pencil in half between his fingers.

"And Howard was saying that was why he liked Colson, because Colson understood that such things are necessary. Colson is an operator and gave immediate approval. He pushed the budget through."

Colson—that made sense, but Ehrlichman? Woodward lined up several neat rows of paper clips on his desk as the witness went on.

"From the comments Howard made, it was apparent that Mitchell was getting typed reports of the wiretaps."

Okay, Woodward thought, that made sense.

"After the Watergate arrests, when Howard was out of town hiding and needed a lawyer, Howard was looking for John Dean, and said, Let *him* get me a lawyer."

Woodward's hand jerked through the neat rows of paper clips, destroying the symmetry.. "John Dean?" he asked.

"That's exactly how Silbert sounded when I told him," the witness said. "He said, 'That's the first time *his* tracks have appeared in this.' "

Woodward took one of his giant paper clips, bent it into a large L and began twirling it in his hand as he read over his notes. At that moment, Bradlee walked by his desk and asked what was up. Maybe a whole lot and maybe nothing, Woodward said, but there was at least one witness who could do some damage to Mitchell, Colson, Ehrlichman and John Dean. Bradlee's eyes brightened. He did a little dance, holding an imaginary towel to his ass and wiggling it back and forth before walking off.

Woodward thought fleetingly of getting in touch with Judge Sirica or one of his law clerks and somehow letting it be known that this witness could answer a few interesting questions. He rejected the notion.

The witness was never asked those questions, but in a later conversation with Woodward he explained why Hunt was staying silent about high-level involvement. "In his lexicon of values," the witness said, "Howard is performing a heroic act. He's like a medieval monk who goes to meditate in a high place in the hope it will get him into Heaven. . . . Howard wants to become the Alger Hiss of the Right."

The trial dragged on. During recesses, Liddy and McCord were accessible and would chat frequently in the corridors with reporters. Liddy delighted in telling little anecdotes like the one about a military plane that accidentally dropped a bomb in the red-light district of a Mexican border town. "So the town officials paid a visit to the military base," he told a dozen reporters one morning, "and they told the base commander that if he would stop bombing the cat houses, they would close them down." Liddy roared at his own story, laughing so convulsively that his face turned bright red.

At one point, after Liddy's lawyer, Peter Maroulis, had another one of his frequent objections overruled by Sirica, Liddy took Woodward aside in the corridor. "Do you know how to play chess?" Liddy asked conspiratorially. Woodward did and told Liddy so. "Well, Peter just

took their queen," Liddy said. What do you mean? Woodward asked.
"Listen, that's all I can tell you, he got their queen." Woodward asked
if that meant that the Judge had committed an error on which the
higher courts would be forced to reverse any convictions. "You're a
good chess player," Liddy said, beaming and bouncing up and down
slightly with his hands in his pockets.

On January 23, the only witnesses from the Nixon committee were
scheduled to testify: Jeb Magruder, Bart Porter, Rob Odle and Hugh
Sloan. Woodward went to listen, and spotted Magruder pacing the
corridors. The tall, 38-year-old former merchandiser of cosmetics,
facial tissues and women's hosiery had an American flag in the lapel
of his conservative suit. Magruder looked at his watch and approached
Silbert. "Earl," he said, "how much longer do I have to wait?" Silbert
smiled deferentially and said something about courts not being run to
meet the schedules of witnesses. Magruder was exasperated. At that
point, Gordon Liddy walked past him and saluted, a big grin on his
face. Reporters in the hallway laughed. Magruder became angrier and
turned and walked back down the hall.

Woodward decided that it was time to meet Magruder. He went up
and introduced himself. Magruder was friendlier than he had expected.
"I only have one objection to what you and that fellow Bernstein did.
That is these visits you paid some of my people at night, banging on
their doors late and not identifying yourselves." Woodward said that
he and Bernstein had always identified themselves and were always
courteous. "Dirty reporting," Magruder said. "Now, it may not have
been you, but Bernstein did. I know."

Always the politician, Woodward thought: Magruder was not willing to confront him, but passed it off on Bernstein, who wasn't there.
Woodward said that visiting people after working hours was not dirty
at all and was necessitated by the unwillingness of Magruder and
dozens of other people to answer questions about Watergate. Magruder
turned to walk away and then looked back to Woodward. "It's none of
your business," he said, summarizing CRP's point of view.

Silbert put Magruder through 33 minutes of tame, respectful questioning. Magruder testified that, as John Mitchell's first assistant, he
was so busy supervising 25 campaign division heads and 250 full-time
employees and spending between $30 and $35 million that he just
couldn't be overly concerned with Gordon Liddy. Magruder said he

didn't even get along with Liddy. Liddy had a different management style. Magruder said it as if a disagreement over management styles was the most serious thing that could ever come between two people, though Liddy had once threatened to kill him. Liddy sat rocking back and forth in his chair while Magruder spoke.

Hugh Sloan, former Nixon campaign treasurer, walked nervously into the courtroom and took the stand. He looked even thinner—"He's down to skin and bones," his mother told a reporter from the *New York Times*. Silbert's perfunctory questioning was cold and distant. Sloan said that he had paid out about $199,000 in cash to Liddy. Silbert did not ask who had ordered Sloan to hand out the money.

After Silbert finished his interrogation, Sirica sent the jury from the courtroom and asked Sloan 41 questions of his own. To one, Sloan replied that he had been worried about the large disbursements to Liddy. So he had checked with Maurice Stans, who in turn had verified the expenditures with John Mitchell, who in turn had said that Liddy should be given the cash.

"You verified it with whom?" Sirica asked.

Sloan repeated his answer.

Before completing his questioning, Sirica made it clear he didn't believe Sloan's testimony that he had given out so much money without asking the purpose of the expenditures. Amazed at Sloan's apparent naïveté, Sirica asked, "You're a college graduate, aren't you?"*

During Silbert's closing argument, Liddy sat in his chair rocking slowly, a smile on his face, as the prosecutor pictured him as the "Mr. Big" of Watergate. Liddy—the ex-FBI agent, the former prosecutor who had made a career of cops-and-robbers. This time the cop had turned robber. Silbert paused, obviously pleased with the sound of his words. Liddy gave a quick, animated wave to the jury, exactly like the one he had given the first day of the trial.

It took the jury less than 90 minutes to find Liddy and McCord guilty of all counts against them. Liddy stood impassive with his arms folded defiantly as the court clerk read the jury's verdict, repeating the "guilty" six times. McCord stood stoically as the word was pronounced

---

* Several weeks later, in a post-trial hearing, Sirica would say flatly that he didn't believe Sloan had been truthful. But he had picked on the wrong person. Sloan was the one CRP witness who had cooperated fully with the investigation. Sirica didn't ask a single question of Magruder or Bart Porter, the CRP scheduling director. Both would later acknowledge committing perjury at the trial.

eight times, once for each count. Sirica ordered both jailed without bond. Before he was escorted out of the courtroom, Liddy embraced his attorney Peter Maroulis, patted him on the back affectionately, and gave one last wave to the spectators and the press before he was taken away.

Bernstein and Woodward wrote a lengthy news analysis summarizing the trial. Under the headline "Still Secret: Who Hired Spies and Why," they noted that the 16-day trial was marked by questions that were not asked, answers that were not given, witnesses who were not called to testify, and some lapses of memory by those who were.

The reporters were convinced that the prosecutors had not thrown the case. More likely, they had been lied to, they had fallen victim to the subtle pressures exerted through the White House and Justice Department. Most of all, they had failed to understand the workings of CRP and the White House and the style of the President's men.

Three days after the verdict, Judge Sirica held a hearing in his courtroom and set bond for Liddy and McCord at $100,000 each. He sternly criticized Silbert. "I have not been satisfied, and I am still not satisfied that all the pertinent facts that might be available—I say *might* be available—have been produced before an American jury."

Defending his own conduct, he said: "I don't think we should sit up here like nincompoops. I'll put it this way—I have great doubts that Mr. Sloan has told us the entire truth in this case. I will say it now and I indicated that during the trial.

"I felt that neither of you—government or defense—asked Mr. Sloan any questions. I had a right to question him to see that all the facts were brought out.

"Everyone knows that there's going to be a congressional investigation in this case. I would frankly hope, not only as a judge but as a citizen of a great country and one of millions of Americans who are looking for certain answers, I would hope that the Senate committee is granted the power by Congress by a broad enough resolution to try to get to the bottom of what happened in this case. I hope so. That is all I have to say."

12

Now, WOODWARD NEEDED to signal Deep Throat for a meeting. Shortly after the election, he had moved from his cramped efficiency apartment to a two-bedroom flat in a restored building two blocks from the *Post*. He had told Deep Throat at their last meeting that the new apartment had no balcony for the flower pot and flag. Worse, the neighbors said that people were forever having their newspapers taken from in front of their doors. Woodward had taken the apartment only after he had thoroughly inspected the building's less obvious assets: back stairways, fire exits and window sills. A new signal system was adopted at the end of the unhappy meeting on Haldeman. It would be a one-way communication, initiated by Woodward, who would place his yellow kitchen wastepaper basket upside down on the fire escape.

But the system hadn't even been tested before serious problems developed. Woodward's upstairs neighbors liked to dance—often between one and four A.M. He banged on the thin ceiling with a broom handle and begged his new neighbors to consider at least a sock hop, but that only rallied the nocturnal dancers. He was not superstitious, but he did believe that in a person's life there were bad cycles which had to be forcefully arrested. His tailspin had begun with the Haldeman story; the frustrations had built during November and December. Better to move than tempt fate further. So, the only time he had turned the trashbasket upside down was in late December and only to tell Deep Throat that he was moving again. Deep Throat was uncommunicative at their brief meeting, advising him to sit tight and see how the Watergate trial developed.

Woodward found a new apartment on the top floor of a high-rise temple of formica-and-parquet luxury in Southwest Washington, near the Potomac; he got himself a new flower pot and was back in business.

Service was inaugurated on January 24, after Woodward had spent several delicious nights reveling in the silence of his new quarters. He went through a basement exit into a rear courtyard and over a wall onto a side street—mindful of Mrs. Graham's warning about surveillance and Deep Throat's increasing apprehension. It took him a half-hour to find a cab, and when he got out about half a mile from the garage, the driver didn't have change for a $10 bill. Angrily, he told the hack to keep the $10.

Deep Throat was waiting. He looked worn, but was smiling. "What's up?" he asked mock-offhandedly, and took a deep drag on his cigarette. Just once, Woodward wished, Deep Throat would really tell him what was up—everything, no questions asked, no tug of wills, a full status report. The reporters had speculated on the reason for Deep Throat's piecemeal approach; they had several theories. If he told everything he knew all at once, a good Plumber might be able to find the leak. By making the reporters go elsewhere to fill out his information, he minimized his risk. Perhaps. But it was equally possible that he felt that the effect of one or two big stories, no matter how devastating, could be blunted by the White House. Or, by raising the stakes gradually, was he simply making the game more interesting for himself? The reporters tended to doubt that someone in his position would be so cavalier toward matters affecting Richard Nixon or the Presidency itself. More likely, they thought, Deep Throat was trying to protect the office, to effect a change in its conduct before all was lost. Each time Woodward had raised the question, Deep Throat had gravely insisted, "I have to do this my way."

That night, it was the familiar pattern. He would respond only to new information; he would not be towed on a fishing expedition about the Plumbers, the guilty pleas in the trial or the riddles of Z.

Afraid he would leave the garage empty-handed, Woodward turned to a subject he and Bernstein were about to write on—Mitchell and Colson. He quickly reviewed the strains of circumstantial detail that seemed to bring the two men close to the conspiracy.

Deep Throat seemed impressed by the groundwork they had done. Suddenly he walked to the front of one of the cars in the garage and, standing erect, placed his gloved hands authoritatively on the hood as if it were a rostrum. "From this podium, I'm prepared to denounce such questions about gentle Colson and noble Mitchell as innuendo, character assassination, hearsay and shoddy journalism. The questions themselves are fabrication and fiction and a pack of absurdities and cometh from the fountain of misinformation."

Woodward, who was very tired, started laughing and couldn't stop. Deep Throat "Ziegler" continued the denunciation: ". . . that small Georgetown coterie of self-appointed guardians of public mistrust who seek the destruction of the people's will—"

The levity was interrupted by a noise. Deep Throat ducked behind a car. Woodward walked up the ramp guardedly. A very convincing old drunk was leaning against the wall, shivering. Woodward made sure he was real, then gave him a $10 bill and told him to find a hotel room. It was brutally cold. Woodward returned to the lower level.

The interruption had unnerved Deep Throat. "Colson and Mitchell were behind the Watergate operation," he said quickly. "Everyone in the FBI is convinced, including Gray [L. Patrick Gray, acting director of the FBI]. Colson's role was active. Mitchell's position was more 'amoral' and less active—giving the nod but not conceiving the scheme.

"There isn't anything that would be considered as more than the weakest circumstantial evidence. But there's no doubt either. 'Insulation' is the key word to understand why the evidence can't be developed."

He outlined four factors that might lead to the "inescapable conclusion" that Mitchell and Colson were conspirators: "One, the personalities and past performance of both. This way of life wasn't new to them. Two, there are meetings and phone calls at crucial times—all of which Colson and Mitchell claim involved other matters. Three, there's the tight control of the money, especially by Mitchell, who was getting details almost to the point of how much was spent on pencils and erasers. Four, there is the indisputable fact that the seven defendants believe they are going to be taken care of. That could only be done convincingly by someone high up, and somehow it has been done convincingly."

How sweeping was the belief that Colson and Mitchell were involved?

"No disagreement anywhere," Deep Throat said. "The White House knows it, the FBI brass knows it." He rubbed his neck and moved the palm of his hand upward across the stiff bristle on his chin. "Involved up to here." The hand went up higher. "But it's still unproven. If the FBI couldn't prove it, I don't think the *Washington Post* can.

"What obviously makes this a Mitchell-Colson operation is the hiring of Liddy and Hunt. That's the key. Mitchell and Colson were their sponsors. And if you check you'll find that Liddy and Hunt had reputations that are the lowest. The absolute lowest. Hiring these two was immoral. They got exactly what they wanted. Liddy wanted to tap the *New York Times* and everybody knew it.* And not everybody was laughing about it. Mitchell, among others, liked the idea."

Deep Throat became contemplative. "Liddy and McCord should realize that no one can help them because it will be too obvious. Any congressional investigation is going to have a big problem unless they get someone from the inside to crack. Without that, you come up with lots of money and plans for dirty tricks but no firsthand account or detailing of what happened at the top." The White House, he said, was developing plans to make sure no congressional investigation could succeed. Part of the strategy would involve a broad claim of executive privilege to prevent investigators from subpoenaing White House and Justice Department records.

What about manipulation of the original Watergate investigation?

"The attempts to separate the Watergate and the espionage-sabotage operation are a lot of bullshit," Deep Throat said. "They amount to the same thing. If the other stuff like [Segretti] had been pursued, they would have found plenty that was illegal."

Woodward asked if Deep Throat thought the reporters had enough for a story on Mitchell and Colson.

---

* The *Los Angeles Times* had reported earlier that Liddy had suggested to White House colleagues that the *New York Times* be wiretapped to learn how it obtained the Pentagon Papers. According to the *L.A. Times* account, Liddy's suggestion had been dismissed out of hand on grounds that he was either crazy or kidding.

"That's for the paper to decide, not me," he said. "But if you do it, it should be done quickly. The longer you wait, the more confident they get that they can attack safely."

This meeting with Deep Throat produced the most serious disagreement between Bernstein and Woodward since they had begun working together seven months earlier. The question was whether a convincing and well-documented account of Mitchell's and Colson's roles could be written. Woodward drafted a story based on the following lead:

> Federal investigators concluded that former Attorney General John N. Mitchell and Charles W. Colson, special counsel to the President, both had direct knowledge of the overall political espionage operation conducted by the men indicted in the Watergate case, according to reliable sources.

Bernstein reworked the story three times, detailing virtually everything they had learned in seven months about Mitchell, Colson and the nature of the federal investigation. Its thrust was that a former Attorney General and a special counsel to the President had escaped prosecution as conspirators because they had insulated themselves well and because the investigation had been tailored to define the conspiracy in the narrowest terms.

Each time Bernstein completed a version, Woodward said he didn't think it should run until they had better proof. Bernstein argued that the story was legitimate, that the newspaper didn't have to offer definitive evidence but, in this instance, could report the conclusions of investigators who reached as high as L. Patrick Gray.

The argument became so heated that they would occasionally retreat to the vending-machine room off the newsroom floor and shout at each other. Bernstein accused Woodward of playing into the hands of the White House by holding back on the story. Woodward accused Bernstein of the same by trying to push a story into the paper that could lead to a damaging attack by the White House. But the old rule applied: If either objected to a story, it did not go into the paper.

Shortly after his meeting with Deep Throat, Woodward got a call from the office of Senator Sam J. Ervin of North Carolina, a 76-year-old constitutional scholar and a formidable power on Capitol Hill. Ervin wanted to talk about Watergate, an aide said.

On January 11, Ervin had acceded to Senate Majority Leader Mike Mansfield's request that he preside over a thorough investigation of Watergate and the 1972 presidential campaign. The agreement seemed to indicate that some investigative machinery would be established on Capitol Hill beyond the preliminary inquiry that Senator Edward M. Kennedy's Judiciary Subcommittee on Administrative Practice and Procedure had been conducting since October 1972.

Unless a congressional subcommittee quickly exercised power of subpoena to obtain records and documents in areas that the federal investigators seemed to be ignoring, Kennedy had told Bernstein in an interview just after the Segretti stories had appeared, the opportunity for a truly comprehensive investigation would probably go down the chute and into the shredder. Kennedy had decided to undertake an investigation. The Senator had professed to know little, if anything, more than what he had read in the papers. "But I know the people around Nixon," he said, "and that's enough. They're thugs."

The White House was circulating the line that Kennedy was out to settle old grudges and launch a 1976 candidacy. Kennedy, face tanned and his hair doing a little back-flip over his collar, tossed it back. His inquiry would be a "holding action." The preliminary investigation would be conducted by both the majority and the minority staffs behind closed doors. It would avoid any suggestion of a witch hunt or a Kennedy crusade. There was no percentage in it for him, Kennedy maintained; the White House would go with everything it had to smear him. Chappaquiddick would be brought up endlessly. He was sure the President's men had a ready store of other information on him, "nickel-and-dime stuff," he said uncomfortably. "They haven't come up with anything really new."

When Kennedy's subcommittee formally began its investigation, the reporters tried to stay in close touch with the Senators and their staff. But Kennedy's ship did not leak. They learned nothing.

Woodward hoped to do better with Senator Ervin, but the Senator was more interested in finding out what Woodward and Bernstein knew.

On the way into Ervin's inner office, Woodward noticed on a

secretary's desk a typed sheet of paper listing the Senator's appointments for the day. Sy Hersh of the *New York Times* had been there several hours earlier. Woodward wondered how Hersh had handled the situation. When was a reporter justified in turning over information to an investigating committee? Or giving advice to a Senator? If the reporter was convinced that he could not make use of a valuable piece of information, was it all right to make a trade?

Bernstein and he seemed to be running out of steam. Could their information help others in the search?

Senator Ervin was sitting behind a heavy wooden desk in the center of his office, a rumpled, hulking figure with a huge ham of a face. He looked as if he would be more comfortable in a front-porch rocker than in the standard-issue beige swivel chair he overfilled. Great heaps of paper were strewn chaotically across the desk. He leaned back and began speaking, head jerking, jowls jiggling, bushy eyebrows twittering—like some great bird of prey trying to lift off without losing his kill.

The moment of truth arrived after a few minutes of gracious comments. "Any leads or sources of information you might be willing to share with us, it certainly would be appreciated and held in the strictest of confidence. I give you my word on that. We'd be mighty grateful for your help," Ervin said.

Information from Deep Throat and Z and some other bits and pieces might help the investigation, conceivably could even send it on its way, Woodward thought. But he couldn't give it. The best he could do would be to suggest possible lines of inquiry.

Identifying sources, he told the Senator, was out of the question. There was one person—not necessarily a source—who had told them he would cooperate with any legitimate investigation: Hugh Sloan. A staff member wrote it down. The reporters' stories, Woodward continued, contained many names and incidents that needed more checking. The key was the secret campaign cash, and it should all be traced; every indication pointed toward a massive Haldeman undercover operation, of which the Watergate break-in and the dirty tricks of the '72 primaries were only parts; unless one of the seven convicted conspirators decided to cooperate, nothing resembling the whole story would come out; the reporters' own stories had only scratched the surface; they did not completely comprehend what had happened, and was still happening, but the enormity of what the President's men had done seemed staggering.

"I'll be content if we discover Mr. Magruder's role," Ervin said wearily. The Senator is an expert on the government's vandalism of people's rights, especially the right of privacy.

Ervin began talking about the separation of powers, his belief that a certain article and certain section of the Constitution meant exactly what it said about the power of Congress. That, he said, was how he intended to investigate Watergate—by getting a resolution passed that would grant a special select committee the broadest possible subpoena power. Then the committee would subpoena whatever documents and people were necessary—in the Executive Branch and elsewhere.

Like whom? Woodward asked.

"Now, I believe that everyone who has been mentioned in your and Mr. Bernstein's accounts should be given an opportunity to come down and exonerate himself," Ervin said. "And if they decline, we'll subpoena them to ensure they have a chance to clear their names." He smiled, barely able to contain himself as his eyebrows danced.

Even the CIA?

Elbows resting on the arms of his chair, Ervin gave a big, affirmative nod.

And the White House? Haldeman? That would be one for the books, the White House chief of staff hauled before the Congress he so despised.

"Mr. Haldeman or Mr. Whomever," Ervin said. "Anybody but the President."

He was serious. Woodward was sure the White House would be equally serious. The first question was whether a resolution granting such power could be passed. Ervin thought it could. Woodward asked if he could write that the Senator planned to subpoena some of the President's top aides.

"If you don't mention names and only say you know my thinking, I don't have any objection," Ervin said. "Just don't quote me directly."*

* This conversation with Woodward was on background, but Senator Ervin later gave permission to be quoted in this book.

Woodward wrote a story outlining Ervin's intention to summon the President's aides and to challenge the claim of executive privilege. The battle lines were being drawn.

On February 5, Senator Ervin introduced a resolution to allocate $500,000 for a Senate Select Committee on Presidential Campaign Activities to investigate the Watergate break-in and related allegations. The powerful Senate Democratic Policy Committee had given the resolution its unqualified support, and the only impediment now would be a last-minute White House–Republican maneuver. The day of the vote, February 7, Woodward arrived on the Hill about 8:30 A.M. to see if one was developing. In the Senate cafeteria, he was chatting with the administrative assistant to a Republican Senator.

What's the White House strategy? Woodward asked.

"What makes you think there is one?" the aide asked. "Don't know who thought up the idea," he added, "but there will be an amendment to broaden the investigation so that it covers the '64 and '68 campaigns."

That figured. "Politics as usual," not for the first time, would be the White House's response.

"They're trying awfully hard," said another Republican aide. "Word came down to make a big push."

Woodward called the White House from a phone booth in the press gallery. "Of course we're doing it," a source there told him. "You'd think those dolts on the Hill would have the sense to do it themselves, but they can't find their way to the john without help. Haldeman's got half the staff here revved up on it. It's the order of the day. We're all supposed to make calls to people we know in the Senate."

Hugh Scott of Pennsylvania, the minority leader, rose to declare that Ervin had introduced the "broadest resolution I've ever seen." He called its charter of authority "wild, unbelievable," and said the resolution could lead to "blackmail" by members of the Senate Watergate committee staff. "There was wholesale evidence of wiretapping against the Republicans" in the 1968 campaign, Scott charged, without citing it. John Tower of Texas and Barry Goldwater of Arizona joined in, but no one offered a concrete example or made a specific charge.

The Democrats voted down every amendment to Ervin's resolution proposed by the minority. When the final vote was called, the Republicans joined their Democratic colleagues and the resolution passed unanimously, 77–0. Veteran Senate reporters told Woodward that the unanimity was merely a Republican recognition of the power of the Democratic majority. Woodward was not so sure. The men on the floor were sharp interpreters of the political winds.

Woodward was exhilarated. The system was showing signs of working. As he left the Capitol, he asked a Republican Senator about a man he had noticed near the floor throughout the crucial tests on the amendments. Oh, the Senator said, that was the Justice Department lawyer the White House sent over to draft the amendments.

The trial, Z's statements and the last meeting with Deep Throat had sent Woodward and Bernstein back to square one—Liddy and Hunt. If they could find out what Hunt and Liddy had done at the White House and exactly what the Plumbers' mission entailed, perhaps they could understand why Hunt and Liddy were willing to go to jail.

Several days after the Senate vote, Woodward headed for a luncheon appointment with a friend of Howard Hunt's at the Hay-Adams Hotel. They met in the lobby and went into the main dining room. Woodward had been trying for months to get this man out to lunch. Now that he had finally succeeded, it would not pay to push him too hard. His value as a source was incalculable now.

Woodward ordered a beer and a hamburger.

The characters in Hunt's novels were always ordering dishes Woodward had never heard of and telling the chef how to prepare them. Hunt's friend, who seemed to share these gourmet tastes, asked the waiter how omelettes were made at the Hay-Adams. Woodward resisted saying, "With eggs." The waiter checked with the kitchen and reported back. The answer was unsatisfactory. The man ordered braised lamb, and broccoli with Hollandaise—providing both were fresh.

He then proceeded to make it clear that he thought Howard Hunt ridiculous. "Once, during the Florida primary, Howard had some fliers printed saying that Mayor [John V.] Lindsay, of New York, was having a meeting and there would be free beer. Howard handed these fliers out in the black areas, and of course there was no meeting or beer, so the blacks would come for their beer and leave hating Lindsay. Howard thought this was the greatest thing since Chinese checkers."

The lamb arrived and was pronounced adequate. "Now we know what Howard's wiretapping squad was really like. Just rank amateur. Well, he told me that he had developed a team of some really heavy people who could conduct electronic eavesdropping—said they could install a sweep-proof bug that was voice-activated and could be picked up a hundred yards away. You know, the Watergate bug was like a crystal set, powered with flashlight batteries—heavy team, my ass. This Hollandaise isn't fresh." He cast his fork angrily on the table and signaled the waiter. "Since June 17, Howard always refers to 'they' when he talks about the White House and Watergate. 'They ordered me to leave town,' 'They wanted this project,' 'They ordered me to come back,' etc. Howard accepted it. But Dorothy [Hunt's late wife] was furious and kept saying, 'They ordered him to do this and it is wrong for them to prosecute him.' "

What projects had Hunt worked on for the White House? Woodward asked.

"Aside from Watergate? Well, Howard once made some vague reference about going to—where was it, where was that woman in the ITT affair? Dita Beard, where did she go?"

Denver, said Woodward.

"Yeah, Denver. Howard went to Denver. It was part of a White House project to show that the ITT memo was a forgery. Dita Beard was in the hospital there in Denver, and Howard went out to talk to her."

What other projects?

"Not too long after he had gone to work at the White House, Howard said that Colson and others had big plans to knock Ed Muskie out of the race and he would be working on that, too."

Hunt's friend was getting a little nervous. He suggested that they get to know each other better before any more information was passed on.

What about research on Teddy Kennedy? Woodward asked. The reporters had already written about that last July.

"Right. Howard said that just after he went to work at the White House he went to Massachusetts—the Boston area, I think—and saw a man who supposedly knew about Kennedy. I just can't remember the fellow's name. Howard went up there and this guy supposedly knew about some of Kennedy's sexual escapades. Howard used his alias, Ed Warren, I remember that, and tape-recorded the interview with this guy."

The man ordered a custard, and as he handed the menu to the waiter, he spilled his glass of water. He glared at the waiter as if it were his fault and told him what the Hay-Adams could do with its Hollandaise.

As they sipped coffee, he snapped his fingers, "Cliff DeMotte," he said. "That was the guy in Boston that Howard saw. He works for the federal government there, some agency. D-E-M-O-T-T-E."

Woodward spent the next two hours on the phone at the office trying to locate Cliff DeMotte. He had the Boston operators check their directories twice, then began calling personnel locators at federal agencies. A woman in the GSA personnel office found it: Clifton De-Motte, GS-12,* assigned to the Navy construction battalion center in Davisville, Rhode Island. Woodward reached DeMotte early the next morning at work and guessed right: the FBI had interviewed DeMotte after finding his number in Hunt's toll-call records.

"That's a confidential interview," DeMotte said, sounding a little shaken. "I'm not supposed to talk about it with the press."

Woodward said he already had most of the information and wanted to review it because the FBI got things screwed up so often.

"I didn't know it was Hunt at the time," DeMotte said. "He used the name Ed Warren. I didn't know it was Hunt until the FBI came and showed me pictures and it sure was Ed Warren, but they said it was Hunt." DeMotte, 41, had been public-relations director for the Yachtsman Motor Inn in Hyannis Port in 1960 when candidate John Kennedy had used the hotel as a press and staff headquarters for his presidential campaign. "Hunt wanted to know if I'd heard of any women-chasing by the Kennedy boys . . . if I'd heard of any scandal-type material. He wanted me to do work on Chappaquiddick. He gave me a book to read to see if it stirred my memory. It didn't." The book was Jack Olsen's *The Bridge at Chappaquiddick,* the same one Hunt had checked out of the White House library. He had visited DeMotte in July of '71, within a week or two of being hired at the White House.

DeMotte had provided Hunt with some "strictly hearsay" informa-

* A civil-service ranking. The grades run from GS-1 to GS-18.

tion about hell-raising by Kennedy staff members. "It was old, from way back in 1956," DeMotte said. "[John] Kennedy had some real swinging parties and used state-police cars to transport these people. Once they sent a police car to get a restock of booze.

"I tried to persuade Hunt that it was a waste of his time. . . . But he said he represented some group that he couldn't tell me about. He said he was a writer. I thought he was a hell of a James Bond operator. . . . We had supper and a drink in the motel. He seemed dedicated to something, either the country, the group or himself. . . . I spent a restless night and tried to find him in the morning for a cup of coffee, but he was gone."

The *Post*'s editions for February 10 carried a story saying that Howard Hunt had investigated Edward Kennedy's personal life during a period when the White House most feared a Kennedy candidacy. This time, Bradlee did not hesitate to put the story on page one.*

The DeMotte story was only a small step in establishing what Hunt and Liddy had done at the White House. The reporters were more

---

* Another apparent indication of the seriousness with which the Nixon forces viewed the threat of a Kennedy candidacy had come to the reporters about one month earlier. Woodward received a call from a woman who said she and a friend had bet an expensive dinner on whether Howard Hunt had been arrested inside the Watergate. He hadn't, which meant that the woman had won the bet; she invited Woodward to share the dinner. He declined.

About 10 days later, the woman visited him in the office. A retired Army major had told her that in March of 1972, at a Republican campaign headquarters in the Washington area, "he saw two campaign commercial spots that had Teddy Kennedy with a buxom blonde sitting on his lap. The woman was spliced or dubbed in." The woman said the retired major's name was Morrison J. Hosley and that he owned a general store in upstate New York.

The next day, Woodward reached Hosley by phone: "Yeah, I saw some cuts about seven months ago that were to be shown in the last 10 days of the campaign, if Kennedy were on the ticket. . . . The cuts looked dubbed. There was no realness to them; you had to put it together in your mind like the anti-Goldwater ads in '64—the ones showing a child walking in the grass and then shifting to a nuclear explosion. Kennedy was shown speaking and then there would be this big-breasted woman on the screen. It would make good TV. . . . But I'm not going to tell you if I saw them in a Republican headquarters or not. You'd better drop it."

Woodward called him back several days later, and was told, "I'm going to say I never told you anything, that it wasn't me who said there is a doctored film. Your source has gone dry."

Then Bernstein tried.

"What I saw, that's history," Hosley said. "I saw a print of it, but maybe I don't want you to have that information."

interested in Hunt's trip to see Dita Beard in Denver. She was the author of the famous memo which showed that there was a connection between ITT's promise of several hundred thousand dollars to help the Republican convention and a favorable anti-trust settlement.

Several days after his lunch with Hunt's friend, Woodward went to the Justice Department for a cup of coffee and some Watergate conversation. After an hour, Woodward asked about Hunt's Denver trip. Some ground had already been cleared. The Long Island paper *Newsday* had just reported that Chuck Colson had sent Hunt to visit Mrs. Beard at a hospital in Denver at the height of the ITT scandal in 1972. *Newsday* had no explanation for the trip.

The Justice Department official walked across the room to a file cabinet and took out a manila folder. He opened it and began reading. Under oath, Colson had acknowledged to Watergate prosecutors that he had sent Hunt to Denver, just before March 17, 1972, to visit Dita Beard. The official was reading from a deposition the prosecutors had taken from Colson in private—to spare the President's special counsel the embarrassment of appearing before the grand jury, he said.

Woodward tried to disguise his surprise. Fortunately, the man was studying another section of the deposition. He looked up at Woodward meekly. "Colson was never asked the reason he sent Hunt to see her. He said it had nothing to do with Watergate, so the matter was dropped. But Hunt used the same alias he used in Watergate—Edward Hamilton—when he saw her in the hospital. And he wore—you're not going to believe this . . ." The official gave a little laugh—"He wore a cheap, dime-store, reddish-colored wig. Apparently, it was the same wig found in the Watergate Hotel the day after the arrests."

At the office that evening, Woodward read the clips on the ITT affair. On February 29, 1972, columnist Jack Anderson had published the Dita Beard memo, sending political shock waves through the White House during President Nixon's visit to China. On March 17, just after Colson had dispatched Hunt to Denver, Mrs. Beard issued a statement from her bed at the Rocky Mountain Osteopathic Hospital in Denver, disowning the memo as a "forgery" and "a hoax." Her statement that evening was the first suggestion that the memo was not genuine, but there was no explanation of why she had waited almost three weeks to disavow it—during which time Richard Kleindienst's nomination as Attorney General was thrown into doubt. Mrs.

Beard had previously confirmed the memo's authenticity, line by line, to Anderson's assistant Brit Hume.

Woodward found three persons who put her denial into a new context—a White House official, a Republican politician with close ties to the White House, and an executive of the private investigative agency Intertel. All told essentially the same story:

Colson had coordinated the united White House–ITT strategy. Initially, both the administration and the corporation had tried to picture Dita Beard as a drunken crackpot and sought to discredit Jack Anderson. The effort had failed. ITT had hired Intertel, which also did work for the Howard Hughes organization, to make a technical inspection of the memo. Intertel established that the memo was probably written on a typewriter in Mrs. Beard's downtown Washington office, but that it would be almost impossible to prove. Robert Bennett, who represented Howard Hughes' interests in Washington, passed this information on to Howard Hunt, his employee, for transmission to Colson.

It was the old "insulation" story. Intertel's findings had cleared the way for the memo to be labeled a forgery. Colson, Hunt's other employer, dispatched Hunt to Denver. Mrs. Beard then issued a statement denying she had written the memo. ("I—and in a greater sense the whole American government—are the victims of a cruel fraud. . . .") Her words got back to the White House, from Hunt to Bennett to Colson. It was like Tinker to Evers to Chance. Colson-Chance then flipped the good news to Hugh Scott, who read Mrs. Beard's denial on the Senate floor that same day.

There was one other person who could tell Woodward more about what had gone on. But Dita Beard was nowhere to be found. Woodward reached her attorney, who said he would pass questions on to Mrs. Beard. A few hours later, the attorney called back to say that Mrs. Beard had recently suffered "a relapse" of the heart ailment that had sent her to the hospital in the midst of the ITT affair. Woodward recalled that she had also suffered a relapse in the midst of her bedside questioning by Senators from the Senate Judiciary Committee in 1972.

Shortly before the attorney's call, Woodward had reached Mrs. Beard's 24-year-old son, Robert, in Denver. Woodward asked if he recalled a visit to his mother by Howard Hunt. Beard said that a "mysterious" man wearing a cheap wig and makeup had visited his mother in the hospital just before she issued her statement. "From pictures I've seen, it could have been Howard Hunt, but I couldn't tell. The man refused to identify himself. He seemed to have inside information about what would happen next. . . . He was very eerie, he did have a red wig on, cockeyed, as if he'd put it on in a dark car. I couldn't have identified my brother like that." Beard added that he would give his mother a message to call Woodward back. If Robert Beard knew of a new "relapse," he didn't mention it.

Shortly before deadline the next evening, Woodward read Gerald Warren the text of a two-column re-examination of the Dita Beard affair based on the new information. The reopening of the ITT controversy so long after the White House had thought the matter disposed of left the President's men uncharacteristically speechless for the moment. Warren took three hours to say, "No comment." Colson was in Russia, on a trade-mission junket. The next day, Robert G. Kaiser, the *Post* correspondent in Moscow, found Colson and told him about the story. "That's a good one," Colson said, flashing a grin and walking away.

If the reporters were to learn what else Hunt and Liddy had done at the White House they would need more on the Plumbers. The first step was to study Egil (Bud) Krogh. Bernstein had met Krogh once, at a ribbon-snipping ceremony. Krogh at the time was the President's adviser on national-capital affairs. He jogged around the Ellipse in a sweatsuit before he went to work mornings, so Bernstein had asked him why the administration couldn't find room in the District budget to build some paths for cycling and jogging. Krogh had made a sympathetically bureaucratic reply about "priorities." He had seemed like a nice enough fellow. Kind of bland, Bernstein had thought. "Nice" was an understatement, the reporters learned as they searched for an explanation of why Krogh had hung around with the likes of Hunt and Liddy. Egil Krogh was the White House Mr. Clean, so straight an arrow that his friends mockingly called him "Evil Krogh." He had been a member of John Ehrlichman's law firm in Seattle, then he had served on the White House Domestic Council staff and coordinated the Nixon administration's worldwide war against drug trafficking. At 33, Krogh had become the youngest undersecretary in the Nixon Cabinet—at Transportation, appointed in February 1973.

Woodward placed a call to Capitol Hill to learn if the record of Krogh's confirmation hearing contained any leads. It didn't. But a congressional investigator who had worked on the hearing provided Woodward with the names of some of Krogh's friends and acquaintances.

The reporters started calling. Soon there was a break: "Bud said . . . that Hunt and Liddy were being routed information from national-security wiretaps," Woodward was told. Krogh's friend could recall no details. Krogh had mentioned it shortly after Hunt and Liddy had been indicted.

Working from a 1972 White House telephone directory, the reporters started calling the people under Ehrlichman's jurisdiction. One former and one current member of the White House staff provided identical versions of the next link in the chain. David Young, the former appointments secretary to Dr. Henry Kissinger and Krogh's deputy on the Plumbers' project, had regularly routed transcripts of wiretapped conversations to Hunt and Liddy in 1971 and 1972. Both sources thought that reporters, and those suspected of leaking information to them, might have been tapped.

Woodward called Kathleen Chenow, the Plumbers' ex-secretary, and asked about the tapped data Young had forwarded to Hunt and Liddy. "I can't talk about that," she said now.

The wiretapping activities—actual and suspected—of the Nixon administration had always been controversial. Under the administration's "national security" wiretap policy, also known as the Mitchell Doctrine, the President's men had claimed unprecedented authority to conduct electronic surveillance. Until the Supreme Court declared it illegal on June 19, 1972—two days after the Watergate arrests—the Justice Department had used electronic eavesdropping without court authorization against those suspected of domestic "subversive" activity. Radicals and civil-libertarians had long insisted that the term "subversive" was a euphemism for those who dissented too vigorously from the Nixon administration's policies. Now the reporters attempted to learn if their colleagues in the news media were among the "subversives" the Justice Department had claimed the right to listen in on.

Judging from the reception their inquiries received, they were coming close to something. Some officials were less than convincing in their denials, others refused to discuss it and some admitted they shared the reporters' suspicions. The reporters had reached a dead end.

Woodward drafted a story based on the bare details. It reported that Hunt and Liddy had received information from national-security wiretaps; that it was routed to them by David Young, Dr. Kissinger's assistant who was also a Plumber. The story noted that the Plumbers were in the business of investigating news leaks. Readers were left to form their own conclusions.

This time, too, Gerald Warren took a few hours to answer with the White House's one-sentence denial: "After thorough checking, we can find absolutely no basis for the report." Tiring of the game, Woodward asked him if that was a flat denial.

Warren, who became cold and formal in such situations, said, "I can't say anything else," and appealed for understanding. The article noted that Warren had not flatly denied the report.

Two weeks later, *Time* magazine published the first detailed account of the Nixon administration's zealous campaign to trace news leaks by tapping the telephones of news reporters and government officials. According to the *Time* account, the phones of half a dozen reporters and twice as many White House and government aides had been tapped by the FBI for reasons of domestic "security." The taps were begun in 1969, under a reluctant J. Edgar Hoover, and were continued under his successor, acting FBI director L. Patrick Gray III, until the Supreme Court decision of June 19, 1972. Hoover, said *Time,* had permitted his agents to install the taps *only* after John Mitchell authorized each tap in writing. In 1971, when the administration had tried to force Hoover to retire, *Time* said, the old bulldog-faced director had successfully resisted by threatening to reveal the details of the wiretapping campaign.

On February 26, the day *Time*'s edition hit the newsstands, Bernstein spent the morning at Justice, trying to confirm the details. Chasing from office to office after *Time*'s work on this one was less than fun. Bernstein got nowhere and took a cab back to the office. Dejected, he stepped into the elevator in the *Post* lobby and suddenly felt his arm grabbed and then his body being pulled back into the lobby. He started to struggle, then heard a female voice.

"Boy, am I glad to see you!" It was Laura Kiernan, a young news aide who had recently been promoted to reporter on the local staff. "There's a guy upstairs in the newsroom with a subpoena for you and your notes. Bradlee doesn't want you up there to get it. He wants you out of here, fast."

Bernstein dashed to a stairwell at the end of the lobby, then up seven flights of steps to the accounting department. Closing the door of an office with an adding machine on the desk, he dialed Bradlee's extension. Woodward was off for a few days in the Caribbean, but they had long before agreed on what to do if they were subpoenaed. Turning over notes or naming sources in either a grand-jury proceeding or a judicial hearing was obviously out of the question. There would be plenty of time to fight that in court. The first thing to do was move their files to a safe place. Bernstein told Bradlee where the files were. They would be moved immediately, he said.

CRP had issued subpoenas for five people at the *Post:* Bernstein, Woodward, Jim Mann (who had worked on some of the initial Watergate stories), Howard Simons and Katharine Graham. Also reporters from the *Star-News,* the *New York Times* and *Time* magazine. Simons and Mrs. Graham, the only non-reporters on CRP's list, had already been served. The subpoenas demanded that those served testify by deposition in CRP's civil suit and bring with them all notes, tapes and story drafts in their possession regarding Watergate. Bradlee told Bernstein he couldn't find the *Post*'s lawyers and he didn't want him served until he'd heard their advice. "Get out of the building," he said. "Go to a movie and call me at five o'clock."

Bernstein went to see *Deep Throat*—the movie version. When he called at five, Bradlee told him to return to the office and explained the strategy. Bernstein would accept the subpoena. Custody of at least some of the reporter's notes would pass to Mrs. Graham.

"Of course we're going to fight this one all the way up, and if the Judge wants to send anyone to jail, he's going to have to send Mrs. Graham. And, my God, the lady says she'll go! Then the Judge can have that on his conscience. Can't you see the pictures of her limousine pulling up to the Women's Detention Center and out gets our gal, going to jail to uphold the First Amendment? That's a picture that would run in every newspaper in the world. There might be a revolution."

That night, Bernstein was at his desk typing when he saw the CRP page hurrying down the middle aisle, arm outstretched. Bernstein continued to type.

"Carl Bernstein?"

Head down, Bernstein raised one hand and picked off the subpoena. But the page stood there silently. Finally, Bernstein glanced up from the typewriter. The page looked about 21, tousled blond hair, wearing a V-necked sweater, very collegiate.

"Hey, I really feel bad about doing this," he said. "They picked me because they thought somebody who looked like a student could get upstairs easier." He was a law student who worked part-time at the firm headed by Kenneth Wells Parkinson, the chief CRP attorney. He promised to keep alert for any information that might be useful to the *Post* and gave Bernstein his home phone number.

13

AFTER WOODWARD RETURNED from the Caribbean later that week, a short, heavy-set young man with a thin beard ringing his face and wearing small, thick glasses arrived in front of his desk. "Tim Butz," he said conspiratorially. He had once worked in Army intelligence, he said. Now he worked with a volunteer group of ex-intelligence types that was investigating people involved in domestic spying activities.

"I think we've found a George Washington University student who spied for CRP," Butz said. "It will take some more work." He told Woodward a rather disjointed tale. Woodward urged him to continue his researches and received almost a dozen telephoned progress reports in the next several days. After about a week, Butz called and said he had found a fraternity brother of the student spy who was willing to tell all. A dinner meeting was set that night, in the coffee shop of the Madison Hotel. When Woodward arrived, Butz was pacing the lobby with a young man he introduced as his "source"—a tall, nervous student named Craig Hillegass. The three went to a booth.

Hillegass described in vivid detail how Theodore F. Brill, his Kappa Sigma fraternity brother, had told him about being paid $150 a week by CRP to infiltrate the group of Quakers who had maintained a 24-hour-a-day vigil in front of the White House for several months. Brill's assignment had been to make regular reports to CRP on the personal lives and plans of the demonstrators, he said, and then to assist in setting them up for arrests on drug charges. Eventually, the Washington police raided the vigil, but found nothing.

Brill, 20, was chairman of the Young Republicans at George Washington University. His job at CRP was terminated two days after the Watergate arrests. "The idea," Hillegass said, thumping his water glass excitedly on the table, "was to create an embarrassment to the Democrats, because any embarrassment to radical groups would be considered an embarrassment to liberal politics and Senator McGovern."

With unrestrained gusto, he went on to describe the James Bond way in which Brill was paid. "Ted said he once was told to meet a woman in a red dress with a white carnation, carrying a newspaper. He exchanged his written report for an envelope containing his pay. Another time, Ted told me, he went to a bookstore on the corner of 17th Street and Pennsylvania [Avenue] and was handed a book by someone with his pay in the book.

"But it was part of a larger network. Ted said there were at least twenty-five others—and the information went to some pretty high-up people at CRP."

Woodward was mindful of Harry Rosenfeld's continuing pleas to find more of the 50 spies mentioned in the October 10 Segretti story. "Where are the other 49?" Rosenfeld would ask every week or two, though perhaps 25 had surfaced by that time. Theodore Brill did not seem exactly like a big-time operator, but—if his fraternity brother was telling the truth—he was part of the pattern.

George Washington University, five blocks from the White House, was on spring vacation. The next night, Woodward reached Theodore Brill at his home in River Edge, New Jersey. Playing the heavy with a 20-year-old history major made Woodward uneasy, but Brill might be one of those unexpected openings to something bigger. Eventually, Brill confirmed his fraternity brother's story and added a few details. He had been hired and paid by George K. Gorton, 25, CRP's national college director. "I was paid five weeks in May and June—once in cash and four times with Gorton's personal check. I learned later that it was a mistake that I got paid in check because there were supposed to be no records kept. I got the impression from Gorton that there were a couple of others elsewhere doing the same work . . . and Gorton said there was someone higher up who knew. I was supposed to go to the convention in Miami to do the same thing there with radical groups."

Why didn't you go? Woodward asked.

"My job was terminated two days after the Watergate bugging broke.

Gorton took me to lunch and said I had to stop because of Watergate. He said the operation was to be considered super-secret. People at the White House were upset," said Brill, neatly undercutting the CRP–White House contention that nobody in either place had divined a relationship between Watergate and other spying and sabotage.

Did Brill have any thoughts about the ethics of his work?

"Ethics?" Brill repeated. He sounded astonished at the question. "Well, not illegal but maybe a little unethical."

Woodward, feeling a bit too pious, thanked him and hung up. He found George Gorton's home number and called. Rock music was blaring in the background and a young man's voice said Gorton was out. After Woodward returned home, he tried again. It was nearly one A.M. More rock music. Gorton came to the phone and Woodward explained the story.

"Are you crazy?" Gorton shouted. "No *Post* reporter would call at one A.M."

Woodward felt slightly wounded. Why didn't people ever say that to Bernstein when *he* called at all hours of the morning? Woodward spelled his name and gave Gorton his home and office phone numbers.

"We'll see," Gorton shouted. "I've got a date here." He slammed down the phone.

Woodward sat at his desk looking out the ninth-floor window at the lights of the capital city. "Creepsters," Nicholas von Hoffman, the *Post*'s iconoclastic columnist, had called them. He stared out the window until he felt his anger subside.

The next morning, he was awakened by the phone ringing. "George Gorton," the voice said. "I just couldn't believe it was you calling in the middle of the night."

Woodward asked him some questions.

"Oh, yeah, Ted Brill did a little work for me. . . . Spying is a funny way to put it. My direction to Brill was only to find out what radicals were doing. It was part of my job to know what all of youth was thinking."

That, said Woodward, was a quaint way to conduct sociological research—planting an undercover agent, essentially an agent provocateur.

Gorton denied that Brill had helped arrange the raid on the Quakers and insisted that Brill's termination had "coincidentally" occurred two days after the Watergate break-in.

Then Gorton, who had been director of the Youth Ball for the President's inaugural, declared proudly that he had people gathering information on radicals in 38 states.

"It was my idea," Gorton said, not too convincingly. He had reported to Kenneth Rietz, director of CRP's Youth Vote Division. "Rietz knew that I could supply him with information on what radicals were thinking. I supplied the information, but Rietz didn't ask where I got it." Then he changed the story, claiming that Brill had been his lone operative.

Ken Rietz, 32, was Haldeman's choice as the next Republican national chairman. He had left CRP for the National Committee to head the 1974 Republican congressional campaigns.

Brill's $150 weekly salary had not been reported under the new campaign disclosure law. After the Brill story appeared, the General Accounting Office audited the CRP books again. The audit helped establish that Rietz had headed a "Kiddie Corps" of young spies for the President.

Around this time, Woodward went to visit a well-placed CRP official. The man seemed disaffected, disgusted with the White House and the tactics that had been used to re-elect the President. "If there was an honest and a dishonest way to do something," he said, "and if both ways would get the same results, we picked the dishonest way. . . . Now, tell me why anyone would do that."

For instance?

"It's hard to think of specifics," the CRP man said. He thought for another moment. "Remember the decision to mine Haiphong about five months before the election? Some of us felt that that decision could make or break the President. We spent $8400 on false telegrams and ads to stir up phony support for the President's decision. Money was used to pay for telegrams to the White House, to tell the President what a great move it was, so that Ziegler could announce that the telegram support was running some large percentage in support of the President. Money also went to pay for a phony ad in the *New York Times*."

He took a copy of the ad out of his desk and handed it to Woodward. Headlined "The People vs. the *New York Times*," the advertisement criticized a *Times* editorial that had opposed the mining.

"Notice," the man from CRP said, "it is signed by about ten supposedly independent people, leaving the impression that citizens are up in arms about the editorial, and are willing to fork over several thousand dollars of their own money to express their opinion. Not so. The ad was paid for by CRP with forty of those $100 bills from the pile in Stans' safe."

A line in the advertisement ran: "Who can you believe—the *New York Times* or the American people?"

Back at the office, Woodward called another CRP official. He said the attempt to drum up support for the Haiphong decision "put the entire staff in overdrive for two weeks. . . . The work included petition drives, organizing rallies, bringing the people in buses to Washington, organizing calls to the White House, getting voters to call their Congressmen."

Bernstein remembered something that tied in. In May 1972, Barker and Sturgis had appeared uninvited at a meeting of Cuban exiles in Miami and attempted to take over plans for organizing a demonstration in support of the mining. Sturgis had driven the lead truck in a parade of support that followed.

Sussman told the reporters to write a story on the campaign of deception surrounding the Haiphong issue. "This hits home," he said. "People understand attempts to tamper with public opinion."

The day the story ran, James Dooley, a 19-year-old former head of the CRP mailroom, came to the *Post* newsroom and said he wanted to talk to someone about the Haiphong mining. Woodward took him into Sussman's office.

"You don't know everything that was done about Haiphong," said Dooley. "We rigged WTTG's poll on whether the people supported the President's decision."

The local Metromedia television station had asked its viewers to send in a card indicating whether they agreed or disagreed with the President on the mining. Sample ballots were placed in advertisements in the *Post* and the *Star*.

"The press office ran the project," Dooley said, "and work ground to a halt. Everyone had to fill out fifteen postcards. Ten people worked for days buying different kinds of stamps and cards and getting different handwriting to fake the responses. . . . Thousands of newspapers were bought from the newsstands and the ballots were clipped out and mailed in."

At a minimum, Dooley said, 4000 ballots supporting Nixon's decision were sent from CRP. WTTG reported that 5157 agreed with the President and 1158 disagreed. Had the CRP ballots not been sent in, the President would, at best, have lost by one vote—1158 to 1157.

"When all the ballots were clipped," Dooley continued, "people became afraid that the newspapers might be discovered, so someone said, 'Shred them.' McCord was in charge of the shredder and he was upset about a ton of newspapers all over the shredder room. . . . But all the newspapers were destroyed as directed."

Woodward called CRP spokesman Devan Shumway and asked if the poll had been rigged. "When you're involved in an election, you do what you can," Shumway replied. "We assumed the other side would do it also. On that assumption, we proceeded. I don't know if the other side did."

Woodward asked if the other side Shumway was referring to was the North Vietnamese.

No, Shumway said, he meant the McGovern forces.

Following it down to the end, Woodward called Frank Mankiewicz, McGovern's former campaign aide. "We didn't do it," he said, somewhat incredulously. "It didn't occur to us, believe me. These guys are something. They assume we have the same sleazy ethics as theirs."

No presidential decision affecting Watergate seemed so ill-advised or left the reporters more perplexed than the White House announcement in February that L. Patrick Gray's name would be submitted to the Senate for confirmation as J. Edgar Hoover's permanent successor. Gray was already the acting FBI director; his confirmation hearings would almost certainly become a congressional inquiry into the FBI's conduct of the Watergate investigation; why risk the possible consequences of a senatorial fishing expedition to make his tenure permanent? The administration officials to whom the reporters posed the riddle seemed no less baffled. Several insiders professed to know only that there had been a mammoth struggle in the innermost Nixon circle.

John Ehrlichman, it was said, had vehemently opposed the nomination, but the President had ultimately rejected his counsel. No one suggested that Gray had been nominated because of ability, or because the White House regarded the hearings as an opportunity to set the Watergate record straight.

Shortly before the hearings were to begin, the reporters decided it was time for Woodward to move the flower pot on his balcony. That night he traveled by foot and cab to the garage. Deep Throat was not there. Deep Throat had said he would leave a message on a certain ledge when he couldn't make an appointment. Woodward, five foot ten, couldn't reach it. He found a section of an old conduit pipe and fished around for it.

There was a small piece of paper on which Deep Throat had typed instructions to meet the next night at a bar Woodward had never heard of. A bar. Had Deep Throat gone crazy? Woodward wondered. Something must be wrong. When he got home, he looked the bar up in the phone book. There was no such listing. From a pay phone in his apartment building, he dialed information. An operator gave him the listing—an address on the outskirts of the city.

At nine the next night, Woodward walked a few blocks before taking a cab to a section of the city in the opposite direction from the bar. He walked another 15 minutes and took a cab to within a few blocks of the bar. It was really a tavern, an old wooden house which had been converted into a saloon for truckers and construction workers. Woodward, who was dressed casually, walked in. No one seemed to pay any attention to him. He spotted Deep Throat sitting alone at a side table and nervously sat down across from him.

Why here? he asked.

"A change," Deep Throat said. "None of my friends, none of your friends would come here. Just a sleepy, dark bar." A waiter came over; they both ordered Scotch.

There has to be more to this new meeting place, Woodward said.

"A little bit classier surroundings," Deep Throat answered. "No chance you were followed? Two cabs and all?"

Woodward nodded.

"How'd the *Post* like its subpoenas?"

Just great, said Woodward.

"That's only the first step. Our President has gone on a rampage about news leaks on Watergate. He's told the appropriate people, 'Go to any length' to stop them. When he says that, he really means business. Internal investigations, plus he wants to use the courts. There was a discussion about whether to go the criminal route or the civil-suit route first. At a meeting, Nixon said that the money left over from the campaign, about $5 million or so, might as well be used to take the *Washington Post* down a notch. Thus your subpoenas, and the others. Part of the discussion was about starting a grand-jury investigation, but that's for later.

"Nixon was wild, shouting and hollering that 'we can't have it and we're going to stop it, I don't care how much it costs.' His theory is that the news media have gone way too far and the trend has to be stopped—almost like he was talking about federal spending. He's fixed on the subject and doesn't care how much time it takes; he wants it done. To him, the question is no less than the very integrity of government and basic loyalty. He thinks the press is out to get him and therefore is disloyal; people who talk to the press are even worse—the enemies within, or something like that."

Woodward took a breath. Deep Throat sipped his Scotch gingerly, then wiped his mouth inelegantly with the back of his hand.

How worried was he?

"Worried?" Deep Throat leaned back and threw his arm over his chair. "It can't work. They'll never get anyone. They never have. They're hiding things that will come out and even discredit their war against leaks. The flood is coming, I'm telling you. So the White House wants to eat the *Washington Post,* so what? It will be wearing on you, but the end is in sight. It's building and they see it and they know that they can't stop the real story from coming out. That's why they're so desperate. Just be careful, yourselves and the paper, and wait them out, don't jump too fast. Be careful and don't be too anxious."

Woodward was anything but reassured by his friend's assessment. He said he needed more details if he was going to tell the others at the *Post* that they were on the menu but weren't going to be eaten. Deep Throat shook his head, indicating that he could not say much more.

What about Gray's nomination? asked Woodward. That didn't make any sense.

Deep Throat said it made all the sense in the world, though it was a big risk. "In early February, Gray went to the White House and said, in effect, 'I'm taking the rap on Watergate.' He got very angry and said he had done his job and contained the investigation judiciously, that it wasn't fair that he was being singled out to take the heat. He implied that all hell could break loose if he wasn't able to stay in the job permanently and keep the lid on. Nixon could have thought this was a threat, though Gray is not that sort of guy. Whatever the reason, the President agreed in a hurry and sent Gray's name up to the Senate right away. Some of the top people in the White House were dead set against it, but they couldn't talk him out of it."

So good Pat Gray had blackmailed the President.

"I never said that," Deep Throat laughed. He lifted his eyes, the picture of innocence.*

What about the *Time* magazine story? Had Gray been aware of taps on reporters and White House aides?

"Affirmative," said Deep Throat, and cautioned that even he did not know all there was to know about the subject. "There was an out-of-channels vigilante squad of wiretappers that did it. Including taps on Hedrick Smith and Neil Sheehan of the *New York Times,* after the Pentagon Papers publication. But it started before that. All the records have supposedly been destroyed." He explained that the wiretapping had been done by ex-FBI and ex-CIA agents who were hired outside of normal channels. Mardian had run the Justice Department end of the operation for the White House. Watergate was nothing new to the administration, Deep Throat continued.

There had been an election strategy session at which Haldeman pushed Mitchell to set up a wiretapping operation for the campaign. Mitchell had been reluctant, but Haldeman was insistent. Mitchell was instructed by the White House chief of staff to move part of the vigilante operation from the White House to the campaign. That meant Hunt and Liddy.

---

* Stephen Sachs, the attorney for Gray, told Woodward in early 1974 that the suggestion that Gray had pressured or blackmailed the President was "outrageously false." "He [Gray] went to the White House expecting not to get the job," Sachs said. "Nixon told him that he should be as ruthless as Hoover in stopping leaks and be aggressive in the use of polygraphs [lie detectors]. . . ." Sachs said that pressuring the White House was "not the way Gray handled himself with those guys. It was plain fear most of the time. . . . Now it makes perfect sense that some of those guys down there would think he might be pressuring because that's the way they operate, but not Gray."

"In 1969, the first targets of aggressive wiretapping were the reporters and those in the administration who were suspected of disloyalty," Deep Throat said. "Then the emphasis was shifted to the radical political opposition during the anti-war protests. When it got near election time, it was only natural to tap the Democrats. The arrests in the Watergate sent everybody off the edge because the break-in could uncover the whole program."

Deep Throat and Woodward each had another Scotch, luxuriating in the unfamiliar comfort of their meeting place. Woodward wondered if his friend was intentionally flirting with the danger of being discovered. Did Deep Throat want to get caught so he would be free to speak publicly? Was there a love-hate dialectic about his government service? Woodward started to ask, then faltered. It was enough to know that Deep Throat would never deal with him falsely. Someday it would be explained.

The drinks were cheap. Woodward put a $5 bill on the table and left first.

The next morning, the reporters studied Woodward's notes. They were now thinking in terms of a report which, like the October 10 story on the massive campaign of spying and espionage, would attempt to put Watergate in perspective. Just as the break-in had been but a small part of a massive election-year campaign of espionage and sabotage, the whole undercover effort to re-elect the President was, in its turn, part of a broader program directed by the President's men, almost from the beginning, against those who they thought threatened the administration.

But the reporters would need more—details, examples, others who could confirm what had happened.

Pat Gray's confirmation hearing was set to begin February 28.

The night before, Bernstein talked to Tom Hart, a young aide to Senator Robert Byrd of West Virginia, who was the Senate Democratic whip and a member of the Judiciary Committee. Hart had compiled a card index of the newspaper and magazine stories and, from these, had filled a loose-leaf binder with lists of contradictions and unanswered questions about Watergate.

The questions were being circulated to selected members of the committee. Until they were answered, and buttressed by evidence from the FBI's Watergate files, Gray would remain on the witness stand, Hart said. Even if the Judiciary Committee reported out a positive recommendation, Byrd would use his considerable influence to oppose the nomination on the Senate floor if the contradictions were not cleared up.

The hearings opened on February 28 with Gray chewing on throat lozenges and insisting that the Watergate investigation had been "a massive special," a "full-court press," with "no holds barred." Then, without being asked, he volunteered that he had turned over the files of the investigation to John Dean and could not guarantee that Dean hadn't shown them to Donald Segretti.

The Senators were astonished. Woodward was relieved that Bernstein wasn't there to hear Gray's testimony. He had been maintaining for months that they should write a story on Dean's receipt of the files. Woodward hadn't thought it important, which was exactly what Gray was presently contending, without much success. He was offering to make the FBI's Watergate files available to the Senators. But the impression that Pat Gray had acted as valet for John Dean, more than 20 years his junior, had sunk in. The Gray hearings were going to become the Dean hearings as well. That was clear.

The next day, Thursday, Bernstein read his file on John Dean. Dean, who had come into possession of the contents of Howard Hunt's safe after June 17, had waited at least seven days to turn them over to the FBI. One notation indicated that two notebooks belonging to Hunt had not been listed in Dean's inventory. A Justice Department attorney told Bernstein that the prosecutors had first heard of them on October 11, when Hunt had filed a motion demanding the return of belongings he had left at his office.

"The White House claimed they never saw the notebooks," Bernstein was told. "We didn't know what to think. We still don't."

He called Hunt's attorney, William Bittman. Bittman confirmed the story and told Bernstein that the notebooks contained names and addresses which the prosecutors had told him might lead to others involved in the Watergate conspiracy. "We thought the FBI had them and had used them in their investigation. I was going to argue that the government's whole case was tainted because their information had come from material [the notebooks] obtained in an illegal search. I was going to call Dean and other people at the White House to show that Hunt was still using his office in June and that he had not abandoned his property in the White House.

"When we found the FBI never got the notebooks, the whole issue became moot," Bittman said. "All I can say is . . . that the whole thing was very strange. I don't know where they went."

Bernstein asked how useful Hunt thought the notebooks would be in building a case against higher-ups.

"I'll let you guess," Bittman said. "Valuable enough for someone to want them to disappear."

On Friday, March 2, at an impromptu news conference, President Nixon announced that he would claim executive privilege against any demand that Dean testify at the Gray hearings. The story of the missing notebooks and Dean's role in turning over the material in Hunt's safe ran with an account of the President's remarks.

Four days later, Gray told the Senators he was "unalterably convinced" that Dean had withheld nothing from Howard Hunt's safe. Almost simultaneously, the White House issued a statement asserting that Dean had turned over all its contents.* But the matter was eclipsed by a more startling development at the hearings.

That afternoon, a group of reporters, including Woodward, filed into Tom Hart's anteroom to pick up copies of documents Gray had supplied in answer to some of the Senator's earlier questions. One was headed "Interview with Herbert W. Kalmbach."

"Mr. Kalmbach said that in either August or September, 1971, he was contacted by Mr. Dwight Chapin and was informed that Capt. Donald H. Segretti was about to get out of the military service and that he may be of service to the Republican Party." It was all there. Kalmbach had admitted, in the interview, that he had paid Segretti for undercover activities, on instructions from Chapin. In one irretrievable step, Patrick Gray had undermined the basic claim of White House innocence. In the process, he had helped establish the credibility of the *Washington Post*.

Bernstein and Woodward had difficulty finishing the Gray story by

---

* In late 1973, John Dean acknowledged that he had destroyed the notebooks, which he had found the previous January in the President's personal financial file. The White House said, "The President did not know the notebooks were in his estate file," and declined further comment.

deadline. Newspapers, networks, radio and television stations were phoning for comments on the *Post*'s "vindication." Almost all the callers used that word.

Bernstein's and Woodward's story reflected 10 months of pent-up anger and frustration. They threw quote after quote of White House denials back at the President's men. But the article was unintentionally packaged like an ax murder. Leading the paper under a three-column head: "FBI Chief Says/Nixon's Aides/Paid Segretti," the text was juxtaposed with oversized pictures of Chapin, Kalmbach and Segretti. The unfortunate combination of their placement running down the side of page and the captions under the pictures made them look like mug shots sent over from homicide. "Chapin: reported Segretti available. . . . Kalmbach: just a disbursing agent. . . . Segretti: linked to Nixon staff." In the excitement, the effect went unnoticed at the *Post*. But not at the White House. The reporters were told by officials there and elsewhere in the administration that the story's treatment had generated as much hatred of the *Post* as anything.

Bradlee, usually sensitive to such things, had been too pleased by the day's events to notice. Between calls for interviews, he raced around the office, pounding Rosenfeld on the shoulder, attempting to exchange a jive handshake with Sussman (who almost lost his pipe) and proclaiming that Pat Gray had rescued the free press.

For the next two weeks, the reporters watched in amazement as, day after day, Gray attested to the ineptitude—if not the criminal negligence—of his supervision of the FBI's investigation. Deep Throat's implicit suggestion that Nixon had been frightened into nominating Gray became increasingly plausible as the nominee demonstrated a dangerous candor.

On March 22, Gray testified that John Dean had "probably" lied when he told the FBI on June 22 that he did not know if Howard Hunt had an office in the White House. The White House issued a statement "unequivocally" denying Gray's charge, and Dean demanded a "correction."

The day before, CRP's subpoenas of the *Post*'s reporters and news executives had been thrown out of court.

14

THE NEXT MORNING, March 23, Woodward was walking down a corridor near the editorial-page offices when Herblock, the *Post* cartoonist, stopped him. "Hey, did you hear about McCord's letter to the Judge? I heard it on the radio."

The last time somebody had brought him news of Watergate from the radio, Woodward thought, the Haldeman story had blown up. No, he hadn't heard, he said, and waited.

"Yeah, McCord's saying there was perjury and pressure to keep quiet, and others are in on it."

As Woodward bounded into the newsroom, Howard Simons, standing near the national desk, was waving a piece of wire copy and shouting.

It was the text of a letter from McCord to Sirica:

"Several members of my family have expressed fear for my life if I disclose knowledge of the facts in this matter. . . . In the interests of justice . . . of restoring faith in the criminal justice system . . ." McCord was coming forward to tell what he knew. Woodward studied the letter's charges: Political pressure had been applied to the defendants to plead guilty and remain silent. Perjury had occurred during the trial. Others involved in Watergate were not identified in testimony.

McCord had requested a meeting with Sirica after sentencing, ". . . since I cannot feel confident in talking with an FBI agent, in testifying

275

before a grand jury whose U.S. Attorneys work for the Department of Justice, or in talking with other government representatives."

Woodward wondered whether McCord could prove his charges. An image of John Mitchell being led off by marshals flashed through his mind.

Simons, jubilant, told Woodward, "Find out what the hell he's talking about—who committed perjury, who else was involved, who applied pressure." He called Mrs. Graham in Singapore.

Bradlee was subdued. The letter might be a giant step, but it was vague.

"Names, fellas, we want names," he said.

That Sunday, both reporters were in the office finding out that Howard Simons' directions were more difficult to follow than to state. If McCord had yet told anybody what he had in mind when he unburdened himself, it was a well-kept secret. The prosecutors doubted that McCord knew much. The White House lid was on tight. The few presidential aides who returned phone calls knew nothing; they called back because they hoped to learn something from the reporters.

In mid-afternoon, Woodward was notified that Samuel Dash, the chief counsel of the Senate Watergate committee, was going to hold a press conference in an hour. Bernstein took a cab to Capitol Hill. Dash was sitting in his office behind a steel-gray desk, waiting for the camera crews to make their final adjustments. Speaking from notes, he said that he had interviewed McCord in two long, tape-recorded sessions over the weekend. McCord had "named names" and begun "supplying a full and honest account" of the Watergate operation. Bernstein could not understand why Dash was holding a press conference. He was not giving concrete details, merely building expectations about whatever it was that McCord had told him. There were going to be public hearings by the Watergate committee at which McCord would certainly testify. The press could blow the Watergate committee's investigation out of the water if McCord's charges leaked and could not be proved.

He went back to the office and unenthusiastically began to see if he could find a committee source who would say what McCord had said. He had made half a dozen unsuccessful calls when the item moved over the *Los Angeles Times* wire. McCord had told Dash that Jeb Magruder and John Dean had had advance knowledge of the Watergate bugging operation and were involved in its planning. The story was by Ron Ostrow and Robert Jackson. Bernstein knew they wouldn't take a flier unless their source was absolutely reliable.

The information about Magruder was no surprise, but there had been no real hint from anyone that Dean had had anything to do with planning the bugging. If the man named by the President to investigate the bugging had been one of its planners, the consequences seemed incalculable. Already, the White House had issued a statement denying categorically the charges against Dean. The statement did not mention Magruder: the Nixon men had cut him loose.

Simons arrived at the office wearing hiking boots. Since receiving the initial tip on the Watergate break-in on June 17, he had been the senior editor most involved in the day-to-day progress of the story.

By evening, Bernstein had called more than 40 people—Senators, members of the Watergate committee staff, lawyers, CRP and White House sources, Justice Department officials, friends of McCord, even his minister. Nothing. He and Simons decided he would write a story quoting the *Times* and noting that the *Post* had been unable to confirm that McCord had made the allegations. Then Simons got a call from a lawyer who said he represented John Dean. He was threatening to file a libel suit if the *Post* ran the allegations about Dean. Simons told Bernstein to quote the threat and name the lawyer.

Simons sensed Bernstein's frustration at the day's events. He told him to get accustomed to being beaten on stories. The days when the *Post* had dominated the Watergate story were over.

The next morning, Bernstein and Woodward searched frantically for confirmation of the *Times* account and came up finally with three people on Capitol Hill who said it was correct. One, a Republican politician, said McCord's allegations were "convincing, disturbing and supported by some documentation."

At the White House, Ron Ziegler announced that the President had personally telephoned Dean and expressed "absolute and total confidence" in him.

Watergate was going to burst. The McCord allegations were only part of the pressures building against the dam which Deep Throat had talked about. The rush was still distant, but it was streaming closer: Dean, Magruder, Mardian, Mitchell and—most important—H. R. Haldeman were likely to be swept away in the flood.

Woodward decided to ask the deputy press secretary, Gerald Warren, for an interview with the President. It was a long shot, an almost embarrassingly long one, but Woodward had always been struck by Richard Nixon's affinity for the unexpected. If the President could open negotiations with Red China, why not with the *Washington Post?*

Woodward phoned Warren and asked if he could come over for a discussion. Warren hesitated then said, "Sure." Woodward didn't have a White House press pass. Warren said he would leave Woodward's name at the gate.

March 27 was a warm, sunny day and Woodward worked up a moderate sweat walking the five blocks to the White House. The press lounge in the West Wing was deserted. He waited in a stiff-backed upholstered chair. After about 10 minutes, Warren came out of a long back hallway and took Woodward to his office; not much bigger than a dressing closet, it was just large enough for his desk and chair and a chair for a visitor. Warren, tall, bespectacled and neatly groomed, is rather scholarly in appearance and demeanor.

"Do you mind if I take notes?" Warren asked, adjusting the glasses on his nose, and flipping to a clean page on his yellow legal-size pad.

Of course Woodward didn't object. He explained that he and Bernstein had information indicating that Watergate was a much broader conspiracy than anyone had yet suggested publicly. The information was going to come out, Woodward said, and the *Post* was not going to be the only agent of disclosure. Perhaps the White House knew of things that might mitigate the effect. The *Post* wanted to explore those factors. The situation had reached a level of gravity where only direct responses by the President might lessen the damage.

Warren occasionally looked up from his note pad and asked for specific facts. Woodward said that he and Bernstein wanted to talk only to the President about the facts and hoped that Warren would consider this a formal request for an interview. Warren said he would, but that he assumed the request would be denied.

"I can tell you," he said, "that it will be a decision I won't make.

I'll forward the request up the line." Woodward imagined it would get about as far as Ziegler, whom he had purposely not called. He tried again.

Judging from their evaluation of the information, Woodward said, the President was going to have to jump ship on the Watergate at some point soon. The *Post* was anxious to discuss specifics before that happened. Woodward said they had information about additional wiretaps, break-ins and other secret operations, all of which was going to come out.

Warren winced a little, and cast a skeptical glance at him. "If you could be more specific, it would help," he said.

Woodward said that he wouldn't go into specific details at that moment, but if the President agreed to be interviewed, then questions would be provided in advance. There would be no attempt to spring something on him.

Woodward felt a hideous rush of nervousness. This wasn't working, he realized. Also, his awe of the Presidency clutched at him. That was part of the reason he was there, sitting in that closet office, he realized. It was to give warning. Warren, too, realized that. But not a threat, Woodward wanted to make clear. It was, in an odd way, friendly, and meant to convey respect and the possibility of a way out. Woodward was seeking an adjustment. He wanted the paper to persuade by facts and good reporting, but he had no wish to build a hostile wall.

Warren smiled as if to say: It doesn't work that way, you either have the goods and print them or you don't. But he sounded sympathetic at times, as if he had wanted to sweep the papers off his desk and say: Right, we've got to talk about this. It could have been Woodward's imagination, and Warren's gentle ways.

When Woodward finished his presentation, Warren laid his pen gently on his pad, stood and extended his hand. "I'll be back to you," he said.

Woodward replied that there was no hurry and shrugged his shoulders to say he knew what the answers would be. As he walked out of the crackerbox office and into the sun, he felt buoyant. He had tried.

Bernstein and he were well aware that they would have far less to do with events than before. Much bigger forces were firmly in charge.

Government investigations were under way, and the instinct for survival could turn some of the President's men into informers.

On Wednesday, March 28, McCord was scheduled to give his first sworn testimony behind closed doors to the seven Senators on the Watergate committee. Bernstein joined dozens of reporters waiting outside the hearing room. The reporters began discussing "leaks" which were bound to come out, and agreed on the dangers of trying to report what would go on inside. It was no longer a matter of "investigative" reporting—evaluating information, putting together pieces in a puzzle, disclosing what had been obscured. They would be merely trying to find out in advance the testimony of witnesses who would eventually take the stand in public. Judging which allegations were hearsay, which firsthand knowledge, and placing them in context would be difficult. Sensational charges and deliberate leaks by interested parties would be hard to evaluate. If some papers or networks searched out leaks, all the reporters would feel bound to compete.

The committee session with McCord lasted four and a half hours. Afterward, Senator Howard Baker of Tennessee, the Republican vice chairman of the committee, announced that McCord had provided "significant information . . . covering a lot of territory."

Bernstein and Woodward began the ritual phone calls, starting with the Senators. "Okay, I'm going to help you on this one," one told Woodward. "McCord testified that Liddy told him the plans and budget for the Watergate operation were approved by Mitchell in February, when he was still Attorney General. And he said that Colson knew about Watergate in advance."

But, in answer to Woodward's questions, he added that McCord had only secondhand information for his allegations, as well as for his earlier accusations that Dean and Magruder had had prior knowledge.

"However," the Senator said, "he was very convincing."

Bradlee was able to get a second Senator to corroborate the story, and Bernstein received the same version from a staff member.

The next day's story, though calling attention to the hearsay nature of McCord's testimony, quoted the unnamed Senator's evaluation.

The flood of "McCord says" stories continued. McCord appeared again on Thursday, and the reporters went through the same exercise.

McCord stated that Liddy had told him that charts outlining the Watergate operation had been shown to Mitchell in February. Three sources gave identical versions of the testimony.

At this point, press secretary Ronald Ziegler announced that the President, seeking to "dispel the myth . . . that we seek to cover up," had ordered members of his staff to appear before the grand jury and testify, if called. The *Star-News* interpreted this as a change of policy and reported that it "appears to be a significant relaxation of Nixon's firm policy of sheltering the staff under the doctrine of executive privilege."

Concerned that the *Post* would make the same error, Bernstein and Woodward went to Dick Harwood, the national editor. Ziegler himself had said that there was nothing new in the policy. Several White House aides had already either testified before or given sworn depositions to the grand jury. The President had never asserted a claim to executive privilege on their behalf to protect them from testifying in *criminal* investigations, but only in congressional hearings.

The reporters suggested strongly to Lou Cannon, a *Post* national-staff reporter who was writing the story, that the newest Ziegler announcement did not represent a change of policy. Cannon's Republican sources were considerable, and he had written some of the *Post*'s finest pieces about the effects of Watergate on the White House and the GOP. Now he was furious. He had discussed the matter with the most experienced members of the White House press corps, and they had agreed that the President had relaxed his position on sweeping executive privilege.

Watergate had been, for some months, a strain on the never very cozy relations between the city and national desks at the *Post*. Bernstein and Woodward were outraged by the tenor of Cannon's story, and also by its position as the lead in the next day's paper.

The next day, their White House sources confirmed that Ziegler's statement was nothing more than a public-relations gesture. But the Senate committee and staff now charged, more importantly, that it was intended to divert attention from the President's claim of executive privilege in the Senate investigation. Senate sources suggested an additional reason for the President's willingness to cooperate with one inquiry and not another—the grand jury's proceedings would be secret, and under the supervision of the administration's Justice Department.

The Senate hearings would be public, and independent of the Executive.

Nine months after Watergate, the White House demonstrated once again that it knew more about the news business than the news business knew about the White House.

If there was one Washington reporter unlikely to be taken in by White House manipulations, Bernstein and Woodward thought it was Seymour Hersh of the *New York Times*. A mutual friend had arranged for Bernstein and Woodward to have dinner with Hersh on April 8.

Hersh, 36, horn-rimmed and somewhat pudgy, showed up for dinner in old tennis shoes, a frayed pinstriped shirt that might have been his best in his college freshman year, and rumpled bleached khakis. He was unlike any reporter they had ever met. He did not hesitate to call Henry Kissinger a war criminal in public and was openly attracted and repelled by the power of the *New York Times*. Hersh had broken the story of the cover-up of My Lai and had spent years reporting on military and national-security bureaucracies. He was uniquely qualified to understand the ramifications of Watergate. "I know these people," Hersh said. "The abiding characteristic of this administration is that it lies."

He could be just as tough on the *New York Times:* "Lies, lies, lies," he remarked of a story written by one of his colleagues.

During dinner, Bernstein and Woodward brought up one of the President's men who was under suspicion in Watergate.

"I'd really love to get that son of a bitch, too, I know him from way before Watergate," Hersh said. "But he'll get no cheap shots from me; either I get him hard, with facts, solid information, evidence, the truth, or I don't touch him."

The three exchanged their sense of some of the witnesses and principals in Watergate, being careful not to tip their hands. Later that evening, Bernstein joshingly asked Hersh what Watergate story he was going to unload when the *Times* front page arrived at the *Post* that night.

"Just a little something," Hersh replied.

Bernstein and Woodward couldn't tell if he was kidding. Woodward called the office. Hersh wasn't kidding. His "little something" was the first report that McCord had testified that the cash payoffs to the Watergate conspirators had come directly from CRP. The connection was one of the keys they had all been waiting for. Since January, everyone had assumed that CRP had bought the conspirators' silence, but now someone was finally saying so from the inside.

Months earlier, Hugh Sloan had told the reporters that the celebrated secret fund had never ceased to exist—even after the Watergate arrests. Bernstein and Woodward had been astonished. Sloan had told them that the money had been transferred from Stans' safe to Fred LaRue. They had not written about it because they couldn't confirm it and didn't know how the money had been spent. Sloan had refused to say how much money was involved. Now it seemed possible that the money had bought the defendants' silence. LaRue had been John Mitchell's deputy and co-director of Watergate housecleaning. He and Mardian were the two CRP officials who had supervised Kenneth Parkinson and the other committee lawyers. McCord's testimony had identified Parkinson and the late Dorothy Hunt, Howard Hunt's wife, as conduits for the payments to the conspirators.

Woodward called a CRP official who had been friendly but unwilling to talk specifics. The man exploded on the phone about the awful state of affairs in the wake of the McCord disclosures:

"John Mitchell still sits there smoking on his pipe, not saying much. . . . I used to take that for wisdom—you know, keeping your mouth shut. Now I realize that it's ignorance. . . . God, I never thought I'd be telling you guys that I didn't hate what you did. It's the way the White House has handled this mess that's undermined the Presidency. . . . I've got friends who look at me now and say, 'How can you have any self-respect and still work for CRP?' I'm sick."

Seeing an unusual opportunity, Woodward said he and Bernstein *knew* that LaRue was involved in the payoffs to the conspirators. Woodward had only seen pictures of LaRue. He was a balding little man with round spectacles, a former Las Vegas casino owner and oil millionaire—the perfect bagman, Woodward had thought.

"I can't answer any questions, but I'll tell you one thing you might have trouble believing," the man from CRP said. "Fred LaRue won't lie under oath. If they ask him, he's going to say he helped pay the men off."

Woodward called Hugh Sloan. LaRue paid off the boys, Woodward announced, then realized how silly he sounded. Sloan was not surprised to hear it. He had always suspected the worst, whatever it was.

How much money was transferred from the fund? Woodward was looking for a ballpark figure.

Sloan wouldn't say.

They played their old game, like two sparring partners who hadn't been in the ring for a while. More than $100,000? More than $50,000? Between $50,000 and $100,000? Which side of $75,000?

"Within $5,000 of that," Sloan said.

That was good enough; it was probably $80,000, but they would use $70,000.

How could CRP continue the secret fund after the Watergate arrests and get away with it?

"It [the transfer] was done in July," Sloan said. "Nothing had come out about the money yet and Secretary Stans approved [it]. It was a way of doing business, having cash around." Sloan presumed that somebody had told Stans to do it, but he didn't know who. He was assuming the worst on that, too.

Do the prosecutors know about this? Woodward asked.

"I don't think so," Sloan said. "I was never asked."*

Woodward called a Justice Department official. Were the prosecutors trying to determine if the conspirators were paid off with the $70,000 LaRue got out of Stans' safe after Watergate?

"The prosecutors are looking at every penny of committee money to see if it went for payoffs, every penny they can find."

Including the money that was in Stans' safe?

"Right."

That tied the knot. The secret fund had brought the reporters full circle—first the bugging, and now the cover-up.

The White House Correspondents Association annual dinner is a

---

* Sloan did say, however, that he had been asked the relevant questions about secret cash when he had testified, a few weeks previously, before a federal grand jury in New York City that was investigating the cash contribution to CRP by Robert L. Vesco, an international financier and accused swindler. Vesco's gift of $200,000 in $100 bills was delivered to the committee in a black attaché case. It had been added to the cash fund in Stans' safe, and had helped finance the Watergate operation and other undercover activities.

formal, overdone, alcohol-saturated event, attended by all those with power—or pretensions to power—in the media and the government. It was held on April 14 at the Washington Hilton and Haldeman, Ehrlichman, Kissinger, and the President (who arrived after dinner flanked by a retinue of POWs) were among those who sat through an evening's entertainment that was interspersed with savage Watergate jokes.

Bernstein and Woodward had been invited because they had received two journalism awards. They spent a good part of the evening pretending they had never before met administration aides who had been sources for them. Some had always been difficult to reach and reluctant to talk. Now, a number of them were themselves shut out, and wanted the reporters to tell them what was happening. "What's going on?" "How bad is it?" "What do you think the President should do?" they were asking the reporters.

In the lobby after the dinner, the reporters saw Attorney General Kleindienst holding court. Kleindienst's public statements had been the backbone of the administration's defense of its investigation; Woodward and Bernstein had never had any access to him. They went up to introduce themselves.

"You two follow the courage of your convictions," Kleindienst said.

What's going on? Woodward asked.

"The Watergate case is going to blow up," Kleindienst said simply.

Woodward said that they should talk. What about the next day—Sunday?

"I have to go to church," said Kleindienst.

Bernstein and Woodward said they were anxious to talk.

"Okay," Kleindienst said, "you go to church with me tomorrow morning and afterwards we'll come back to my house and have breakfast."

Some of the news organizations had rented hospitality suites where drinks were served almost to sunrise. Woodward arrived at the *Wall Street Journal*'s party at about 2:00 A.M. About 20 people, glasses in hand, were gathered in one corner, and a familiar voice was ringing out from the center of the circle. "You son of a bitch!" Unmistakably Bradlee. He was arguing with his former employee, now White House aide Ken Clawson. The subject was Clawson's purported statement confessing he had written the Canuck Letter. But the argument ranged over ancient battles—the press versus the government, the *Washington Post* versus Nixon. Clawson had once told friends that Bradlee was the man he most admired. Now he despised Bradlee, and held him personally to blame for the Canuck Letter story.

Fueled by alcohol, the debate grew hotter and more personal. The two men, in dinner clothes, waved away anyone who tried to join in. Finally, in a ridiculous attempt to be more discreet, they moved into a closet, and left the door open.

"Have they hit each other yet?" one woman asked hopefully.

At the bar, there was another Watergate imbroglio. Edward Bennett Williams, the *Post*'s lawyer and the president of the Washington Redskins, President Nixon's favorite football team, was faced off against Patrick J. Buchanan, a White House speechwriter. Williams' firm also represented the Democratic Party. He was speaking bitterly about the 1972 election.

"You're just a sore loser, Ed," Buchanan was saying.

"But you did it dirty, Pat," Williams said, heaving his large body to one side. "You had to do it dirty. You won, but you had to steal it."

"The Watergate's all you had," Buchanan retorted. "Some Cubans going in to look at Larry O'Brien's mail. . . . You blew it out of all proportion."

"Dirty, Pat, dirty election," Williams said. "Aren't you ashamed? You're a conservative, and all this law-breaking. And the *Washington Post* really sticking it to you. Oh, that must have hurt the most." Williams threw his arm around Woodward. "The *Washington Post* just jamming it up your old ass."

"Sixty-one percent, Ed," Buchanan responded. "Sixty-one percent. Just the biggest landslide in recent history, and if it hadn't been for Watergate, it would have been more."

"You did it dirty."

"A little spying, Ed. That's politics. I'll bet you guys had the binoculars on Shula [the Miami Dolphin football coach] at the Super Bowl. You had the glasses out on the other side of the stadium and you didn't even win."

"You won, Pat, all right, and now everyone is seeing how it stinks." Williams faltered slightly, clutching his drink in both hands.

"How about some of your clients, Ed?" Buchanan responded,

referring, possibly, to former Teamster president James Hoffa and ex-Senate aide Bobby Baker. "You've really handled some fine fellows."

"Pat," Williams said, moving in and planting his bulky frame in front of Buchanan, "I'm surprised at you, Pat. There's one big difference—"

"How about some of those crooks you defended?" Buchanan taunted.

"There's a big difference," Williams boomed, "such a big difference." He bent his head, leaned against the bar, and looked up quietly.

"What's this big difference, Ed?"

"I didn't run any of my clients for President."

The next morning, Woodward and Bernstein slept through church and drove out to Virginia to Kleindienst's house for the breakfast they had been promised.

Mrs. Kleindienst opened the door. "He's been called to the White House and can't discuss the Watergate with you," she said. "He went there for services and had to stay for a meeting. He was sorry."

That Sunday afternoon at dusk, Woodward and a friend were sitting on a grassy ridge in Montrose Park in Georgetown. A short distance away, Woodward saw a couple in intense conversation strolling toward them.

"It's Haldeman," Woodward's friend said. It was indeed Haldeman, wearing light-colored sneakers, casual slacks and a tan windbreaker. He walked slowly, his hands in his pockets. His wife, also casually dressed, was speaking to him with obvious emotion and conviction. Haldeman was silent, occasionally turning his head to her. The sun was setting.

Woodward saw a chance to get past the wall. Here, in a public park, with no guards or police or White House limousines waiting. Haldeman looked subdued. Woodward started to rise, wondering if Haldeman would slug him if he introduced himself.

"Leave him alone," Woodward's friend said quietly. The couple walked by, engrossed in private conversation. Woodward didn't move.

Kleindienst called the reporters at their office on Monday morning to apologize for the canceled breakfast. There had been an urgent meeting at the White House, he said cryptically. It would all be out in a few days.

That evening, the *Post*'s night city editor called Woodward at home. The *Los Angeles Times* was predicting on its front page that the White House would make a dramatic Watergate admission in a few days: one or more high-level officials not identified in the story would be named as directing or condoning political espionage and sabotage activities without approval from the President.

Woodward made an emergency call to Deep Throat. The procedure involved making a call from a pre-designated phone booth, saying nothing and then hanging up after 10 seconds. Woodward had to wait for almost an hour by the phone booth before the call was returned.

No meeting was possible that night, Deep Throat said. "You don't have to tell me why you called."

The whole town is going crazy, what's going on? Woodward asked.

"You'd better hang on for this," said Deep Throat. "Dean and Haldeman are out—for sure."

Out? Woodward repeated, dumbfounded.

"Out. They'll resign. There's no way the President can avoid it."

Could the *Post* publish that?

"Yes. It's solid," Deep Throat said.

What should we do? Woodward asked.

"Someone's talking. Several are talking—go find out. I've got to go. I mean it—find out." Deep Throat hung up.

When Woodward arrived in the newsroom at about eleven the next morning, April 17, Bernstein, Sussman, Rosenfeld, Simons and Bradlee were in Bradlee's office trying to figure out what to do next. Bernstein had just talked to a White House official who said the place was chaotic, but that nobody seemed to know what was going to happen, or when.

Woodward rushed into Bradlee's office, blurting out Deep Throat's message. The others were stunned.

It was solid, Woodward said. Deep Throat had been sure. They all realized that the house of cards was crumbling.

"Can we go with it?" Bradlee asked, staring out the window.

Yes, said Woodward. But he was concerned that a story might delay the resignations.

Bernstein worried that a story in the *Post* might even kick the decisions the other way.

Rosenfeld suggested politely that perhaps the reporters and the *Post* as well were overrating their importance. If Dean and Haldeman had to go, the President had more to worry about than whether the *Post* got the satisfaction of reporting it first.

Bradlee was recalling that he had been badly burned on a resignation story once, and the experience had left him with a healthy fear of the whole genre.

"I wrote a cover story for *Newsweek* on J. Edgar Hoover, saying the search was finally under way for his successor at the FBI," he said. "Moyers [Bill D. Moyers, Lyndon Johnson's press secretary] said, 'We've finally got the bastard. Lyndon told me to find his replacement.' So that was the lead, without Moyers' name: 'The search is finally under way for J. Edgar Hoover's successor.' Johnson—the next day, I think—held a press conference at which he appointed Hoover director of the FBI for life. And as he went in before the television cameras, he said to Moyers, 'You call up Ben Bradlee and tell him, "Fuck you." ' Well, for years people said, 'You did it, Bradlee. You did it, you got him appointed for life.' "

Bradlee said he didn't know what to do with this one about Haldeman and Dean. He wanted to go, but he was afraid of it.

A decision became unnecessary for the moment. A news aide brought a piece of wire copy into the room. The President had scheduled an announcement for that afternoon in the White House press room.

The reporters decided Bernstein should go in case the President agreed to answer questions from the floor. He called Ziegler's office —Bernstein didn't have a White House press pass either.

The room was already jammed when he arrived. Bernstein was surprised at what he judged to be a very different attitude among the

White House press corps, old and young. There were a lot of angry people in the room. Gallows humor was the order of the day. The President was running late.

"He's out getting a cocker spaniel and a cloth coat for Pat," said one senior reporter.*

"Nixon's going to waive executive privilege for Manolo and finally throw him to the wolves," said another. Manolo Sanchez was the President's valet.

Somebody theorized that they were about to hear the administration's prison-reform message. "Yeah," replied another, "they're going to move the White House to Leavenworth."

A few members of the press corps, including Helen Thomas of UPI, thought the President was going to announce Bob Haldeman's resignation. An hour passed and the television lights were turned off. Gerry Warren appeared and said the President would be out as soon as possible. Warren looked grim.

There was some discussion as to whether Warren's appearance meant that Ziegler was finished and going to be replaced. If the President admitted any White House involvement in Watergate, someone said, Ziegler deserved to be finished. He deserved to be finished no matter what, someone else added, and there was a good deal of laughter.

Helen Thomas thought the President had become so emotionally wrought at what he was going to have to announce that he couldn't pull himself together to go through with it. That would explain the delay, she said.

Warren appeared again and said it wouldn't be too much longer. The lights went back on.

At 4:40 P.M., Ziegler, looking grimmer than Warren, emerged from the hallway in the West Wing. "Ladies and gentlemen, the President of the United States."

The President was very tanned, but he looked older than his pictures. His hands were shaking, Bernstein noticed.

"On March 21," he said, "as a result of serious charges which came

* The remark referred to Nixon's famous Checkers speech in 1952, when he was running for Vice President. In the speech, he defended his campaign finances and a secret fund.

to my attention, some of which were publicly reported, I began intensive new inquiries into this whole matter. . . . I can report today that
there have been major developments in the case concerning which it
would be improper to be more specific now, except to say that real
progress has been made in finding the truth."

There were to be no resignations that day. Instead, the President
announced that he would suspend "any person in the Executive
Branch or in government" who was indicted in the case.

The President had become the investigator who would see justice
done where others had failed. These were the much reported "major
developments." Nixon had met on Sunday with Attorney General
Kleindienst and Assistant Attorney General Henry E. Petersen "to
review the facts which had come to me in my investigation and also
to review the progress of the Department of Justice investigation." So
that was why Kleindienst couldn't have breakfast on Sunday morning.

Richard Nixon was now also the prosecutor and had expressed "to
the appropriate authorities my view that no individual holding, in
the past or at present, a position of major importance in the administration should be given immunity from prosecution."

The President, reversing his earlier position, was now agreeing
to permit his aides to testify under oath before the Senate Watergate
committee, he said. Though they might still claim executive privilege
on particular questions. John Ehrlichman was working out the details
with the committee.

The President's announcement lasted about three minutes. His
hands did not stop shaking. Most of the time he looked past the
reporters in front of him, his eyes fixed on the television cameras on
a platform at the rear of the room, or on the paper he was reading from.

Then he forced a smile—more like a grimace—and hurried from
the room. Bernstein asked some of the regulars if his hands always
shook like that. Only recently, they said.

The mood in the press room turned ugly after the President left.
The reporters were going to beat and flail Ziegler into submission.

At first Ziegler's resistance was firm. There were no contradictions
between the President's latest statement and what had been said before,
Ziegler insisted. The previous statements from the White House had
been based on "investigations prior to the President's action" and on

"the previous investigation" and on "information available at the time." Now "new information" had led to the latest "standing statement of position."

But the reporters wanted more. On the eighteenth blow, Ziegler yielded.

"This is the operative statement," he said. "The others are inoperative." For a moment, there was a splendid silence.

It was after six when Bernstein returned to the office and began writing. Any story about Haldeman's and Dean's resignations would have to await further confirmation. Ziegler had filled several pages of transcript dodging that question. But Woodward had already written an insert that helped put the President's statement in perspective. He had been told by officials at Justice and the White House that several presidential aides would soon be indicted by the Watergate grand jury—Mitchell, Magruder and Dean were the most likely candidates. They were not named in the story.

When he read the story, Harry Rosenfeld gave Bernstein a good-natured look which said, "You should know better," and crossed out the reference to the President's shaking hands.

The reporters began to search for the exact reasons behind the President's abrupt turnabout. The next morning, April 18, Woodward called a man from CRP and asked him who was talking to the prosecutors.

"Why don't you come over to my office about four this afternoon? I might have something for you," he said.

It was a long, warm walk, not very pleasant because the Metro subway construction had ripped up many of the streets and sidewalks along the way. The sound of jackhammers and piledrivers was deafening. Woodward could still hear the noise outside as he sat in a chair across the desk from the CRP man.

"Magruder is your next McCord," he said. "He went to the prosecutors last Saturday [April 14] and tucked it to Dean and Mitchell."

Woodward was surprised. He had regarded Magruder as a super-loyalist. Things must have been very bad, he said.

"Bad, shit," the man said. "The walls were coming in on him—

walls, ceiling, floor, everything." He threw his arms in front of his face for emphasis.

Woodward asked what Magruder had pinned on Dean and Mitchell.

"The whole mess," the man said, "the bugging plans and the payoff scheme . . . those meetings, or at least one meeting, in Mitchell's office when everything was discussed with Liddy before the bugging."

Woodward took a cab back to the office and called a White House official.

We know Magruder is talking, Woodward said.

"You've got pretty good information, then," the official answered.

How extensive was what Magruder told the prosecutors?

"The works—all the plans for the bugging, the charts, the payoffs . . . This is no hearsay like McCord. It will put Dean and Mitchell in jail."

Woodward called Magruder's lawyer, James J. Bierbower, and told him that the *Post* was aware that his client had gone to the prosecutors.

"Now wait, now wait," Bierbower said, "I'm not even confirming that he is my client."

Woodward said the *Post* was going to report that Magruder had accused Dean and Mitchell on both the bugging and the cover-up.

"I'll call you back in fifteen minutes," Bierbower said.

Half an hour later, he told Woodward, "I will confirm that he will testify before the grand jury when he is called."

Woodward called a Justice Department official and told him what he had.

"That's not all." The official sounded positively cocky. "Other people will testify that Mitchell and Dean were in on the arrangements for the payoffs."

Bernstein reached a White House source who confirmed Deep Throat's information that Haldeman and Dean were finished there. Dean's resignation had already been typed out and Haldeman's was in the works.

Woodward was finishing the first page of the story when Bradlee arrived at his desk. He had brought a sheet of his two-ply paper with him and sat down at a typewriter behind Woodward. Their backs were to each other. Woodward heard Bradlee say something about "the story I've been waiting for." Then Woodward heard the sound of the typewriter. Bradlee's first paragraph was out in about a minute flat and he asked Woodward to turn around and look.

Woodward protested mildly that Bradlee had failed to attribute the story to any sources. It read as if Magruder's allegations had come from nowhere and landed in the *Post*'s lap.

Bradlee was undeterred. "You can do that later," he said, and started typing again. By the end of the third paragraph, he had more or less solved the attribution problem and filled the two-ply.

Except for titles, middle names and initials, the three-paragraph lead was Bradlee's.

> Former Attorney General John N. Mitchell and White House Counsel John W. Dean III approved and helped plan the Watergate bugging operation, according to President Nixon's former special assistant, Jeb Stuart Magruder.
>
> Mitchell and Dean later arranged to buy the silence of the seven convicted Watergate conspirators, Magruder has also said.
>
> Magruder, the deputy campaign manager for the President, made these statements to federal prosecutors Saturday, according to three sources in the White House and the Committee for the Re-election of the President.

The entire story filled half of the front page, the most space ever devoted to a single Watergate story.

The New York Times edition for the same day, April 19, carried a five-column headline on Watergate. Attorney General Kleindienst had disqualified himself from handling the case because of "persistent reports" that three or more of his colleagues would be indicted. Sy Hersh had written that the grand-jury inquiry had shifted emphasis from the Watergate bugging itself to the obstruction of justice by administration officials thought to be involved in the cover-up. John Dean was said to be ready to implicate others, if indicted.

That morning, Bernstein called Dean's office. Dean's secretary was crying. She didn't know where her boss was, or if he worked at the White House any more. She gave Bernstein the names of several friends and associates of Dean's who might be helpful. All were unreachable.

15

IN THE LATE MORNING, when Dean's secretary had regained her composure, she called back and read Bernstein a statement that had been issued in Dean's name.

> To date I have refrained from making any public comment whatsoever about the Watergate case. I shall continue that policy in the future. . . . It is my hope, however, that those truly interested in seeing . . . that justice is done will be careful in drawing any conclusions as to the guilt or involvement of any person. . . . Finally, some may hope or think that I will become a scapegoat in the Watergate case. Anyone who believes this does not know me, know the true facts, nor understand our system of justice.

Bernstein read the statement twice. A threatening, defiant John Dean was something new. He called the White House press office to check the statement. The White House would have no comment on "unauthorized" statements by John Dean.

The *Post*'s White House reporter, Carroll Kilpatrick, called Bernstein from the White House press room. Ziegler, in his daily news conference, had made no effort to defend Dean. The President's counsel was "in his office . . . attending to business of some sort." The President was searching "for the truth, not scapegoats."

Bernstein reached a friend of Dean's whom he had talked to once before. Their previous conversation, brief and unfriendly, seemed forgotten. Now, Bernstein was told: "The truth of the matter is fairly long and broad and it goes up and down, higher and lower. You can't make a case that . . . this was just John Mitchell and John Dean. If Jeb's saying John Dean had prior knowledge of the bugging, John has a different story. John welcomes the opportunity to tell his side of the story to the grand jury. He's not going to go down in flames for the activities of others."

The friend would not say which others. But the message, loud and clear, confirmed that those who had once served Richard Nixon as one, and had forged the superstructure of rigid White House discipline and self-control, were in open warfare with one another.

Bernstein reached one of the associates suggested by Dean's secretary. The man sounded cordial when Bernstein introduced himself. Bernstein decided to make a proposal:

The *Post* had been very rough on John Dean, he said, but the facts had justified it. Now the case was blowing wide open. Dean had been in a unique position to understand the whole of Watergate. Others in and out of the White House were obviously gunning for him—Ziegler today and Magruder yesterday—and would try to discredit Dean before he could do them any more damage. If the *Post* knew what Dean had to say—if he would talk to the reporters, and if they thought he was telling the truth—the paper could foil the attacks. But only with facts. The reporters had enough sources to check out his allegations and substantiate them. It could work to Dean's advantage. Unless he lied.

The associate said that Dean respected the *Post*'s Watergate coverage. Just what they needed, Bernstein thought, an endorsement from John Dean.

Dean "doesn't think you've been unfair to him. There's no reason for him to take it personally. Hell, he didn't take a step without somebody telling him what to do in this thing. He didn't make the decision to try to beat you. He was against it. He'd like nothing better than to sit down with you and tell you the whole story. But that's not what he needs now. If he ever testifies, he has to be able to say under oath that he did not talk to the press first. That doesn't mean that you and I can't do a little visiting with each other. After you check out a few things and there gets to be some trust built up both ways, we'll both know better where we're going."

Not knowing what to expect, Bernstein asked where he should begin.

"You might start with the P's statement," the associate said. (It took Bernstein a moment to realize that "the P" was the President.) "Find out what happened on March 21—who it was that brought all those 'serious charges' to the P's attention."

John Dean?

"Well, I'm not saying who it was, but your thinking is on the right track. Check it out. It sure wasn't John Ehrlichman who walked into the Oval Office that day and said, in effect, 'There has been a cover-up and it's worse than you think it is, Mr. President.' That would be a pretty good reason to make somebody a scapegoat if you were, say, H, wouldn't you think?"

Haldeman?

"And others. From June 17 on, John Dean never did a thing unless H or somebody else told him first to do it—including the arrangements for hush money."

Who else?

"Let's see how you do with checking this out first."

What about before June 17?

"John Dean would tell the grand jury that, yes, he went to a meeting at which the bugging was discussed, and that he said he wouldn't have anything to do with it, and that he said anybody else who did was crazy."

John Dean seemed to have answers for everything. If Dean had been at that meeting, how did he explain the "Dean Report"? And the President's assurance that Dean and his report had convinced the President that his close aides did not have advance knowledge of the bugging?

"The so-called report of the investigation was more or less whole-cloth—a concept, or a theory, that was passed on to the P."

By whom?

"Not John Dean. He had never even discussed Watergate with the P as of August 29."

Then what was the report?

"God damn, I thought you guys were supposed to be smart," he laughed. "There never was a report. Dean was asked to gather certain facts. The facts got twisted around to help some other people above him. Now those people plan to cut their losses and shore up by implicating John Mitchell and John Dean. It's wishful thinking on their part if they think they can get away with that."

Why didn't Dean go public right away, if he was so interested in the truth?

"One, because nobody would believe him if he walked out today and said everything he knows. This didn't start with Watergate. It was a way of life at the White House. He's got to establish gradually that he's reliable, that he won't lie. Because he knows things that nobody else is ever going to talk about willingly. Almost everything can be checked out. But before he goes public, he's got to convince everybody —the prosecutors, the press and Senator Sam's people on the Hill— that he's telling the truth. Otherwise the White House will cut his balls off before he has a chance."

Which was why John Dean was willing to do business with the *Washington Post,* correct?

"Look, you asked me the right questions and I gave you some leads. The *Washington Post* isn't about to go out on a limb for John Dean. Check it out and we'll visit again tomorrow."

Bernstein didn't know what to think. Of all the Watergate principals, he probably had the least regard for John Dean. At least John Mitchell was his own man. Colson's intellect was first-rate, somebody to respect at the poker table, regardless of what you thought of him. Haldeman was an enigma, sometimes brilliant, often pitifully shortsighted, often cruel, sometimes appealingly human. But Dean had not seemed to have any substance, a WASP Sammy Glick who hadn't even been very imaginative about the way he climbed to the top. On the other hand, Dean would be the kind Haldeman would rely on and then cut loose. He had to know a lot.

Bernstein called back Dean's associate. What he was going to ask was unusual, but it might be a good test of how straightforward the man was going to be. Bernstein asked him why he should trust him— who his friends were, whom he had worked with, his politics, how he had come to know John Dean, why he was convinced Dean was telling the truth, who didn't like him, and even what he did in his spare time.

They talked for more than half an hour, and Bernstein found himself answering a few questions about himself. The man sounded like somebody he would like. And, it developed, they had a mutual acquaintance, somebody whose judgment Bernstein respected.

He called the acquaintance. John Dean's friend came very highly recommended, especially with regard to honesty and trustworthiness.

Behaving like a Scoutmaster had left Bernstein feeling a little preposterous, but relieved. If Woodward or he could now find someone else to whom Dean had made the same allegations, they could write the story.

Woodward called the man from CRP.

Not only had Dean told him all the same things, but he had firsthand knowledge of some of the allegations. "There never was any 'investigation' by the President until John Dean told him everything that day [March 21]," he said. Dean had been "just a runner" in the cover-up. There was virtually nothing about the cover-up, including the payments to the conspirators, which Haldeman hadn't approved. And Dean wanted to tell everything to the grand jury if he could arrange a deal with the prosecutors.

Bernstein called the first friend of Dean's he had talked to briefly earlier that afternoon. Dean had told him the same story.

Bradlee was uneasy about printing allegations that Dean wasn't willing to make publicly or confirm personally. The reporters, with help from Rosenfeld and Sussman, tried to convince him that they were too important to ignore. Dean's "scapegoat" statement made little sense otherwise. They recounted the precautions they had taken.

But Bradlee's final decision was based primarily on something they had all forgotten about: Deep Throat's call to Woodward. If Haldeman was out, said Bradlee, he had to be in so much trouble that the President could no longer afford to protect him.

"Okay," he said.

The same morning the *Post* reported John Dean's charges, the headline in the *New York Times* signaled that John Mitchell's blithe dismissals of his own complicity had ended. Only a few days earlier, when Jeb Magruder's allegations had appeared in the *Post*, Mitchell had said: "This gets a little sillier as it goes along, doesn't it? I've had a good night's sleep and haven't heard any of this nonsense." Now the *Times* reported, Mitchell had told "friends" that in three meetings during 1972 he had listened to proposals to bug the Democrats and had rejected the plans on each occasion. Dean, too, had rejected the idea, Mitchell had told these "friends." But he had his doubts about Jeb Magruder.

For reporters, the new game in town was to find an "associate" or "friend" of a Watergate player who would anonymously disclose his principal's version of events. That morning, Bernstein reached a Mitchell "associate" who confirmed the *Times* account. Mitchell was due to appear before the Watergate grand jury at 12:30 P.M. Bernstein asked about his state of mind.

"For a ruined man, he's holding up very well," the associate said. "He's resigned to the likelihood that he's going to jail. He can't go out because of the press, that's the main problem. He just sits in the apartment all day watching television or working on his defense. He hits the sauce every once in a while, but nothing serious. He's still got all his marbles. Martha yells at him all day long that he ought to take every damn one of them down, including Nixon. Anything he knows about the President being involved, though, he's keeping to himself. He says the answer is no. But that would be his answer regardless. He's too proud to even call Nixon, much less ask him for help or advice. 'That's for Haldeman and Ehrlichman to do,' he says. He'll stay loyal, no matter what it costs him, or how much he hates the others."

Which others?

"Ehrlichman more than anybody. Haldeman. And Colson, too, but that's a little different. He thinks Colson's crazy, all those insane schemes to booby-trap anybody that shows up on the six-o'clock news criticizing Nixon.

"Ehrlichman and Haldeman he hates for different reasons and a lot more. He thinks they ruined the President, poisoned his mind, especially Ehrlichman. A lot of it's personal because they shut him off from Nixon. He maintains they were out to get him for months and that Watergate was just the excuse they were waiting for, plus Martha. Somehow Pat [Nixon] got in on the act, too, he says, back in January or so when she smelled liquor on his breath at a ceremony. Hans and Fritz [Haldeman and Ehrlichman] got wind of it, and all three were jumping on the poor guy's back, telling the President he had to go."

Mitchell, grayer and thinner, left the grand-jury room shortly after three o'clock and met outside the federal courthouse with reporters.

For the first time, he publicly acknowledged attending meetings at which plans to bug the Democrats were discussed when he was Attorney General. "I have heard discussion of such plans. They've always been cut off by me at all times, and I would like to know who it was that kept bringing them back and back. . . . The electronic surveillance was turned down, and turned down, and that was disposed of." He had approved "an entire intelligence-gathering program" aimed at obtaining "every bit of information that you could about the opposing candidates and their operations." Through wiretapping? he was asked again. "No, no, no, no. Wiretapping is illegal, as you know, and we certainly were not authorizing any illegal activities."

Woodward called another Mitchell associate whom he knew to be reliable. The man said Mitchell had told the grand jury that he approved paying the seven original Watergate conspirators with CRP funds. But he had insisted under oath that the money was intended to pay the conspirators' legal fees, not to buy their silence. He had testified that he vetoed the bugging proposal for the third and final time during a meeting with Magruder in Key Biscayne. He believed Magruder had gone over his head and obtained approval for the Watergate operation from somebody at the White House.

Who?

"He thinks it was Colson, but he didn't mention any names to the grand jury. He's got no hard evidence."

Bernstein was still in pursuit of Dean. Dean's associate said over the phone that Dean had squirreled away "documentary evidence" which would, among other things, establish the involvement of his superiors in both the bugging and the cover-up. "Up to now, John Dean has been a true-blue soldier for the White House, and now the White House has decided they can send him up the river for being a good soldier. Well, he's going to take some lieutenants and captains with him."

A lawyer involved in the case told Bernstein he had seen Chuck Colson in the U.S. Attorney's office that afternoon, a Friday. Woodward was able to establish that Colson had turned over documents from his files implicating John Dean in the cover-up. Things were happening fast. Bernstein was handed Jack Anderson's latest Sunday column. Anderson was getting grand-jury transcripts and printing excerpts verbatim. Gordon Strachan, Haldeman's political aide, had testified that, immediately after the election, Haldeman had ordered him to turn over to Fred LaRue $350,000 in CRP funds—which had been kept in a Virginia bank safe deposit box since April.

Now Woodward found a LaRue "associate." It was payoff money, the associate said, added to the original $80,000 which LaRue had received from Sloan and funneled to the conspirators. A Justice Department official confirmed to Bernstein that the grand jury was operating under the assumption that both the $350,000 and $80,000 bundles, in $100 bills, had been used to pay off the conspirators.

Haldeman had been cornered outside his house by ABC and asked to confirm or deny reports that he would resign.

"I can deny them," he said.

Flatly?

"Yes, sir, uh-huh."

Returning a phone call from the night before, a mid-level White House official described the situation there to Woodward—old loyalties shattered, little work getting done, confusion about who on the staff might be indicted, who ordered what and who ordered whom, who would resign and who would be saved. "It's every man for himself—get a lawyer and blame everyone else."

The President had met with his Cabinet. "We've had our Cambodias before," he said. Then, accompanied only by Ziegler, he flew off to Key Biscayne.

Bernstein and Woodward wanted to catch up on some sleep, and on Sunday neither arrived at the office until early afternoon. The newsroom was quiet, with only a dozen or so reporters there. It was relaxing. They read the Sunday papers. Hersh, too, had the grand jury looking into the Haldeman-Strachan-LaRue transfer, as well as the possibility that Haldeman had received wiretap transcripts. They had written about the latest charge by Dean's associate—that Ehrlichman was involved in the cover-up ("E was the action officer, not H," he had said). Haldeman and Ehrlichman had hired the same lawyer, who was also meeting with the President. News that would have occasioned banner headlines a few weeks ago was now simply mentioned within a larger story: Gordon Strachan had testified that Haldeman had approved the hiring of Donald Segretti. They had written a single paragraph on it.

The reporters began calling around town, looking for associates of the three principal characters as yet unheard from: Colson, Haldeman and Ehrlichman. Woodward found a Colson surrogate who sounded eager to talk. He was worried. "John Dean got to Sam Ervin and the prosecutors on roller skates and tried to do a number on us. Among other things, he said he would deliver on Colson—if they come across with immunity."

What did Dean tell them about Colson? asked Woodward.

"Who knows? I'm not so dumb that I think I'm going to convince you that Chuck Colson is a virgin. He's no saint and that place isn't the Sistine Chapel. But my man doesn't break the law."

Instead of covering up on Watergate, he insisted, Colson had tried to find the truth. Then he had sounded the alarm.

"Colson went right in to the President as early as December and laid it on the line—warned Richard Nixon that some of his people were part of Watergate in a big way and had an organized cover-up going. He warned Nixon about Dean and Mitchell. The President said, 'The man [Mitchell] has denied it to me; give me some evidence.' And there are two other people who went to Tricky and said, 'Cut yourself off from Dean and Mitchell.' Tricky wouldn't budge. . . . It's too fucking bad if it makes the President look bad. He was told that John Dean and John Mitchell were betraying him."

Woodward called a White House source. On at least three different occasions that winter Colson had told the President that he should "get rid of some people" because they were involved in Watergate. So had others. Most of the warnings focused on Dean and Mitchell, the source said.

Woodward called Colson. He denied "warning" the President about Dean or Mitchell or about a cover-up.

What, then, had he told the President on the subject?

"I will not discuss private communications between myself and the President," Colson said. "Not with anyone—you, the press in general, with the grand jury or the Senate committee."

A few minutes later, Woodward received a call from a second Colson associate. "Don't pay any attention to Chuck's denial," he advised. He, too, confirmed that Colson had explicitly told the President there was evidence that his men were involved in both the bugging and the cover-up. The associate said there were two reasons for Colson's denial: to avoid acknowledging that the President was forewarned, and the fear that John Dean might "retaliate" by implicating Colson before the grand jury.

The White House had no comment on that Monday's lead story in the *Post:* "Nixon Alerted to Cover-up in December."

The next Thursday, April 26, Bernstein made his daily call to John Dean's principal associate early in the afternoon. Bernstein again raised the question of what had happened between Dean's meeting with the President on March 21 and the President's announcement on April 17.

"I think we lost the highest-stakes poker game in the city's history," the associate said.

Bernstein guessed out loud that the President had thrown in his chips with Haldeman and Ehrlichman against John Dean.

"It looks that way now. But nobody will tell him anything for sure. He's like a prisoner. . . . For a while, John was feeling very high because he felt they were all going to do the right thing. It was his understanding that an agreement had been reached. Then it collapsed because the German shepherds said they didn't think they had to go to the doghouse with John Dean."

Haldeman and Ehrlichman didn't think . . . ?

". . . that they had to be indicted to save the situation."

What exactly had Dean told the President on the 21st?

"John went in and said, 'Mr. President, there is a cancer eating away at this office and it has to be removed. To save the Presidency, Haldeman and Ehrlichman and I are going to have to tell everything to the prosecutors and face the consequences of going to jail.' That was the gist of it. The President sat down in his chair stunned, like somebody had hit him in the head with a rock."

Then what happened?

"He told him everything—even gave him a list of who would probably have to go to jail. It was a very long list. John told him that the shepherds had known the whole story since the beginning, that he kept them informed of everything there was to know and carried out their orders, and that, from the beginning, they had told John not to discuss anything with the President, that they would handle that end of it."

What was the President's reaction?

"Mostly he listened. Then he told John that he must be under a lot of strain. So he sent him up to the Mountaintop to put his thoughts in order and get it all down on paper. . . . John came down from Camp David expecting that everybody would stand up and say, 'Yes, we were responsible and the President knew nothing about this. We are prepared to accept the consequences and will cooperate with the grand jury investigation.'

"But when John got back to the White House, it became obvious that the President had been persuaded by the German shepherds to keep his losses to a minimum . . . to sacrifice John Dean while trying to discourage the indictment of Haldeman and Ehrlichman. Instead of agreeing to cooperate, they are still telling the P that John should walk the plank for all of them. The P is ready to give John the final shove."

Bernstein asked if Dean now believed the President was involved in the cover-up himself.

"See what other people say about this first," he replied. "Then we can visit again."

Woodward called his man from CRP. "Dean said in March he wanted to blow this up. Dean has attempted to be honest, but he was taking orders from Haldeman and Ehrlichman. Honesty and following orders were inconsistent, so Dean broke ranks."

The reporters began another round of calls to the White House. Dean's version of the events since March 21 was surprisingly easy to confirm. The grip of fear that Haldeman and Ehrlichman had once exercised seemed to have been broken. Haldeman and Ehrlichman had acknowledged to certain of their colleagues in the White House that they had authorized widespread undercover activities and knew of payments to the convicted conspirators but maintained that they had never specifically approved or ordered anything illegal.

About 7:45 that night, Woodward got a call from a Capitol Hill source with an even bigger story: The *New York Daily News* would be on the streets in a few minutes, he said, saying that Acting FBI Director Gray had destroyed documents taken from Howard Hunt's White House safe. The documents reportedly destroyed had been in two folders. One contained bogus State Department cables fabricated by Hunt to implicate President John F. Kennedy in the 1963 assassination of South Vietnam President Ngo Dinh Diem. The second was a dossier stuffed with information collected by Hunt on Senator Edward Kennedy. The source said the *News* story was accurate.

Woodward called a Senate aide on the Watergate committee. He confirmed the *News* account. John Dean had told Assistant Attorney General Henry Petersen about it 10 days before.

About 9:30, the phone at Woodward's desk rang. "Give me a number to call you on," Deep Throat said.

Woodward gave him the number of one of the main city-desk lines. The call came at once.

"You've heard the Gray story?" Deep Throat asked. "Well it's true. On June 28, in a meeting with Ehrlichman and Dean, Gray was told the files were—quote—'political dynamite' and should—quote—'never see the light of day.' He was told, quote, 'they could do more damage than the Watergate bugging itself.' In fact, Ehrlichman had told Dean earlier in the day, 'You go across the river every day, John. Why don't you drop the goddamn fucking things in the river?' Gray kept the files for about a week and then he says he threw them in a burn bag in his office. He says that he was not exactly told to destroy the files, but understood it was absolutely clear what Dean and Ehrlichman wanted."*

Bernstein reached Dean's associate.

"You ever hear the expression 'Deep Six'?" he asked. "That's what Ehrlichman said he wanted done with those files."

The story was solid. Howard Simons ordered the front page remade for the second edition.

Bernstein was more shaken by all this than by anything since June 17. It was the language and the context of Ehrlichman's remark to Dean that troubled him. Just as if they were a couple of Mafiosi talking to each other in a restaurant, the President's number-two assistant had said to the President's *consigliere: Hey, Joe, we gotta dump this stuff in the river before the boss gets hurt.*

Howard Simons slouched in a chair, drawing deeply on a cigarette,

---

* Before the Senate Watergate committee, Gray corrected this. He said then that he had kept the files at his Connecticut home for nearly six months, and had burned them with the Christmas trash in December 1972.

the color gone from his face. "A director of the FBI destroying evidence? I never thought it could happen," he said quietly.

In the late afternoon of April 27, Bernstein and Woodward were called over by one of the editors to look at a story that had just come across the Associated Press wire as a bulletin.

It was another Watergate. In Los Angeles, at the trial of Daniel Ellsberg, Judge Matthew Byrne had announced that he had learned from the Watergate prosecutors that Hunt and Liddy supervised the burglary of the office of Ellsberg's psychiatrist in 1971.

Bernstein reached John Dean's associate for their daily conversation.

"Carl, how do you think they learned about that little bag job on the coast?" the associate asked.

Dean again?

"You ask the prosecutors who told them about that. . . . John's got some stories to tell. Ask them about his credibility. Everything he's told them has checked out . . . and there is still a lot more he hasn't told them yet that they want to know about. Don't forget: John Dean was over there at the White House a long time, and there were lots of projects. John has knowledge of illegal activities that go way back."

How far back?

"Way back . . . to the beginning."

More wiretapping?

"I wouldn't challenge that assumption."

Burglaries?

"Would you keep a squad of burglars around the house for years if you only wanted them for one or two jobs? . . . H and E are upset about what has come out so far. There are documents . . ."

About burglaries?

"About a lot of things. You might think about the story of Patrick Gray destroying those documents. There is only one way this whole story will ever come out. . . . You didn't see E run down to the prosecutors and tell how he broke the law. Has H been down there? I don't expect the P to walk down Pennsylvania Avenue to the courthouse. That leaves one person. John Dean again. . . . We are laying a foundation to protect ourselves.

"Haldeman and Ehrlichman have been trying to get John to take a dive and convince the P that he should save their skins and blame it all on John. The P has agreed."

Is Dean going to implicate the P?

"There were lots of meetings. . . . The P was there. The cover-up was being discussed."

The next evening, Woodward went to the White House. He had asked a senior presidential aide for an interview to talk about John Dean. Woodward sat in one of the colorfully decorated offices in the old Executive Office Building and drank coffee out of a cup bearing the Presidential Seal.

Haldeman and Ehrlichman were finished, the man said.

And, yes, it was coming. John Dean was going to implicate the President in the cover-up. The aide had a pained expression on his face.

What did Dean have?

"I'm not sure. I'm not sure it is evidence. . . . The President's former lawyer is going to say that the President is . . . well, a felon." The man's face trembled. He asked Woodward to leave.

16

AT THE OFFICE, Bernstein and Woodward discussed the statements of both men. They were convinced that Dean was going to implicate the President. Bradlee and Simons thought it would be premature to print that. They wanted specifics, a look at the documents Dean supposedly had, Dean's recollections of conversations with the President himself—something that would enable them to evaluate whether Dean was telling the truth.

Instead of the Dean story on the President, the reporters put together a Sunday story which said that senior White House aides had concluded that Haldeman and Ehrlichman were involved in the cover-up.

The next morning, April 30, word came in slowly. There was a phone call from Capitol Hill. Then, a tentative confirmation from a reporter at the White House. Bradlee came out of his office to tell Woodward: It's happening today. Four of them: Haldeman and Ehrlichman have resigned; Dean has been fired; Kleindienst has also resigned. Elliot Richardson is moving over from the Defense Department to become Attorney General. Bernstein came in a few minutes later and Simons told him the news. He went to his desk and sat down. James McCartney, a national correspondent for Knight Newspapers who happened to be in the office writing an article on the *Post* for the *Columbia Journalism Review,* came over and wanted to talk to Bernstein. Bernstein said he didn't want to talk just then.

Just before noon, the White House made an announcement, and

the resignation letters arrived in the office and were Xeroxed. That made it real. The Haldeman letter referred to "various allegations and innuendoes" and "the flood of stories" which made it "virtually impossible under these circumstances for me to carry on my regular responsibilities in the White House." Ehrlichman said that "regardless of the actual facts, I have been a target of public attack . . . repeated rumor, unfounded charges or implications and whatever else the media carries."

McCartney's article, which appeared in the July-August 1973 issue of the *Columbia Journalism Review,* recorded Bradlee's reaction to the official news:

> It was 11:55 A.M. on April 30, and Benjamin Crowninshield Bradlee, 51, executive editor of the *Washington Post,* chatted with a visitor, feet on the desk, idly attempting to toss a plastic toy basketball through a hoop mounted on an office window 12 feet away. The inevitable subject of conversation: Watergate. Howard Simons, the *Post*'s managing editor, slipped into the room to interrupt: "Nixon has accepted the resignations of Ehrlichman and Haldeman and Dean," he said. "Kleindienst is out and Richardson is the new attorney general."
>
> For a split second, Ben Bradlee's mouth dropped open with an expression of sheer delight. Then he put one cheek on the desk, eyes closed and banged the desk repeatedly with his right fist. In a moment he recovered. "How do you like them apples?" he said to the grinning Simons. "Not a bad start."
>
> Bradlee couldn't restrain himself. He strode into the *Post*'s vast fifth-floor newsroom and shouted across rows of desks to . . . Woodward . . . "Not bad, Bob! Not half bad!" Howard Simons interjected a note of caution: "Don't gloat," he murmured, as *Post* staff members began to gather around. "We can't afford to gloat!"

Bradlee came through the city room, whooping. "Never," he kept saying. "Never, never, never, never." Bernstein and Woodward sat at the desks. Woodward suggested they take a walk.

That night at nine, the President addressed the nation on network television. Bernstein and Woodward went into Howard Simons' office to watch the speech with him and Mrs. Graham.

"The President of the United States," the announcer said solemnly.

Nixon sat at his desk, a picture of his family on one side, a bust of Abraham Lincoln on the other.

"Oh, my God," Mrs. Graham said. "This is too much."

The President began to speak: "I want to talk to you tonight from my heart. . . . There had been an effort to conceal the facts both from the public, from you, and from me. . . . I wanted to be fair. . . . Today, in one of the most difficult decisions of my Presidency, I accepted the resignations of two of my closest associates. . . . Bob Haldeman and John Ehrlichman—two of the finest public servants it has been my privilege to know. . . . The easiest course would be for me to blame those to whom I delegated the responsibility to run the campaign. But that would be a cowardly thing to do. . . . In any organization, the man at the top must bear the responsibility. That responsibility, therefore, belongs here in this office. I accept it. . . . It was the system that has brought the facts to light . . . a system that in this case has included a determined grand jury, honest prosecutors, a courageous judge, John Sirica, and a vigorous free press. . . . I must now turn my full attention once again to the larger duties of this office. I owe it to this great office that I hold, and I owe it to you—to our country.

". . . There can be no whitewash at the White House. . . . Two wrongs do not make a right. . . . I love America. . . . God bless America and God bless each and every one of you."

The day after the President's April 30 speech, Bernstein was at his desk reading the *New York Times* and the *Washington Star*. A copy aide dropped a UPI wire story:

> White House Press Secretary Ronald Ziegler publicly apologized today to the *Washington Post* and two of its reporters for his earlier criticism of their investigative reporting of the Watergate conspiracy.
>
> At the White House briefing, a reporter asked Ziegler if the White House didn't owe the *Post* an apology.
>
> "In thinking of it all at this point in time, yes," Ziegler said, "I would apologize to the *Post,* and I would apologize to Mr. Woodward and Mr. Bernstein. . . . We would all have to say that mistakes were made in terms of comments. I was over enthusiastic in my comments about the *Post,* particularly if you look at them in the context of developments that have taken place. . . . When we are wrong, we are wrong, as we were in that case."

As Ziegler finished he started to say, "But . . . " He was cut off by a reporter who said: "Now don't take it back, Ron."

Bernstein took the copy and laid it on Woodward's desk. Later, Woodward called Ziegler at the White House to thank him.

"We all have our jobs," Ziegler replied.

Bernstein and Woodward had been sitting on the Dean story for a week; they had not been able to develop information on exactly what Dean was going to say about the President's involvement in the cover-up. On Saturday, May 5, they had just finished writing a story about the mood of uncertainty and lack of morale in the White House when a long teletype message came from the wire room. It was a press release from *Newsweek*. Woodward assumed the worst—the news magazines put out a press release on Saturday night only when they had an exceptionally important story.

The *Newsweek* story said that Dean was prepared to describe two incidents in the previous year that led him to conclude that Nixon knew about the Watergate cover-up. The first was in September 1972, after the Watergate indictments had been returned, and they had gone no higher than Liddy. Dean was summoned to the Oval Office by Haldeman and found the President and his chief of staff "all grins." Dean quoted the President as saying, "Good job, John, Bob told me what a great job you've been doing." The second occurred in December, Dean alleged, when Ehrlichman told him the President had, in effect, approved executive clemency for Howard Hunt.

Simons, Rosenfeld, Sussman and Woodward gathered around Woodward's desk. Bernstein was out of town. Woodward said that he thought he could confirm the story easily. He called a senior White House aide. Reluctantly, the aide said that Dean had given substantially the same account to him. A little later, a senior Senate committee aide told him, "That's Dean's story, or part of it."

The disclosure that Hunt and Liddy had supervised the burglary of Daniel Ellsberg's psychiatrist's office had inextricably linked Watergate and the Ellsberg trial in Los Angeles. In the newsroom, the two stories were often referred to as Watergate East and Watergate West. In early May, Bernstein and Woodward decided to go with a story saying that two *New York Times* reporters' telephones had been wiretapped as part of the investigation of the Pentagon Papers leak. Months before, Deep Throat had told Woodward their names—Neil Sheehan and Hedrick Smith—but, even now, the reporters could not find a second source, so the names weren't used. They did find, however, that there was a possibility that Ellsberg had been overheard on a tap. That figured, since Ellsberg had leaked the papers to Sheehan.

At Ellsberg's trial, the prosecution was insisting there were no taps involving Ellsberg. Now Judge Matthew Byrne asked the government to search its records again for evidence that Ellsberg might have been overheard on any wiretap.

The new acting FBI director, William D. Ruckelshaus, found one. The logs were missing, but Ruckelshaus had been told by his aides that Ellsberg had been overheard at least once—not on Sheehan's phone, as it turned out, but on the home telephone of Morton Halperin, a former member of the National Security Council staff of Dr. Henry Kissinger. Ruckelshaus' announcement that Halperin's phone had been tapped for 21 months was the first confirmation that the administration had used wiretaps to investigate news leaks. Moreover, it established that the government had illegally failed to disclose all its wiretap information to Ellsberg's defense attorneys.

Several days later, on May 11, Judge Byrne dismissed all the charges against Ellsberg. Government misconduct, he stated, had "incurably infected the prosecution."

The next Monday, May 14, Ruckelshaus announced that, as part of the administration's search for news leaks, 17 wiretaps in all had been ordered in 1969–71. The missing logs had been located; they had been in John Ehrlichman's safe in his White House office. Ruckelshaus did not disclose the names of the 13 government officials and four reporters whose phones had been tapped. The question was—who had authorized it?

Woodward placed a direct call to a top FBI official. The official was not oblique: some of the wiretap authorizations had come to the FBI either orally or by letter from Henry Kissinger.

Incredulous, Woodward called a former FBI man.

"I know Kissinger gave some authorizations," he said.

The White House switchboard put Woodward directly through to Kissinger's office. It was about 6:00 P.M.

"Hello," the familiar voice said in a heavy German accent.

Woodward explained that they had information from two FBI sources that Kissinger had authorized the taps on his own aides.

Kissinger paused. "It could be Mr. Haldeman who authorized the taps," he said.

How about Kissinger? Woodward asked.

"I don't believe it was true," he stated.

Is that a denial?

A pause. "I frankly don't remember." He might have provided the FBI with the names of individuals who had seen or handled various documents which had been leaked. "It is quite possible that they [the FBI] construed this as an authorization. . . . In possible individual cases it is possible that I pointed out who handled what document to my deputy [General Alexander Haig], who in turn would have passed on the information to the FBI."

Woodward said that two sources had specified that Kissinger had *personally* authorized the taps.

A brief pause. "Almost never," he said.

Woodward suggested that "almost never" meant "sometimes." Was Kissinger then confirming the story?

Kissinger raised his voice angrily. "I don't have to submit to police interrogation about this," he said. Calming down, he went on, "If it is possible, and if it happened, then I have to take responsibility for it. . . . I'm responsible for this office."

Did you do it? Woodward asked.

"You aren't quoting me?" Kissinger asked.

Sure he was, Woodward said.

"What!" Kissinger shouted. "I'm telling you what I said was for background."

Woodward said they had made no such agreement.

"I've tried to be honest and now you're going to penalize me," Kissinger said.

No penalty intended, Woodward said, but he could not accept retroactive background.

"In five years in Washington," Kissinger said sharply, "I've never been trapped into talking like this."

Woodward wondered what kind of treatment Kissinger was accustomed to get from reporters.

Kissinger had an effective way of moving back and forth from anger to tranquility. "I talked in order to be helpful," he said next. And then, angrily, "What conceivable motive would I have had in granting you an interview?"

Woodward said that he would check with the *Post*'s diplomatic reporters to see if different rules about background and on-the-record conversations were observed.

"You've totally violated any procedure I've ever had with any reporter," Kissinger announced, and said goodbye.

Woodward consulted Murrey Marder, the *Post*'s chief diplomatic reporter. Did reporters usually allow Kissinger to determine, after an interview, whether it was going to be on the record, off the record or only for background.

Well, yes and no, Marder said. Technically, Woodward was right, but most reporters who covered Kissinger regularly let "Henry" place statements on background after the conversation. Half an hour later, Marder came by Woodward's desk to say that Henry had called him to complain bitterly about his interview with Woodward. Marder, Bernstein and Woodward went into Howard Simons' office to discuss what had happened.

Marder took a middle line, joking, "Henry may blame the collapse of Paris negotiations on us."

Simons' phone rang. He picked it up, gave a few grunts and switched the call to the speaker phone so everyone could hear.

"Tell the assembled multitude, Bennie," Simons said.

It was Bradlee, speaking from his home in a stiff German accent. "What are you guys doing?" he asked. "I just got a call from Henry. He's mad."

Simons explained.

"You decide what to do," Bradlee said. "I'll play reporter and read you what Henry said and you can use it if it will help."

Simons smiled. "Is it on background?"

Kissinger, moving up the line from Marder to Bradlee, was doing what is known in diplomatic circles as "hardening your position." His statement to Bradlee was that it was "almost inconceivable" that he could have authorized the wiretapping.

"Almost inconceivable" is not a denial, Woodward noted, and argued for the story.

But it was nearly eight, too late for the first editions. Simons decided to hold it a day.

Woodward was angry. He felt the editors had waffled on the story because of Kissinger's position. Bernstein disagreed. The information from the FBI sources had come so easily—perhaps they were part of an effort to shift responsibility from Haldeman and Ehrlichman to Kissinger. It was worth waiting a day to find out.

As it turned out, though, the story could not wait a day. Sy Hersh had it. A day later, he wrote in the *Times* that Kissinger had played a role in fingering some of his aides as possible leaks. Marder did the story for the *Post* a day after that.

Nearly everyone at the *Post* involved in reporting Watergate had reached a state of perpetual exhaustion. No one had been enthusiastic about a somewhat ambiguous story that would take a whole evening to coordinate and write.

On May 17, the Watergate hearings were scheduled to begin. During the preceding week, the reporters put together a long story that included details they had been collecting for months. The disclosure of the 17 wiretaps and the burglary of Ellsberg's psychiatrist were two more incidents in the pattern of White House vigilante activities Deep Throat had talked to Woodward about.

The undercover work went back to 1969, and included these operations: the Secret Service had forwarded information on the private life of a Democratic presidential candidate to the White House; Senator Eagleton's health records had arrived in John Ehrlichman's office before they were leaked to the press; Haldeman personally ordered an FBI investigation of CBS news correspondent Daniel Schorr in 1971. It added up to a broad campaign of illegal and quasi-legal operations. The account appeared on May 17.

The night of May 16, on the eve of the hearings, Woodward set out for a meeting with Deep Throat. It would be the first since Haldeman and Ehrlichman had resigned, and Woodward figured his friend would be in a good mood. At their last meeting, Deep Throat had told him they could meet earlier, say about 11:00 P.M.

Cabs were easier to find at that hour, and the trip did not take as long as usual, but Deep Throat was in the garage when Woodward arrived. He was pacing about nervously. His lower jaw seemed to quiver. Deep Throat began talking, almost in a monologue. He had only a few minutes; he raced through a series of statements. Woodward listened obediently. It was clear that a transformation had come over his friend. Woodward had dozens of questions, but Deep Throat held up his hand.

"That's the situation," he said when he had finished. "I must go this second. You can understand. Be—well, I'll say it—be cautious."

He stepped away and hurried from the garage.

Woodward got out his notebook and wrote it all down. When he got back to his apartment a little after midnight, he called Bernstein.

Can you come over? Woodward asked.

Sure, Bernstein said. At Woodward's apartment building, he rang the outside buzzer. Woodward met him at the elevator.

What's up? Bernstein asked.

Woodward put his finger over his lips to indicate silence.

Bernstein wondered if Woodward had gone crazy or if it was some gag. They walked down the hall to Woodward's apartment. Once inside, Woodward put on some music. A Rachmaninoff piano concerto. Bernstein noted what awful taste Woodward had in classical music. Woodward then drew the draperies over the large windows overlooking the city to the east. At his dining-room table, Woodward typed out a note and passed it to Bernstein.

Everyone's life is in danger.

Bernstein looked up. Has your friend gone crazy? he asked.

Woodward shook his head rapidly, indicating to Bernstein not to speak. He typed another note.

Deep Throat says that electronic surveillance is going on and we had better watch it.

Bernstein signaled that he wanted something to write with. Woodward gave him a pen.

Who is doing it? Bernstein wrote.

C-I-A, Woodward mouthed silently.

Bernstein was disbelieving. While the Rachmaninoff piano concerto played on, Woodward began typing as Bernstein read over his shoulder:

Dean talked with Senator Baker after Watergate committee formed and Baker is in the bag completely, reporting back directly to White House. . . .

President threatened Dean personally and said if he ever revealed the national security activities that President would insure he went to jail.

Mitchell started doing covert national and international things early and then involved everyone else. The list is longer than anyone could imagine.

Caulfield* met McCord and said that the President "knows that we are meeting and he offers you executive clemency and you'll only have to spend about 11 months in jail."

Caulfield threatened McCord and said "your life is no good in this country if you don't cooperate. . . . "

The covert activities involve the whole U.S. intelligence community and are incredible. Deep Throat refused to give specifics because it is against the law.

The cover-up had little to do with the Watergate, but was mainly to protect the covert operations.

The President himself has been blackmailed. When Hunt became involved, he decided that the conspirators could get some money for this. Hunt started an "extortion" racket of the rankest kind.

Cover-up cost to be about $1 million. Everyone is involved— Haldeman, Ehrlichman, the President, Dean, Mardian, Caulfield and Mitchell. They all had a problem getting the money and couldn't trust anyone, so they started raising money on the outside and chipping in their own personal funds. Mitchell couldn't meet his quota and . . . they cut Mitchell loose. . . .

CIA people can testify that Haldeman and Ehrlichman said that the President orders you to carry this out, meaning the Watergate cover-up . . . Walters and Helms† and maybe others.

Apparently, though this is not clear, these guys in the White House were out to make money and a few of them went wild trying.

* John J. Caulfield, a former New York City policeman, was a White House undercover agent and investigator.

† Richard M. Helms and General Vernon A. Walters were the director and deputy director of the CIA.

Dean acted as go-between between Haldeman-Ehrlichman and Mitchell-LaRue.

The documents that Dean has are much more than anyone has imagined and they are quite detailed.

Liddy told Dean that they could shoot him and/or that he would shoot himself, but that he would never talk and always be a good soldier.

Hunt was key to much of the crazy stuff and he used the Watergate arrests to get money . . . first $100,000 and then kept going back for more. . . .

Unreal atmosphere around the White House—realizing it is curtains on one hand and on the other trying to laugh it off and go on with business. President has had fits of "dangerous" depression.

Bernstein sat down at the table, smoking a cigarette. He had been told that week by one of his Justice Department sources to watch out for "surveillance." He and Woodward motioned to each other about leaving the apartment and going for a walk. In Woodward's hall, they stopped and decided that they had better tell someone.

Who? Woodward asked.

Bernstein said that they had better go straight to Bradlee. Now, Bernstein said. It was after 2:00 A.M.

They got into Woodward's car. They decided not to talk in the car, either. Several blocks from Bradlee's house, they called him from a pay phone. He says come over, Bernstein said.

The reporters had never been to Bradlee's house, and they had wondered how the boss lived. The streetlights created a half-dark atmosphere. As they approached the porch, a barking dog charged out. A man stepped out of the dim shadows. It was Bradlee, his hair combed, his voice and eyes sleepy.

"Come in," he said and the three stepped into a comfortable living room filled with books and rustic antiques.

Woodward passed Bradlee a copy of the memo. Bradlee began reading and started to ask a question. The reporters both stopped him and asked that he finish reading first.

Bradlee finished and looked up.

Let's walk outside, Bernstein suggested.

Bradlee gazed bemusedly about his living room, then he stood up and walked out the front door. The three moved into the center of the small yard. The chill was biting. None of them wore a coat or sweater.

Bradlee said with a touch of mockery that it was unlikely that his front yard was bugged. "What the hell do we do now?" he asked.

Bernstein suggested mobilizing a group of reporters to check out each item on the memo. Woodward suggested that the *Post* hire private detectives to help. They spent half an hour on the front lawn, bouncing around to keep warm, reviewing Deep Throat's statements. Bradlee said he had never seen anything like this before. Skeptical but shaken, he said that the problem was no longer just journalistic. He mentioned something about the state and the future of the country. He said he would call a meeting of key editors and reporters the next morning.

It was Bradlee who seemed to be prolonging the discussion, repeating himself and letting the reporters repeat themselves. None of his usual impatience showed.

"Okay," he said finally, looking at Woodward. The reporters left at 4:00 A.M. They had no idea whether Bradlee thought the early morning visit was called for.

The next morning at the office, Woodward and Bernstein passed copies of the memo to Simons, Rosenfeld and Sussman, gesturing that it should not be discussed in the office.

Just before noon, Bradlee called a meeting on the *Post*'s roof garden outside Mrs. Graham's office. Bradlee, Simons, Rosenfeld, Sussman, national editor Richard Harwood, Bernstein and Woodward sat around a large wrought-iron table under an umbrella. Harwood found the entire story implausible. His questions indicated concern that the *Post*'s Watergate coverage was nearing the edge of fantasy.

Bradlee said that he wasn't interested in the logic of it. "We've seen some pretty illogical things in the last year." He just wanted to find out what might be true.

The meeting ended inconclusively. Bernstein and Woodward had a lunch appointment with one of Dean's associates who they thought might know about some of the information they had received. They met him in a relatively remote restaurant, and over a long, leisurely lunch he confirmed most of the major points in the Deep Throat memo.

According to typed notes of the discussion, the source "didn't think

RMN [Nixon] used the word 'jail' when he threatened Dean on national security, but confirms the conversation took place and the President made it clear 'in the strongest terms' that he wouldn't stand for Dean revealing undercover activities. Dean was very shook after that meeting. . . ."

But he confirmed that Dean believed Senator Baker was in the bag and helping the White House, and that Hunt was blackmailing the White House.

"Beginning in February, RMN began dealing with Dean directly. By then blackmail scheme well into effect and stakes rising. RMN in one meeting asks Dean how much the total price will be for silence, asks for estimate. Dean says $1 million and the President says it can be accommodated, that there would be no problem getting the money . . . doesn't think as much as $1 million already doled out, that being the figure for whole package."

Bradlee called another meeting in a large vacant office in the old, remodeled portion of the *Post* building. The same group gathered behind a glass panel which looked out on the desks of the Style section of the paper.

The editors and reporters paced back and forth as Bernstein and Woodward described what they had learned at lunch. It was the most concrete evidence so far that the President knew about the cover-up and was a willing participant.

Harwood shifted gears; he thought the story was important and should run. Bradlee and Simons were nervous. "This was new to us," Simons said later. "We had been told that our offices might be bugged, that lives could be in danger. Anyone who could do that might consciously set us up on a story. There was no reason to rush."

It would be two weeks before Bernstein and Woodward wrote about Dean's allegation concerning the President's involvement in the $1 million estimate of the cover-up cost, and two weeks more before they had confirmed and written the story that Howard Hunt had blackmailed the White House. But, in the following months, almost all the items on the Deep Throat memo appeared in the public record as a result of the work of news organizations, the Senate committee and statements from the White House.

For several days after Woodward's meeting with Deep Throat,

Bernstein and Woodward behaved cautiously. They conferred on street corners, passed notes in the office, avoided telephone communications. But it all seemed rather foolish and melodramatic, so they soon went back to their normal routines. They never found any evidence that their telephones had been tapped or that anyone's life had been in danger.

At the trial in January, the Justice Department had contended that low-level officials like Gordon Liddy were the moving forces behind the Watergate conspiracy. The first hint that Justice was considering the President's involvement came during a lunch with a high department official in May.

In the week before the President's April 17 announcement, the official told Bernstein, the prosecutors had informed Assistant Attorney General Petersen that they were on the verge of indicting several of the President's closest aides—present and former. The prosecutors had insisted that the President be told personally of the impending indictments. Petersen did so. The prosecutors had expected the President to announce the resignations of Ehrlichman and Haldeman immediately. Instead, he had resisted for almost two weeks. They had asked that he order the cooperation of members of his staff. It never came. The prosecutors had been confused and disturbed about the President's actions ever since.

In late May, Bernstein talked about this on the phone with another Justice Department attorney. He had decided that the best way to get at it was to suggest that the department was going easy in its investigation. Why wasn't it dealing with allegations against the President?

"What makes you think we aren't?" the lawyer replied, angrily.

We know that your theory of the case is a closed conspiracy that ends with Haldeman, Bernstein said.

"You just showed me you don't know it," the attorney said. He paused. "If you're taking notes, that is not saying one way or the other."

Then you're investigating the President?

"Come on, you're not going to get me to answer that."

Bernstein listed some of the evidence against the President.

"You don't know what you're talking about," the lawyer said impatiently. "Evidence has nothing to do with it. Talk to some lawyers. What does the Constitution say about the President? Think about it. Can he be indicted? Even assuming one had a case that showed he was guilty of obstruction?"

Bernstein asked why the prosecutors were unwilling to call the President before the grand jury.

"Who said they wouldn't?"

You *haven't,* Bernstein said.

"Talk to some lawyers," the attorney said disgustedly.

Bernstein did that, and when he finished he understood what had happened. The question of the President's involvement had been discussed at some length in Justice. Attorneys researching the problem had come to believe that the Constitution precluded the indictment of an incumbent President. If the President could not be indicted, the lawyers reasoned, he could not be called before a grand jury.

Bernstein went to a well-placed source who said, "There is no bombshell tucked away. There is an evidentiary pattern . . . raising questions about the President's role."

Bernstein suggested to another Justice Department attorney that if it had been anyone other than the President, such a pattern of evidence would have meant that person would have been called before the grand jury. The attorney agreed.

Working with a Justice Department phone directory, Woodward found a lawyer in the Criminal Division who said, "The Watergate investigation has run smack into the Constitution. We now must deal with the question of how the President can be investigated."

Bernstein went back to the angry attorney who had first suggested the constitutional problem. "Of course the President can't be called," he stated, "and of course it would be justified." That was the prosecutors' view, too, he added.

The story was headlined: "Prosecutors Say Quiz of Nixon Can be Justified." The White House was outraged. Ziegler said the President would not testify before the grand jury or the Senate committee because "it would be constitutionally inappropriate" and "would do violence to the separation of powers." The *Post* story, Ziegler said, recounted "a shocking and irresponsible abuse of authority on the part of federal prosecutors. Grand jury proceedings are by law secret." The White House asked Attorney General Richardson and Harvard law professor Archibald Cox, who had been appointed special prosecutor in May, to find the sources for the story. If an investigation was ever opened, the sources were never found.

The first week of June, Bernstein was talking to a source he hadn't called for several weeks. He asked if there had been any other burglaries.

"There was one *proposed* . . . but I don't think it ever came off. The Brookings Institution. John Dean turned it off."

Bernstein called Dean's associate. "I'm not sure you have the right word, friend," he said. "Somebody must have misspoken himself. Chuck Colson wanted to rub two sticks together."

Maybe Bernstein's mind was jumping too fast. Colson wanted to start a *fire?*

"You might say that."

It couldn't have been serious, Bernstein said.

"Serious enough for John Caulfield to run out of Colson's office in a panic. He came straight to John Dean, saying he didn't ever want to talk to that man Colson again because he was crazy. And that John better do something to stop him before it was too late. John caught the first courier flight out to San Clemente to see Ehrlichman. That's how serious it was."

Why Ehrlichman?

"Because he was the only one with enough influence to stop it at that point. And he was not happy to see John Dean. Dean wasn't supposed to know about it. But once he flew out there to make a big deal about it, E didn't have any choice but to shut it down. John stayed in the room and listened while E called Colson. The whole time he was on the phone, E just glared at him like he was a traitor."

Dean's associate explained the purpose of the operation to Bernstein: Morton Halperin, Daniel Ellsberg's friend whose telephone was among the "Kissinger taps," was believed to have kept some classified documents when he left Kissinger's staff to become a fellow at the Brookings Institution (a center for the study of public policy questions). The

White House wanted those documents back, and since security at the institution was too tight to risk a simple burglary, it was conjectured that a fire could cover a break-in at Halperin's office.

Bernstein located someone who had heard the whole story from Caulfield. "Not just a fire, a *firebombing*," the man said. "That was what Colson thought would do the trick. Caulfield said 'This has gone too far' and [that] he didn't ever want anything to do with Colson again in his life." Both Dean and Caulfield had told the story to investigators, he said.

Woodward was afraid it might be a set-up.

Bernstein checked his sources again and the investigators. Absolutely solid, he told Woodward. A firebombing.

Woodward then called Colson.

"There's no question about that," Colson told him. "There is one mistake. . . . It was not the Brookings but the *Washington Post*. I told them to hire a wrecking crane and go over and knock down the building and *Newsweek* also."

Woodward said that he was serious, the allegation was deadly serious and not a joke.

"It was the *Washington Post*, I'm telling you. He had an explicit assignment to destroy the *Washington Post*," responded Colson, his tone perfectly straight. "I wanted the *Washington Post* destroyed."

Woodward didn't doubt it, but he said the allegation about the Brookings Institution was going into the paper.

"Explicitly," Colson replied, "it is bullshit. I absolutely made no such statement or suggestion. It is ludicrous. The story you have told me is a flight of fantasy, the outer limits—this one has gone too far."

He called Woodward back several hours later. "Are you serious about this story?"

Woodward said that he was.

Colson's tone was altered. "I was asked about this by the federal prosecutors. I was aware that there was a discussion about how to get highly classified documents back. . . . There is always a possibility that I might have said it. . . . It is characteristic of me . . . but I never made it and certainly never meant it."

The story ran on June 9.

About a week before John Dean testified before the Senate committee in June 1973, Woodward was talking about Howard Hunt with a

Senate attorney. The attorney felt that Hunt held a key to still more undercover work. Hunt had been brought to Capitol Hill from jail for long interviews. And he had disclosed an instruction he claimed to have received from Colson about an hour after Alabama Governor Wallace was shot.

"Hunt said Colson wanted him to fly to Milwaukee immediately and break into Arthur Bremer's apartment," the attorney said, "and bring back anything that might help in connecting Bremer to left-wing political causes."

Wallace had been shot by Bremer in a Maryland shopping center on May 15, 1972, at about 4:00 P.M. By 6:30, a *Post* editor had learned the name of the would-be assassin from White House official Ken Clawson. Clawson had said that it was clear from literature found in Bremer's dingy Milwaukee apartment that the assassin was connected to leftist causes, possibly the campaign of Senator George S. McGovern. Woodward had been working on the story, and he had rejected the idea. There had, in fact, been both left-wing and right-wing propaganda in the apartment. But several reporters from Milwaukee had told him they had been permitted to enter Bremer's apartment during a 90-minute period right after the shooting in Maryland. Many reporters had carried off papers and other effects. Two reporters for Milwaukee papers had told Woodward that they had gone into Bremer's apartment after FBI agents had been there once and left. An hour and a half later, the agents had come back and sealed off the apartment. The FBI had never offered any explanation as to why they had permitted Bremer's belongings to be looted.

Back in late 1972, before the first Watergate trial, Howard Simons had summoned some of the editors and Bernstein and Woodward into his office. "You know, there's one thing we've got to think about," he had said. "The ultimate dirty trick."

Bernstein and Woodward had mentioned it to each other more than once. Woodward had had an anonymous call saying that one of the Watergate suspects had gone to Milwaukee to meet with Arthur Bremer. And it had been rumored that Bremer was carrying $100 bills while he was stalking Wallace. Simons wanted the rumors checked.

Woodward and Bernstein had been skeptical and Simons had agreed. But, as he pointed out, many once-unthinkable things had occurred.

The reporters never found any evidence to substantiate a connection between Bremer and the suspects. Months later, a *Post* reporter went to Milwaukee, but he too turned up nothing.

Now Woodward was being told that Colson had ordered Hunt to break into Bremer's apartment. The next morning, he called Hunt's attorney, William O. Bittman. "There is no question that there was testimony about that," Bittman said. "Colson asked him [Hunt] to go to Milwaukee and go into Bremer's apartment. . . . I don't have a clear recollection of the reason why he was to go out there. I don't recall whether the word 'break-in' was involved."

About four that afternoon, June 19, 1973, Woodward went to Colson's law office to see David Shapiro, Colson's law partner and his chief legal adviser for Watergate matters. The new law firm of Colson & Shapiro had offices in a modern building a few blocks from the White House. Shapiro greeted Woodward heartily, offering him a thick, chubby hand and an overstuffed, light brown leather chair. It was ridiculous, Shapiro said, even to think that Colson would do such a crazy thing. A bespectacled young attorney in the firm named Judah Best* was brought in by Shapiro to meet Woodward. He told him it would be unfair to write a story even mentioning such a flimsy allegation. Working his hands heavily, Best frowned and grimaced as he maintained that Howard Hunt was under pressure and clearly unstable. Shapiro and Best worked on Woodward for about 45 minutes, trying to plant the seeds of doubt. Shapiro then went to his desk, called his secretary and instructed her to tell "him" to come in. Moments later, the door opened and in came Colson, wearing blue pin-striped pants, dark blue shirt and blue polka-dot tie. He had a gigantic pot belly. He looked wounded and tired as he shook hands with Woodward. He didn't say much, but just stared at Woodward.

"You can't do this to this man," Shapiro said, standing behind his desk. Colson said nothing. He looked like he was about to weep. There was none of his usual overbearing manner. "You're out to destroy him," Shapiro said.

Woodward said he was not out to destroy anyone.

"Come on, you can admit it," Shapiro said.

The lawyers argued that it would have been illogical for Colson to

---

* In less than two months, Best would get a new client—Vice President Spiro T. Agnew—and would successfully bargain Agnew's office away to keep him out of jail.

order Hunt to burglarize Bremer's apartment because Colson was in close contact with the FBI that night. They said Colson had urged the Bureau to make a speedy, thorough investigation.

"Would it have been logical for me to push in the FBI and simultaneously order Hunt to Milwaukee?" Colson asked.

Woodward figured the tape recorder was going and he chose every word. He remarked that the Watergate case was already crowded with illogic.

"The charge is absolutely untrue and I'll swear it is untrue under oath," Colson said.

Colson seemed hurt by Woodward's unwillingness to accept his statement as definitive proof.

Woodward recorded Colson's denial in his notebook.

Shapiro then produced copies of a report about a lie-detector test Colson had voluntarily taken that vindicated him of complicity in the Watergate bugging. Woodward was also handed a "Memorandum for the File," dated June 20, 1972, the day the *Post* had first identified Howard Hunt as a suspect. Memoranda for the file are often called "cover-your-ass memos." The one handed to Woodward, with the subject heading "Howard Hunt," said in part: "I talked to him [Hunt] on the telephone the night Governor Wallace was shot simply to ask him for his reactions on what he thought might have been the cause of the attempted assassination. Hunt was known as something of an expert on psychological warfare and motivations when in the CIA." In a covering memo, Colson had noted, however, "I cannot be sure that my memory is all that precise."

Shapiro gave Woodward two more memos unrelated to the Colson-Hunt-Bremer story. One was dated October 11, 1972, the day after Bernstein's and Woodward's major espionage-sabotage story. The memo was written by Ken Clawson and addressed to Colson. Referring to the mention of his name in connection with the Muskie Canuck Letter, Clawson had written that he would spend the second Nixon administration "paying back the *Washington Post*." The other memo indicated that Haldeman had tried to blame Colson, not Clawson, for authorship of the letter.

Woodward asked for copies of the two memos on the Canuck Letter. There was a long silence.

Woodward repeated his request.

Another silence. Then one of the lawyers said something about being able to work out something and Woodward would be able to get copies in the near future.

Were they offering a deal? It was not explicitly stated, but the suggestion of a trade was in the air. What would happen if Woodward said there would be no story on the Bremer allegation? Would one of the attorneys say it would then be possible to let him have copies of the memos? Maybe Woodward was listening for it because he was pretty certain that this was the way Colson did business. Woodward wanted to turn off any such suggestion. He said it sounded like something was being offered, but that he *knew* it wasn't.

All three spoke at once. Of course, they wouldn't think of that. They would never do that, it would be an insult to think so or imagine so.

Woodward saw how they operated. If he hadn't been listening for it, he wouldn't have realized that a trade had been offered. That is the way bribes must work, Woodward thought, so that only someone listening for it would hear it. He couldn't test the situation. If he were to step close to a deal, they could destroy him.

Shapiro and Colson started grinding on Woodward again. That was the price he had to pay, Woodward guessed. He had to listen; maybe there was a reason, maybe he would be convinced. He got in a question occasionally. Why were you in touch with the FBI so much? he asked Colson.

"The President was agitated and wanted the political background on Bremer," Colson said. Informed of the shooting, the President became deeply upset and voiced immediate concern that the assassin might have ties to the Republican Party or, even worse, the President's re-election committee. If that were the case, Colson noted, it could have cost the President the election.

The meeting with Shapiro and Colson had taken almost two hours, and there wasn't time to get the story into the paper that day. Just before deadline the following evening, Woodward called Shapiro and told him that the story was going. Woodward had promised to let him know.

Later that night, Colson called Bernstein to protest. The allegation was "an utterly preposterous one," he insisted, and added that he did "not believe that it could be an accurate report of any testimony that the Senate committee has received."

Bernstein told him it was accurate.

Even if it accurately reflected Hunt's testimony, Colson said, it would be irresponsible to print it because Hunt had been under "great duress" when he met with the Senate committee.

Bernstein said he would include Colson's observations in the story.

Colson played heavily on what he described as Bernstein's civil-libertarian instincts, pleading with him to keep the story out of the paper. When Bernstein said no, Colson called him a "vicious hypocrite."

Since June 17, 1972, the reporters had saved their notes and memos, reviewing them periodically to make lists of unexplored leads. Many items on the lists were the names of CRP and White House people who the reporters thought might have useful information. By May 17, 1973, when the Senate hearings opened, Bernstein and Woodward had gotten lazy. Their nighttime visits were scarcer, and, increasingly, they had begun to rely on a relatively easy access to the Senate committee's staff investigators and attorneys. There was, however, one unchecked entry on both lists—presidential aide Alexander P. Butterfield. Both Deep Throat and Hugh Sloan had mentioned him, and Sloan had said, almost in passing, that he was in charge of "internal security." In January, Woodward had gone by Butterfield's house in a Virginia suburb. No one had come to the door.

In May, Woodward asked a committee staff member if Butterfield had been interviewed.

"No, we're too busy."

Some weeks later, he had asked another staffer if the committee knew why Butterfield's duties in Haldeman's office were defined as "internal security."

The staff member said the committee didn't know, and maybe it would be a good idea to interview Butterfield. He would ask Sam Dash, the committee's chief counsel. Dash put the matter off. The staff member told Woodward he would push Dash again. Dash finally okayed an interview with Butterfield for Friday, July 13, 1973.

On Saturday the 14th, Woodward received a phone call at home from a senior member of the committee's investigative staff. "Congratulations," he said. "We interviewed Butterfield. He told the whole story."

What whole story?

"Nixon bugged himself."

He told Woodward that only junior staff members had been present at the interview, and that someone had read an excerpt from John Dean's testimony about his April 15 meeting with the President.

"The most interesting thing that happened during the conversation was very near the end," Dean had said. "He [Nixon] got up out of his chair, went behind his chair to the corner of the Executive Office Building office and in a barely audible tone said to me he was probably foolish to have discussed Hunt's clemency with Colson." Dean had thought to himself that the room might be bugged.

Butterfield was a reluctant witness. He said that he knew it was probably the one thing that the President would not want revealed. The interrogators pressed—and out floated a story which would disturb the presidential universe as none other would.

The existence of a tape system which monitored the President's conversations had been known only to the President himself, Haldeman, Larry Higby, Alexander Haig, Butterfield and the several Secret Service agents who maintained it. For the moment, the information was strictly off the record.

The reporters were again concerned about a White House set-up. A taping system could be disclosed, they reasoned, and then the President could serve up doctored or manufactured tapes to exculpate himself and his men. Or, having known the tapes were rolling, the President might have induced Dean—or anyone else—to say incriminating things and then feign ignorance himself. They decided not to pursue the story for the moment.

All Saturday night, the subject gnawed at Woodward. Butterfield had said that even Kissinger and Ehrlichman were unaware of the taping system. The Senate committee and the special prosecutor would certainly try to obtain the tapes, maybe even subpoena them.

Kissinger doesn't know, Woodward reflected. And he thought, Kissinger probably knows *almost* everything, and he wouldn't like the idea of secret taping systems plucking his sober words and advice out of the air—whether for posterity or some grand jury. How will foreign leaders feel when they learn of hidden microphones? Woodward thought about knowing something that Kissinger didn't know. Ziegler was also in the dark, apparently.

Woodward called Bradlee. It was about 9:30 P.M. and Bradlee sounded as if he might have been sleeping. Woodward outlined Butterfield's disclosures. As he read, his voice tripped several times. Maybe he was overreacting. Bradlee was silent.

"I just wanted you to know," Woodward said, "because it seems important. We'll go to work on it if you want."

"Well, I don't know," Bradlee said with slight irritation.

"How would you rate the story?" Woodward asked.

"B-plus," Bradlee said quickly.

B-plus, Woodward thought. Well, that isn't much.

"See what more you can find out, but I wouldn't bust one on it," Bradlee said.

Woodward apologized for calling on a Saturday night.

"No problem," Bradlee said cheerfully. "Always glad to hear what's up."

They hung up. Woodward concluded that he'd been too anxious.

The Senate committee moved quickly. On Monday, on national television, Butterfield reluctantly laid out the whole story of the tapes before the Senate committee, and the country.

"Okay," Bradlee said the next morning. "It's more than a B-plus."

17

IN THE FIRST WEEK of November, Woodward moved the flower pot and traveled to the underground garage. Two weeks earlier, the President had fired special Watergate prosecutor Archibald Cox, who had subpoenaed nine presidential tape recordings. Attorney General Eliot Richardson and William Ruckelshaus, his deputy, had resigned. In the shattered inner circle of the White House, the President's aides were saying that the special prosecutor had been fired because the President feared that Cox was going to prosecute him. Then, with Cox gone, the President bowed to public opinion and a court order and surrendered seven of the tapes. Two had never existed, his lawyers said.

Deep Throat's message was short and simple: one or more of the tapes contained deliberate erasures.

Bernstein began calling sources at the White House. Four of them said they had learned that the tapes were of poor quality, that there were "gaps" in some conversations. But they did not know whether these had been caused by erasures. Ron Ziegler told Bernstein there were no gaps or erasures in the tapes. A story that asserted the opposite would be "inaccurate." Bernstein proposed that the story could be held if Ziegler would pledge, on his honor, that he was absolutely sure. "We deal in facts, not honor," Ziegler replied.

The story quoted anonymously Deep Throat's remark that there were gaps of "a suspicious nature" which "could lead someone to conclude that the tapes have been tampered with."

On the afternoon of November 21, Ziegler phoned Bernstein back. The President's lawyers had announced in Judge Sirica's courtroom that one of the tapes contained an 18½-minute gap. "I'm giving you my word that I didn't know about this when we had our other conversation."

Bernstein and Woodward did not disbelieve him. They knew from a number of sources that the President had refused for months to let any of his White House aides listen to all the tapes—even while he was claiming that their full disclosure would vindicate him.

Richard Nixon, his subordinates were saying, had become a prisoner in his own house—secretive, distrustful even of those who were attempting to plead his cause, combative, sleepless. One of the men who had been closest to him throughout his presidency told Woodward helplessly, "The only people he will talk to candidly about Watergate are Bebe Rebozo and Bob Abplanalp"—the millionaire businessmen who were his long-time personal friends.

At Disneyworld in Florida, the President told an audience of editors on national TV, "I am not a crook."

On December 28, General Alexander Haig, the White House Chief of Staff, reached Katharine Graham by telephone in a Washington restaurant. He was calling from San Clemente to discuss two of the reporters' stories on the *Post*'s front page that morning. The first said that Operation Candor, the name given the campaign by the President to defend himself, had been shut down, and that two of the President's most trusted advisers, who had steadfastly maintained his innocence, were no longer convinced of it. The second story said that the President's lawyers had been supplying attorneys for H. R. Haldeman and John Ehrlichman with copies of documents and other evidence that the White House was submitting to the special prosecutor's office.

Haig characterized the stories as "scurrilous," accused the *Post* of "disservice" to the nation, and appealed to Mrs. Graham to stop publishing such accounts.

Haig himself, the reporters soon learned, had come to doubt the wisdom of the President's course. For more than six months he and Henry Kissinger had been urging the President to cut his ties with the three former aides who had been the closest to him and were now the primary targets of the special prosecutor's investigation—Haldeman, Ehrlichman and Colson.

Instead, the President had built his legal defense in concert with the three, and had continued to meet with them and talk with them on the telephone. During the summer of 1973, Kissinger had tried to persuade the President to disavow his former aides publicly and to accept a measure of responsibility for Watergate. The suggestion had been angrily rejected by Ron Ziegler. "Contrition is bullshit," he had responded to the presidential speechwriter who brought him Kissinger's recommendation.

By late February 1974, the special Watergate prosecution force had obtained guilty pleas from Jeb Magruder, Bart Porter, Donald Segretti, Herbert Kalmbach, Fred LaRue, Egil Krogh and John Dean. Eight corporations and their officers had pleaded guilty to charges of making illegal contributions to CRP. In Washington, Dwight Chapin was under indictment for perjury. In New York, John Mitchell and Maurice Stans were on trial, charged with obstruction of justice and perjury.

On March 1, the Washington grand jury that had indicted the original conspirators and burglars of the Democratic National Headquarters in 1972 handed up its major indictments in the Watergate cover-up case. It charged seven of the President's former White House and campaign aides with conspiracy to obstruct justice: Haldeman, Ehrlichman, Colson, Mitchell, Strachan, Mardian and lawyer Kenneth Parkinson.

A week later, a second Washington grand jury handed up indictments in the conspiracy to burglarize the office of Daniel Ellsberg's psychiatrist. Those charged were Ehrlichman, Colson, Liddy and three Cuban Americans, including Bernard Barker and Eugenio Martinez, who were among the original Watergate break-in defendants.

Acting for the full House, to which the Constitution gives the "sole power to impeach," the House Judiciary Committee had begun the first investigation in more than one hundred years into such possible action against a President. The chief Watergate grand jury turned over to Judge Sirica, in addition to the seven indictments, a briefcase containing a report and the accompanying evidence of what Deep Throat, and others, assert to be a staggering case against the President.

Since the prosecutors had argued strongly that the Constitution precludes the possibility of indicting an incumbent President, the grand jurors recommended that both be turned over to the House committee.

On January 30, the President had delivered his annual State of the Union Message to a joint session of the House and Senate, the justices of the Supreme Court and the members of the Cabinet, as well as to other guests and a national TV audience. "One year of Watergate is enough," he declared at the conclusion, and he implored the country and the Congress to turn to other, more urgent, matters.

To those who will decide if he should be tried for "high crimes and misdemeanors"—the House of Representatives—

And to those who would sit in judgment at such a trial if the House impeaches—the Senate—

And to the man who would preside at such an impeachment trial —the Chief Justice of the United States, Warren Burger—

And to the nation . . .

The President said, "I want you to know that I have no intention whatever of ever walking away from the job that the American people elected me to do for the people of the United States."

Index

Books on the Presidency
from Touchstone

☐ **The Final Days**

By Bob Woodward and Carl Bernstein

The classic, behind-the-scenes account of Richard Nixon's last days in the White House. "An extraordinary work of reportage on the epic political story of our time."　　　　　　*—Newsweek*
64645-1　　　$7.95

☐ **Exile**
The Unquiet Oblivion of Richard M. Nixon

By Robert Sam Anson

Exile picks up where *The Final Days* left off, describing Nixon's life after being driven from office: his private anguish, legal and financial struggles, the Ford pardon, the David Frost interviews, and his relationships with Presidents Reagan, Carter, and Ford. "An extraordinary story."
　　　—The Washington Post Book World
60566-6　　　$8.95

☐ **Eisenhower, Volume One**
Soldier, General of the Army, President-Elect: 1890-1952

By Stephen Ambrose

The first volume of the definitive two-volume biography offers startling new insights into Eisenhower's early years, his command of WWII operations, his thoughts about the war, and his relations with family, friends, and world leaders. "Outstanding . . . complete, and objective."
　　　—The New York Times Book Review
60564-X　　　$12.95

☐ **Eisenhower, Volume Two**
The President

By Stephen Ambrose

The concluding volume of Ambrose's definitive biography fully covers the Eisenhower presidency: the President's rejection of advice to use atomic weapons, his thinking on defense policy and the Cold War, his actions on civil rights, and his views on communism and Joseph McCarthy.
60565-8　　　$12.95

☐ **FDR**
A Biography

By Ted Morgan

The best single-volume biography ever written of Roosevelt the man and the President—from FDR's patrician upbringing, early career and struggle with polio to the New Deal and World War II. "A fascinating three-dimensional portrait. . . . A vivid contribution."
　　　—The New York Times Book Review
62812-7　　　$12.95

☐ **The Power To Lead**
The Crisis of the American Presidency

By James MacGregor Burns

Burns attributes the current crisis of confidence in the presidency to an outmoded Constitution and party system, media trivialization, and the overly personalized presidency. He offers bold proposals for revitalizing our political system. "Original and courageous."　　　*—The Washington Post*
60462-7　　　$8.95

- - - - - **MAIL THIS COUPON TODAY—NO-RISK 14-DAY FREE TRIAL** - - - - -

Simon & Schuster, Inc.
200 Old Tappan Road
Old Tappan, NJ 07675. Mail Order Dept. PM87

Please send me copies of the above titles. (Indicate quantities in boxes.)
(If not completely satisfied, you may return for full refund within 14 days.)

☐ Save! Enclose full amount per copy with this coupon. Publisher pays postage and handling; or charge my credit card.

☐ MasterCard　☐ Visa

My credit card number is _____Card expires _____

Signature _____

Name _____
　　　　　　　　　(Please Print)

Address _____

City _____State _____ Zip Code _____
or available at your local bookstore　　　　　Prices subject to change without notice